LEARN TO TALK MALAY

A COURSE FOR ADULT BEGINNERS,
WITH GRAMOPHONE RECORDS,
BASED ON EIGHT SCENES OF
EVERYDAY LIFE IN MALAYA

Works by the same author

Published by MACMILLAN

A HANDBOOK OF MALAY SCRIPT

TRANSLATION AND COMPOSITION EXERCISES
FOR MALAY STUDENTS

with MOHAMED HASHIM BIN MAT PIAH
CHE' UMAR ANAK-bĕRANAK

Published by the ENGLISH UNIVERSITIES PRESS

TEACH YOURSELF MALAY

Best wishes to Paddy
from Michael.

R.M.N. Barracks.   Dec. 1956.
Singapore.

Tak 'kan pisang berbuah dua kali.

Bananas won't fruit twice.

——— · ———

LEARN TO TALK
MALAY

by
M. B. LEWIS
Lecturer in Malay, School of Oriental and African Studies,
University of London

SCRIPT
by
SULAIMAN BIN HAMZAH
Lecturer in Malay, The Malayan College, Kirkby, Liverpool

RECORDS
by
"HIS MASTER'S VOICE"

MACMILLAN AND CO. LIMITED
ST. MARTIN'S STREET, LONDON
1954

MACMILLAN AND COMPANY LIMITED
London Bombay Calcutta Madras Melbourne

THE MACMILLAN COMPANY OF CANADA LIMITED
Toronto

ST MARTIN'S PRESS INC
New York

PRINTED IN GREAT BRITAIN

PREFACE

This course is an attempt to present the Malay language through the medium of contemporary conversational material. But in spite of the fact that a spoken tongue, because of the additional range given to it by the play of intonation, has to a certain extent a grammar of its own, it is nevertheless interesting to note that this 'everyday' twentieth-century Malay is not appreciably different in structure from the sixteenth-century literary Malay which is accounted the high-water mark of Malay prose. If dialect variations were taken into account there would be much to add on the subject of vocabulary and pronunciation, but there would still not be many marked changes of structure to note. Those changes are to be found not in the colloquial language but in those levels of the written language which have felt most sharply the impact of western idiom, that is to say the prose of translation and of journalism.

I have been fortunate in finding in Ĕnche' Sulaiman bin Hamzah a collaborator whose interested and sensitive co-operation has made the work of compiling the course a pleasure. Its inception was due to the need which both of us felt for livelier teaching material to present to our non-Malay students, but the many enquiries for such a course which I have received from time to time encourage me to hope that the book and the accompanying records may prove of interest to a wider public, more particularly since the vocabulary and pronunciation used approximate to a standard which is widely acceptable. On this point the script-writer speaks for himself in the two paragraphs which follow.

M. B. LEWIS

London
June 1954

SA-PATAH KATA

Pĕrchakapan Mĕlayu yang tĕrpakai di-dalam buku ini bukan-lah pĕrchakapan mana-mana satu daerah di-Tanah Mĕlayu mĕ-

v

lainkan ia-itu pĕrchakapan yang di-tutorkan oleh orang Mĕlayu
yang datang dari bĕrlainan daerah. Di-maktab-maktab, di-
sĕkolah-sĕkolah, di-tĕmpat latehan mata-mata, di-tĕmpat latehan
askar, di-majlis mĕshuarat dan di-lain-lain tĕmpat pĕrkumpulan
orang Mĕlayu yang datang dari bĕrlainan daerah pĕrchakapan
sapĕrti ini-lah yang biasa-nya dapat di-dĕngar. Ada juga orang
yang bĕrchakap bagini di-rumah-nya atau di-kampong-nya
sĕndiri. Yang dĕmikian itu pada biasa-nya kĕrana di-rumah
tangga-nya ada orang bĕrasal dari bĕrlainan daerah atau pun
kampong-nya itu baharu sahaja di-diami oleh orang dari bĕrbagai-bagai daerah, bĕlum ada mĕnĕrbitkan pĕrchakapan
daerah yang bĕrsĕndiri.

Pada pĕndapatan saya pĕrchakapan chara ini-lah yang boleh
di-katakan Pĕrchakapan Umum.

Pĕnuntut-pĕnuntut Mĕlayu yang awal bĕlajar di-maktab ini
tĕlah mĕnolong dĕngan banyak-nya di-dalam kĕrja mĕngarang
pĕrbualan ini. Mĕreka itu datang dari bĕrbagai daerah di-
Tanah Mĕlayu. Sa-tĕlah bĕrunding dĕngan mĕreka itu bĕbĕrapa
kali baharu-lah saya mĕngambil kĕputusan sapĕrti yang tĕrsĕbut
di-atas tadi. Saya uchapkan bĕrbanyak-banyak tĕrima kaseh
kapada mĕreka itu sakalian-nya.

Translation

The Malay used in this book is not the dialect of any one
particular state of the Malay Peninsula, it is the language used
between Malays who come from different states. In colleges and
schools, in police depots and soldiers' barracks, in Councils of
State and other assemblies where Malays from various parts of
the Peninsula come together, this is the sort of Malay that is to
be heard. In some cases, too, it is the Malay that is talked in the
home and in the village, the reason usually being that husband
and wife are natives of different states, or that the villagers are
new-comers who were born in different parts of the Peninsula and
have not yet developed a local dialect.

In my opinion, this is what may be called ' Standard
Malay '.

The Malay students of the first training course held at this
College gave considerable help in the preparation of these con-

versations.   They came from all the different states of Malaya, and it was after prolonged consultation with them that I came to the conclusion which I have stated above.   To them all I offer my thanks.

SULAIMAN BIN HAMZAH

The Malayan College
Kirkby, Liverpool
June 1954

RECORDS
H.M.V. Nos. JO 426–429

Names of Speakers, with birthplace

Che' Mahmud: Sulaiman bin Hamzah, Raub, Pahang.

Che' Normah: Zan binti Haji Muhamad, Kalumpang, Selangor.

'*Mr. Martin*': Alias bin Shamsuddin, Kuala Kangsar, Perak.

Zaharah: Sofiah binti Mat Yit, Batu Gajah, Perak.

CONTENTS

INTRODUCTION

The Language

Malay is the most widely spoken of a group of languages (*Malayo-Polynesian* or *Austronesian*) which covers most of the equatorial islands from Madagascar to Easter Island. From a comparative study of these languages scholars have postulated an '*Original Indonesian*' from which they have all developed, but no trace of that parent language remains to-day. Modern Indonesian (*Bahasa Indonesia*) is an adaptation of Malay which is being fashioned to serve as a common language for the various peoples of the Indonesian Republic, whose mother-tongues (such as Javanese, Sundanese, Madurese, Balinese, Achinese, Minangkabau, Batak, etc.) have grown from the same stock.

Malay is the mother-tongue of the Malays of the Malay Peninsula and of certain coastal districts in some of the islands.

The Records (H.M.V. Nos. JO 426–9)

The lines printed in bold type are to be heard on the records.

Malay pronunciation (as well as vocabulary) varies considerably according to locality, but there is a growing tendency among educated Malays to cultivate, in addition to their own dialect pronunciation, a 'standard' pronunciation which is intelligible wherever Malay is spoken.[1] With the exception of a few words here and there, that is the pronunciation to be heard on these records. It is, indeed, the way in which these speakers would converse among themselves, since they come from three different states of Malaya.

When you have listened to the first record several times over, read through the following paragraphs and see if you agree with the points made in them.

Malay Sounds

A PRELIMINARY NOTE ON STRESS

Nearly all root-words in Malay are of two syllables. When

[1] See *Sa-Patah Kata*, p. v.

the first of these syllables is open (*i.e.* ends in a vowel), it is that syllable which takes the stress (e.g. *sákit*).[1] When the first syllable is closed (*i.e.* ends in a consonant, as in *sambut*), the stress is almost even, often with a rising intonation on the final syllable. Thus the stress-pattern of most Malay words is covered by the two English words 'sofa' and 'rough-shod'.

But stress in Malay is much weaker than it is in English,[2] and as long as you resist the temptation to put a marked stress on the final syllable of words such as *panas, kasut, parang*[1] (thus reducing the open penultimate *a* to a neutral vowel) you need not give much thought to it.

THE VOWELS

You will note that the romanized spelling uses six vowels: *a, i* and *e, o* and *u*, and *ě*, as well as the two final diphthongs *-au* and *-ai*. Each of these symbols, as you would expect, has to serve for a range of gradations varying according to position in the word, to dialect peculiarities, and to personal idiosyncrasy, but the following points are of general application:

   (*a*) The letter *a*

      i. in an open penultimate syllable, *i.e.* stressed, *e.g.* as in *sakit*:

        This is the Malay sound which, above all others, stamps an 'English accent' as such, unless care is taken at the outset to eliminate the southern English front vowel heard in *cat, bag*, etc. (I.P.A.[3] æ). That is a sound which is never heard in a Malay word. Its only occurrence on the records is in I. 86 (**Penang**), where Zaharah immediately corrects her guest's English pronunciation. When Malays adopt an English word which contains this sound

---

[1] *a.* When a suffix is added the stress is sometimes moved on, to fall on a newly-created open penultimate, *e.g. káta* may become *katá-nya*, but the change is not obligatory, and there is little uniformity of practice.

    b. When the open penultimate syllable has the indeterminate vowel *ě* (see (*d*) below), the stress falls on the final syllable (*e.g. běsár*).

[2] It is, moreover, impossible to discuss stress accurately without taking into account the effect of intonation.

[3] I.P.A. = International Phonetic Alphabet.

they usually change it into a short *e*, turning 'bank' into *beng*.[1]

The Malay sound is the back-vowel, the broad *a* used in the north of England, in Scotland and in Wales (I.P.A. ɑ), which a southerner might feel tempted to describe as *aa*. But it is the quality of it that is different, not the length. It is not the *r*-lengthened *a* of *cart*. Thus the Malay word *kata* ('say') does not rhyme with *patter*, nor yet with *carter*[2]; it is nearer to *cutter* than to either of these, but the first vowel is more open.

ii. in an open final syllable, *i.e.* unstressed (unless the penultimate has the neutral vowel *ě*), *e.g.* as in *kita*:

In this position the *a* is usually sounded as if it were the neutral vowel indicated by *ě* (I.P.A. ə), but it varies according to locality. With northern speakers it retains its *a* sound, and with some southern speakers it becomes almost as close and as far forward as the *eu* in French *feu* (I.P.A. ɸ). But the pronunciation used in the records (*i.e.* the neutral vowel, like the final *a* in *Java*) is acceptable everywhere.

iii. in a closed syllable:

a. penultimate

When it is in the closed first syllable of a two-syllabled word (*e.g.* in *sambut*) the *a* is almost as open as in an open penultimate syllable (*e.g.* in *sakit*). From the point of view of pronunciation it is advisable to think of the word as being divided after the vowel, rather than between the two consonants, *i.e.* it is sounded *sa-mbut* rather than *sam-but*.

This happens constantly, not only with *a* but also with the other vowels. If you look through several consecutive lines of text you will see that

[1] Malay does not tolerate two consonant sounds at the end of a word.
[2] Note how both voices refuse the English pronunciation of *Martin* in I. 5, and I. 40.

when you do have two consonants in the middle of a Malay word the first one of them (except for an occasional *r*, often in a Sanskrit word) is always a nasal (*m*, *n*, *ng*[1]), that is to say, it is merely a glide, leading the tongue to the initial consonant of the second syllable rather than closing the vowel of the first syllable. The result of this is that Malay abounds in gently accented open syllables (*sa-*, *si-*, *se-*, *su-*, *so-*; *ba-*, *bi-*, *be-*, *bu-*, *bo-*, etc.), which contribute largely to its soft-flowing modulation that is much nearer to the melody of Italian speech than to the more staccato enunciation of southern English.

b. final

When *a* occurs in a closed final syllable, there is greater variety of pronunciation. It tends to become a little closer, almost like the vowel in the English word *cup*. This is particularly noticeable when the final syllable is stressed, *e.g.* in *kějap* I. 69, *tahan* III. 42, *děpan* [2] III. 71, *faham* V. 38.

Before the velar nasal *ng* it tends to be itself nasalized (I.P.A. ã), *e.g.* in *datang* in I. 72.

Whatever the vowel pronunciation in this closed final syllable, the syllable itself is *never* telescoped as a final unaccented syllable so often is in English (*e.g.* in *cotton*, *brazen*, *curtain*). It retains its correct vowel sound and its proportionate weight as a syllable, *e.g. macham* in I. 68 does *not* become *mach'm*.

iv. in an antepenultimate syllable (*i.e.* before the stress) *a* is usually pronounced as the neutral vowel (I.P.A. ə), *e.g.* in *halaman*, where the first syllable is frequently dropped altogether. Such trisyllables

---

[1] *ng*, *ny* and *ch* are *single* sounds, though the romanized script represents them by double symbols.

[2] The diphthong in the final syllable of *děpan* in line I. 74 is a dialect pronunciation. Cf. the diphthong in *Rah* in the previous line.

are rare, but the effect is seen in compound words such as *bagitu* III. 83, and in duplicated words, *e.g.* in *barang-barang* in I. 92 the first two *a*'s are sounded as neutral vowels, the third (an open penultimate, which takes the stress) is the broad open *a* of the first syllable of *kata* in section i above, and the fourth is the slightly nasalized *a* referred to in section iii *b*.

Similarly, the prefixed words *ka-* and *sa-* are always reduced to the neutral vowel (*kě-* and *sě-*) in speech, because they come before the stress, since nearly all Malay root-words have two syllables.

The prefixed word *di-*, in the same way, is usually dimmed to *dě-* in speech.

At this point you are advised to play through the first record again, concentrating on the pronunciation given to the letter *a* in its various positions. It will pay you to take trouble over this letter; a glance at any page of the text will show you that it is the preponderant vowel-symbol,[1] and as such will do much to make or mar your Malay accent.

(*b*) The letters *i* and *e*

These vowel-symbols are treated together because they are sometimes interchangeable. The romanized spelling has been fixed, for the written word, but pronunciation varies; *e.g. běrsila* is pronounced *běrsela* by two different speakers in II. 93 and V. 25.

> *i*: this vowel presents little difficulty. It has its continental, not its English, value (*i.e.* it is never like the diphthong in the English word *fine*).
>
> In an open syllable (*e.g.* in *ini*) it is longer than the vowel sound in the English word *feet*, and the lips are more spread in producing it.

---

[1] A count of two dozen lines taken at random (lines 3 to 27, excluding English words) gives the following result: the vowel-symbol *a*, 134 occurrences; all other vowel-symbols combined, 132 occurrences.

In a closed penultimate syllable (*e.g.* in *tinggal*) it has much the same value as in an open syllable (see (*a*) iii. *a*. above).

In a closed final syllable unstressed (*e.g.* in *sakit*) it tends to be shorter, though never quite as short as in the English word *kit*.

When the closed final syllable is stressed (*e.g.* in *jěrit*, see footnote 1*b*, page xii) it is a little longer.

e : this vowel has its continental value, varying from the *é* of the French word *café* to the open *e* of the English word *get*.

It is always a pure vowel, not a diphthong, *i.e.* it NEVER has the double sound of the *a* in 'cake' (= *é* + *ee*).

(*c*) The letters *u* and *o*

As with *e* and *i* above, these two vowel-symbols are treated together because they are sometimes interchanged; *e.g.* the word *rumah* is pronounced *romah* in I. 91, and *pokok* is pronounced *pukuk* in I. 87; *boleh* in I. 87 has the *u* sound, in I. 82 it has the *o* sound.

The *u* and the *i* tend to be heard in the north, the *o* and the *e* in the south of the Peninsula.

u : this sound presents no difficulty.

In an open syllable (*e.g.* in *bukan*) it is like the *oo* of 'boot', but with lips well-rounded and pushed forward.

In a closed penultimate syllable (*e.g.* in *tumpang*) it has much the same sound as in an open syllable (See (*a*) iii. *a*. above).

In a final closed syllable (*e.g.* in *ikut*) it has a shorter sound, but it is seldom quite as short as the *oo* in 'foot'.

The Malay *u* is never like the English vowel in 'but'; it is the Malay *a* that sometimes gives that sound (See (*a*) iii. *b*. above).

The Malay *u* is never like the English vowel in

'cute'; in Malay that double sound is represented by *iu* as in *siul*.

o : this vowel has its continental, not its English, value.

It may be half-open, almost as in 'hot', or close as in French '*eau*' but it is always a pure vowel, not a diphthong, *i.e.* it NEVER has the double sound of the *o* in 'coke' (= *o* + *oo*). Once again, as with open *a* and open *e*, it is the northern English, or the Welsh, not the southern English sound that will help you. Learn to say 'Don't put the cake in your bag' with a South Wales accent, and you will be saved from 'cat' and 'cart' and 'cake' and 'coke', which are all non-Malay vowels.

In a final syllable closed by the nasal consonant *ng* (*e.g.* in *kampong*) the vowel itself tends to be nasalized as well, *i.e.* it rhymes with French '*long*' rather than English 'long'.

(*d*) The neutral vowel, marked *ĕ* (called *pĕpĕt* in Malay)

This is the indeterminate sound which is heard in the unaccented first syllables of such words as 'catastrophe', and 'parabola', that is to say it is without quality of its own, but it serves to keep the consonants apart.[1]

This symbol never occurs in the final syllable of a Malay word; the word *pĕpĕt* itself, with a neutral vowel in the final syllable, is Javanese.

In an open syllable, when the following sound is *r* or *l* the *pĕpĕt* sound is reduced to a minimum, and at times disappears altogether, *e.g.* in *k(ĕ)reta* in line 69, *b(ĕ)lakang* in line 73, and *k(ĕ)lapa* in line 77 (but on the other hand, in *tĕrok* in IV. 59, and *tĕrus* in VIII. 37 the first syllable carries almost as much weight as the second).

When the next syllable begins with any other consonant than *l* or *r* the *pĕpĕt* syllable, though not taking the stress, is usually as deliberate in pronunciation as the final syllable, *e.g.* in *tĕngah* (I. 25), *kĕjap* (I. 69), *dĕngan*

[1] In I. 81 the *pĕpĕt* has a dialect pronunciation, *a*.

(I. 73), *sĕdap* (I. 82), *pĕdas* (II. 109), *pĕnoh* (III. 25), *pĕsan* (VI. 57), *gĕnap* (VI. 85), etc.

When the penultimate *pĕpĕt* syllable is closed, the two syllables are always evenly stressed, *e.g.* in (*tĕr*)*hĕmpas* (IV. 36), and *bĕntang* (V. 75).

Note.

i. When the closing consonant is *r* the pronunciation is more often -*rĕ*- than -*ĕr*-, *e.g.* *krĕbau* rather than *kĕrbau*, but this merely represents *kĕrĕbau* (which would be a more accurate romanization) with the *pĕpĕt* that comes before the *r* reduced to a minimum.

ii. In the word *pĕrgi* the *r* is usually omitted in speech.

iii. The prefix *bĕr-*, is frequently reduced to *b-*.

iv. As an initial syllable the *pĕpĕt* sound is scarcely to be heard at all, *e.g.* (*ĕ*)*mbun* (III. 12), and (*ĕ*)*mak* (I. 26).

(*e*) The final diphthong -*au*

This is merely a combination of the sounds *a* and *u*, resulting in the same diphthong as is heard in the English word 'now'.

(But note that when the two letters come together in the middle of a word the two sounds are pronounced separately, producing a dissyllable, *e.g.* *daun* (VI. 36) = *da* + *oon*.)

(*f*) The final diphthong -*ai*

This is a combination of the sounds *a* and *i*, resulting in the same diphthong as is heard in the English word 'fine'.

(But note that when the two letters come together in the middle of a word the two sounds are pronounced separately, producing a dissyllable, *e.g.* *lain* (VI. 7) = *la* + *een*.)

THE CONSONANTS

Roughly speaking, the consonants have the same values as in English, but there are some points of difference to be noted.

1. *c*, *q*, *v* and *x* are not used.

2. *f*, *kh* and *z* occur only in words of Arabic origin. In speech, *f* is usually changed to *p* (*e.g.* in *fasal* I. 9), and *kh* is frequently changed to *k* (*e.g.* in *khabar* I. 57 and *khemah* V. 19, by two different speakers. But a third speaker, in *khabar* I. 47, gives it the Arabic scraped sound like the *ch* in 'loch'.).

3. *k* at the end of a word is pronounced (in the Malay Peninsula) as a glottal stop, *i.e.* the vowel in front of it is cut off abruptly by a closing of the windpipe, and no click is heard for the *k* (*e.g.* *ĕmak* I. 7 and *dudok* I. 73).

   In some words this sudden check is denoted by an apostrophe (*e.g.* *ta'* I. 3, and *Che'* I. 47).

   As an initial or medial consonant *k* is not aspirated. (See 10 and 11 below.)

4. *g* is always hard, as in 'go'; it never has the *j* sound, as in 'gentle' (*e.g.* *pĕrgi* I. 21).

5. *ng* is a *single* sound, the sound heard in 'singer'.

   Warning. Do not be tempted to pronounce a *g* after the *ng* unless it is *there in print*. The English word 'finger', if spelt Malay fashion, would be 'fingger'. Listen carefully to the following words in Scene I: *ingat* I. 3, *dĕngan* I. 7, *tengok* I. 8, *jangan* I. 11, *mĕngapa* I. 17. Then compare them with *tinggal* I. 7, the only *ngg* in the same fourteen lines.

6. *s*, in all positions, is always hissed, as in 'sat'; it never has the *z* sound, as in 'has' (*e.g.* *masa* I. 6, *sakit* I. 9).

   Note. A final *s* is sometimes pronounced like an *h*, and the quality of the preceding vowel is slightly changed in consequence, *e.g.* in *kupas* II. 39, and *lĕpas* II. 89.

7. *h*, as an initial letter, is sometimes scarcely heard at all,[1] *e.g.* in *hari* I. 5 and IV. 44, and (*tĕr*)*hĕmpas* IV. 36.

   As a medial letter, *h* is scarcely heard if it comes between two unlike vowels, *e.g.* in *tahu* I. 90. But when

---

[1] In some Arabic words, *e.g.* *hal* I. 90 and III. 38, the *h* is never dropped in Malay pronunciation because it transliterates a different *h* in the Arabic alphabet.

it comes between two like vowels (mostly two *a*'s) it is clearly heard,[1] *e.g.* in *tahan* III. 42.

As a final, *h* is sometimes clearly pronounced (*e.g.* in *Rah* I. 3, *-lah* I. 69, *sireh* I. 90), but often it is not heard at all, particularly in the enclitic particles *-lah* and *-kah*. When this happens, the unprotected *a* is often reduced to the neutral *pĕpĕt* sound.

Note. *h* is the only final consonant which effects a liaison with a following initial vowel, *e.g.* the pronunciation of such a phrase as *buah itu* gives the impression that the second word is *hitu*.

8. *l.* The Malay *l* is never like the English final *l* (*e.g.* in 'all', 'until'), which is a 'dark' sort of sound, with much *u* in it. The Malay *l* is nearer to the English initial *l* (and medial) in 'little', 'lenient', with a suspicion of *i* in it. The tongue is more spread as it presses against the palate so that more air is squeezed out on either side of it.

Note. In some words a final *l* following an *i* is habitually pronounced as a glottal stop, *i.e.* as if it were written *k*, *e.g.* *mĕngambil* I. 69, and *kĕchil* IV. 10. (In the north of the Peninsula a final *l* following *a* or *u* becomes *i*, and combines with the preceding vowel to form a diphthong.)

9. *r.* This letter varies considerably. In these records the general pronunciation is the uvular (*i.e.* the throat) *r* (I.P.A. R), but the rolled *r* is used by many speakers.

In the south, final *r* is sometimes not heard (*e.g.* *gambir* and *kapor* I. 91).

10. *p* and *t.* These letters, like the other two voiceless plosives *k* and *ch*, are not aspirated as are the corresponding English sounds. Note how much 'gentler'

---

[1] There are several three-syllabled words, with *h* as second consonant, which are habitually reduced to two syllables, so that the *h* is cut out in speech : *sahaya* is now usually written as well as pronounced *saya*, *sahaja* is pronounced *saja*, *dahulu* is usually *dulu*, and *baharu* usually *baru* (but *not* with the stress on the last syllable as is heard so often, incorrectly, in the place-names *Kota Bharu* and *Johore Bahru*).

the Malay word *kata* sounds than the same two syllables in the English word 'catapult'.

As finals, *p* and *t* are not exploded,[1] or else are exploded so lightly that the explosion is audible only to the speaker himself. Contrast the final sound in *kĕjap* I. 69 with the final sound in the English word 'cup', and the final sound of *Ingat* I. 9 with the final sound of English 'hat'.

Note. Since a final *t* is not exploded, it does not make a liaison with a following initial vowel or *h*. Indeed, the contrary is the case, for instead of reaching forward to the vowel it jerks back and becomes almost a glottal stop, *e.g.* in *saki(t) hati* I. 9.

11. *ch* and *j*. These two sounds are not quite the same as the English sounds in 'chain' and 'Jane'. They lack the slight movement of friction (a suspicion of *sh*) that follows the plosives in the English words. Contrast the initial sounds of *chĕritakan* I. 89 and of 'cherry', of *jangan* I. 11 and 'jungle', and the medial sounds of *kĕchil* V. 10 and 'kitchen', *tunjok* I. 92 and 'injure'.

The above notes have given only the outstanding differences between Malay and English sounds. There are many other minor differences, and, as has been said, there are wide divergences in dialect pronunciation, but if you imitate closely the pronunciation of, say, 'Che' Mahmud', you will be understood in any part of the Malay Peninsula.

The chief points to remember are the following:

1. Pure vowels for *e* and *o*; northern English *a*.
2. Unaspirated voiceless plosives (*i.e.* no *h*-sound after *p*, *t*, *k*, *ch*).
3. Unexploded final plosives *p* and *t*.
4. Light stress, usually on the open vowel of a penultimate syllable.

---

[1] An unexploded final *t* is heard in English in such phrases as 'at the', 'I don't know', where the tongue makes contact with the palate (for the *t*) but does not click away from it before going on to the next sound. In the same way, the tongue must make contact with the palate for the Malay final *t*. Merely to 'leave it out' will not do.

Finally, speak smoothly and evenly. Malays usually converse in gently undulating tones that accord well with one of their many proverbs enjoining moderation in all things:

> *Biar tĕrlĕtak, jangan tĕrhĕmpas.*
> Lay a thing down, never fling it down.

Intonation

The difference in intonation between English and Malay is of first importance, but it is too complicated a subject to be treated briefly. Listen, and imitate, and where possible make a record of differences noted; such for instance as the 'up–down' ending (preceded by a run of monotone syllables) which is so frequently heard, *e.g.* in *boleh* I. 62, *ini* I. 81, *Pinang* I. 87, *kasut* II. 14, *dapor* II. 45, *dudok* II. 51, *Martin* II. 71, *api* II. 72, *balek* II. 89, etc.

Indonesian Romanization

This differs in the following respects from the romanization of the Malay Peninsula:

1. Hyphens are not used before the enclitic words *-lah*, *-kah* and *-nya*; nor after the proclitic words *di-*, *ka-* and *sa-* (the two last being spelt *ke* and *se*).
2. The *pĕpĕt* vowel is not marked, but the *e* vowel is usually indicated by an acute accent or a length-mark.
3. *ch* becomes *tj*, and *j* becomes *dj* (*e.g. macham* is written *matjam*, and *jangan* is written *djangan*).
4. *y* becomes *j* (*e.g. yang* is written *jang*).
5. *kh* becomes *ch* (*e.g. khabar* is written *chabar*).
6. *sh* becomes *sj* (*e.g. mĕshuarat* is written *mĕsjuarat*).

The Scenes

In the matter of type and arrangement all considerations have been subordinated to the main objective, namely, that the spoken word should jump to the eye. Since bold type demands liberal spacing, it will be found that in a few of the longer speeches the italic lines of the literal translation and the roman lines of the free translation run away from their Malay originals.

It is hoped that where this occurs the reader will find the necessary clues in the full stops and the proper names.

Names of speakers have all been reduced to their first three letters in order to preserve the alignment.

It will be noted that the word-for-word method is not strictly adhered to in the literal translation when it is not considered to be helpful. For instance, English adjectives are put before their nouns once the point has been made that Malay adjectives follow their nouns. Such transpositions are indicated, in the earlier pages, by a hyphen between the transposed words. Commas are used freely to indicate thought-breaks, without which much of the literal translation is apt to become nonsense.

The Notes, Stock, and Sentence Patterns

It is the spoken word that is the subject of this teaching course. There may be some readers who will prefer to rely entirely on repetition and imitation of what they hear on the records, accepting the two translations, literal and free, as sufficient elucidation. But there are others who will feel happier if they are able to break down what they hear and to satisfy themselves that they understand the shape of the sentences spoken. It is for such students that the Notes have been written. In them an attempt has been made to deduce the grammatical principles which underlie the language; to hold up a mirror, as it were, in which the student may watch the language at work.

The material thus gathered is sorted and re-presented in tabular form in 'Taking Stock'.

Finally, sentences which are examples of commonly-recurrent constructions are used as models for variations on the same basic pattern.

It is hoped that this threefold presentation of the same material may enable the student to acquire a fairly wide range of idiomatic constructions without undue drudgery.

The Setting

The following paragraph introduces you to the Malay family around whom the Scenes are centred. At this stage, read only the free translation given below, and come back to the Malay

paragraph after you have finished studying all the Scenes. By
that time you will have formed some idea of the difference
between spoken and written Malay from the notes on the 'stage-
directions' (which are in written Malay), and from points which
you will have gleaned when consulting the vocabulary.

KETĚRANGAN

Che' Mahmud sa-orang Mělayu dudok di-Kuala Lumpur,
ia-itu sa-orang yang boleh di-katakan běrada juga. Pada masa
Kěmahkotaan dalam tahun 1953 ia tělah pěrgi ka-London
běrsama-sama děngan istěri-nya Che' Normah sěrta anak pěrěm-
puan-nya Zaharah. Zaharah itu běrumor sa-puloh tahun.
Di-London měreka běrkěnal-kěnal děngan Mr. Martin dan tělah
diam di-rumah-nya sa-lama tiga hari. Mr. Martin ada běranak
sa-orang nama-nya Peter. Peter itu tělah běrkawan baik děngan
Zaharah walau pun hanya tiga hari běrmain sama-sama. Lima
bulan sa-tělah balek dari London itu Che' Mahmud tělah měně-
rima surat daripada Mr. Martin měngatakan ia tělah měndapat
kěrja dalam sa-buah sharikat běsar di-Tanah Mělayu dan akan
sampai ka-Kuala Lumpur dalam tempoh sa-bulan. Pada masa
měnulis surat itu ia sibok bělajar bahasa Mělayu děngan těkun-
nya pada tiap-tiap hari. Guru-nya sa-orang pěnuntut Mělayu
dari Ipoh. Dan lagi ia měngatakan ia akan tiba děngan kapal
těrbang dan juga ia tělah di-tětapkan tinggal di-sa-buah hotel
sěměntara bělum měndapat rumah. Dalam tiga ěmpat hari
sa-bělum mula běkěrja ia minta Che' Mahmud měnunjokkan
kapada-nya apa-apa yang patut di-kětahui-nya běrkěnaan
děngan hal orang Mělayu. Che' Mahmud tělah měnjawab
surat itu měngatakan ia běrsětuju měnunaikan pěrmintaan-nya
itu.

Translation

Che' Mahmud is a fairly prosperous Malay who lives in
Kuala Lumpur. At the time of the Coronation, in 1953, he
went to London with his wife Che' Normah and his daughter
Zaharah, who is ten years old. In London they became friendly
with Mr. Martin and stayed three days at his house. Mr.
Martin has a son called Peter. Peter and Zaharah became great

friends, although it was only for three days that they played together.   When they had been back from London five months, Che' Mahmud received a letter from Mr. Martin saying that he had got a job with a firm in Malaya and would be arriving in Kuala Lumpur in about a month's time.   At the time of writing he was having Malay lessons every day and working very hard at the language.   His teacher was a Malay student from Ipoh. He said, too, that he would be arriving by air and that arrangements had been made for him to stay at an hotel until he could get a house.   He asked Che' Mahmud if he would show him the various things that he ought to know something about, in connection with Malay life, during the few days before he began work. Che' Mahmud answered the letter, saying that he would willingly comply with his request.

SCENE I

DI-PADANG KAPAL TĔRBANG

AT THE AIRPORT

Pada hari Mr. Martin akan tiba, Che' Mahmud dudok bĕrbual-bual anak-
bĕranak.

*On day Mr. Martin going-to-arrive, Che' Mahmud sits chat-chatting parents-and-
child.*

On the day on which Mr. Martin is to arrive, Che' Mahmud is sitting
chatting with his wife and daughter.

MAH. **Rah ingat ta' Peter?**
Rah remembers, (or) not, Peter?
Do you remember Peter, Rah?

ZAH. **Peter mana, abah?**
Peter which, daddy?
Which Peter, daddy?

MAH. **Peter anak Mr. Martin. Kita dudok di-rumah dia**
Peter, child of-Mr. Martin. We live at-house of-him three days,
Mr. Martin's little boy. We stayed with them for three

tiga hari masa kita di-London hari itu.
time we in-London, days those.
days when we were in London.

NOR. **Rah tinggal dĕngan dia masa abah dĕngan ĕmak**
Rah stay with him, time father with mother go see Coronation that.
You stayed at home with him while daddy and I went to

pĕrgi tengok Coronation itu.
see Coronation that.
see the Coronation.

ZAH. **O, Peter itu. Ingat. 'Tapi Rah sakit hati fasal ta'**
Oh, Peter that. Remember. But Rah sore of-heart about not-go
Oh, that Peter. Yes, I remember him. But I'm sad to

pĕrgi tengok Coronation itu.
see Coronation that.
think that I didn't go and see the Coronation.

MAH. **Jangan-lah**[1] **macham itu. Bukan-kah**[1] **Peter pun**[1]
Don't like that. Is-it-not Peter remain also? More-still, Rah,
You mustn't talk like that! Peter stayed at home too,

---

[1] The particles *-lah*, *-kah*, and *pun* are explained in the notes.

I

12 **tinggal juga? Lagi pun Rah bukan ta' tengok**
not-the-case not-see in television.
didn't he? Besides, you *did* see it on television.

13 **dalam T.V.**

14 NOR. **Tengok dalam T.V. lagi sĕronok. Dapat tengok**
See in television more enjoyable. Able see all. Mother with
It was better, seeing it on television. You could see it all.

15 **sĕmua. Ĕmak dĕngan abah dapat tengok pĕrara-**
father able see procession only.
Daddy and I only managed to see the procession.

16 **kan sahaja.**

17 ZAH. **Mĕngapa abah tanya Rah ingat-kah tidak Peter itu?**
Why father ask Rah remember (or) not Peter that?
Why did you ask me whether I remembered Peter, daddy?

18 MAH. **Abah dia 'nak tiba hari ini.**
Father of-him going-to arrive day this.
His daddy is coming to-day.

19 ZAH. **Ka-Kuala Lumpur? Dia dudok di-rumah kita?**
To-Kuala Lumpur? He live in-house of-us?
To Kuala Lumpur? Is he going to stay with us?

20 MAH. **Ka-sini-lah. 'Tapi dia tidak dudok di-rumah kita.**
To-here. But he not live in-house of-us. He live at-hotel. Rah
Yes, he's coming here. But he won't be staying with us.

21 **Dia dudok di-hotel. Rah hĕndak ta' pĕrgi sambut**
want, (or) not, go receive him evening this?
He will stay at an hotel. Would you like to go and meet

22 **dia pĕtang ini?**
him this afternoon?

23 ZAH. **Hĕndak. Dĕngan apa dia datang?**
Want. With what he come?
Yes, I should. How is he coming?

24 MAH. **Dĕngan kapal tĕrbang. Kapal tĕrbang itu tiba**
With ship-flying. Ship-flying that, arrive strike four. Strike
By air. The plane gets in at four o'clock. At half-past

25 **pukul ĕmpat. Pukul tiga sa-tĕngah Rah siap-lah**
three-one-half, Rah make-ready with mother-in-question, able we
three, you get ready with your mother and we'll go to the

děngan ěmak-nya, boleh kita pěrgi ka-padang kapal
go to field of-ship-flying.
airport.
těrbang.

Měreka anak-běranak sampai ka-padang kapal těrbang pada pukul ěmpat pětang. Tiada běrapa lama lěpas itu nampak-lah sa-buah kapal těrbang běsar datang běrkěliling hěndak turun. Zaharah tiada lěpas mata-nya daripada měmandang kapal těrbang itu. Nyata běnar ia běrasa suka hati. Kapal těrbang itu běransor sa-makin rěndah.
They child-and-parents arrive to-field of flying-ship at strike four, afternoon. There-is-not so-much length-of-time after that, there is seen one-unit flying-ship large, come circling going-to come-down. Zaharah not let-go eyes-of-her from watching the flying-ship. Clear, truly, she feels joyful of-heart. The flying-ship gradually more-and-more low.

They arrive at the airport at 4 p.m. Soon afterwards, a large aeroplane appears and circles round, preparing to land. Zaharah keeps her eyes fixed on it. It is easy to see that she is delighted. The plane gradually comes lower and lower.

ZAH. **Itu dia agak-nya kapal těrbang-nya abah, 'dah turun.**
That (is) it, the guess-of-it, (the) flying-ship-in-the-case, father,
There's the plane, isn't it, daddy, coming down.
has-become descending.

MAH. **Agak-nya itu-lah dia.**
The guess-of-it, that, indeed, (is) it.
Yes, that's it, I think.

ZAH. **O. Běsar-nya kapal těrbang itu! Ěmpat kipas-nya.**
Oh. The bigness of-it, that flying-ship. Four (the) fans of-it.
Oo! What a big plane! It's got four propellers.

MAH. **Memang-lah, kapal těrbang dari England.**
Naturally, flying-ship from England.
Of course it has. It has come all the way from England.

Kapal těrbang itu sudah běrhěnti bětul.
The flying-ship has stopped truly.
The plane comes to a standstill.

ZAH. **Boleh kita pěrgi děkat 'bah?**
Able we go near, father?
Can we go up to it, daddy?

MAH. **Ta' boleh. Kita nanti-lah sahaja di-sini.**
Not able. We wait only at-here.
No, no. We'll just wait here.

40 NOR. **Orang 'dah turun 'dah. Mana dia Mr. Martin?**
People having got-down (is) completed. Which (is) he, Mr.
The passengers have all got out. Which is Mr. Martin?
Martin?

41 ZAH. **Ha! Itu dia, yang běrtopi kělabu itu.**
Ah! That (is) he, (one) who (is) be-hatted grey, the.
Ah! There he is! The one with the grey hat.

42 MAH. **Ia. Itu-lah dia Mr. Martin. Choba kita lambai,**
Yes. That-indeed (is) he, Mr. Martin. Try we wave, allow-
Yes. That's Mr. Martin. Let's wave, so that he'll see us.

43 **biar dia nampak kita.**
that he see us.

44 NOR. **Ta' měmandang dia. Jangan-jangan pěning lagi.**
Not directing-his-eyes-this-way, he. May-it may-it not (be),
He isn't looking this way. I hope he isn't feeling airsick still.
dizziness still.

45   Mr. Martin sampai ka-těmpat měreka měnanti.
      Mr. Martin arrives to-place of-them-waiting.
      Mr. Martin reaches the spot where they are waiting.

46 MAH. **Hullo, Mr. Martin!**
Hullo, Mr. Martin!

47 MAR. **Hullo! Apa khabar Che' Mahmud? Che' Normah**
Hullo! What (is the) news (of) Che' Mahmud? Che' Normah,
Hullo! How are you, Che' Mahmud? And Che'

48 **apa khabar? Zaharah pun ada juga!**
what news? Zaharah is-present too!
Normah? And Zaharah's here too!

49 ZAH. **Chakap Mělayu pula! Dahulu ta' pandai.**
Speech Malay if-you-please! Before, not skilled.
He's talking Malay! He couldn't when we last saw him.

50 MAR. **Ia. Saya 'nak bělajar chakap Mělayu. Mahu-kah**
Yes. I want learn Malay speech. Willing Zaharah teach me?
Yes. I want to learn to speak Malay. Will you teach me,

51 **Zaharah ajar saya?**
Zaharah?

52 ZAH. **Mahu. 'Tapi Rah ta' pandai.**
Willing. But Rah not skilled.
Yes, I will. But I'm not very clever.

MAR. **Ini bĕtul-bĕtul, Che' Mahmud, bukan main-main.**
This (is) true-true, Che' Mahmud, not play-play. With Che'
I really mean it, Che' Mahmud. I'm not joking. I want
Dĕngan Che' Mahmud saya mahu bĕrchakap Mĕlayu
Mahmud I wish speak Malay only. Can?
to talk only Malay with you. May I?
sahaja. Boleh-kah?

MAH. **Boleh. Saya lagi suka. Normah pun suka, bukan?**
Can. I more pleased. Normah, too, pleased, is-it-not-so?
By all means. I shall be delighted. And so will you,
Normah, won't you?

NOR. **Tĕntu-lah. Apa khabar Mrs. Martin dĕngan Peter?**
Sure. What news Mrs. Martin with Peter?
Yes, of course. How is Mrs. Martin, and Peter?

MAR. **Khabar baik. Tĕrima kaseh. Dia dĕngan Peter ta'**
(The) news (is) good. Received favour. She with Peter not
Quite well, thank you. She and Peter weren't able to
dapat datang sa-kali dĕngan saya.
manage come one-time with me.
come with me.

ZAH. **Peter pun 'nak datang juga? Bila?**
Peter going-to come too? When?
Peter is coming too? When?

MAR. **Ia. Tiga bulan lagi. Bila saya dapat rumah.**
Yes. Three months still. When I succeed-in-getting house.
Yes. In three months' time. When I can get a house.

ZAH. **Dudok di-rumah Rah pun boleh.**
Live at-house of-Rah can.
You could stay with us.

MAH. **Barang-barang Mr. Martin mana?**
Things of-Mr. Martin where?
Where is your baggage, Mr. Martin?

MAR. **O, ta' banyak. Ini sahaja. Bag satu lagi sudah saya**
Oh, not much. This only. Case one, still, there-has-been me-
Oh, I haven't much. Only this. My other suit-case I
suroh hantar ka-hotel. Barang-barang yang lain
bidding send to-hotel. Things which other, I send with sea-ship.
have told them to send to the hotel. I've sent the rest of

66   **saya hantar dĕngan kapal laut. Lambat sadikit**
Slow a-little the arrival-of-them. No-knowing, two three weeks
my baggage by sea.   It will take a good time to arrive.

67   **sampai-nya. Ĕntah dua tiga minggu lagi agak-nya.**
still, the guess of-it.
Another two or three weeks, perhaps.

68 MAH.   **Kalau macham itu mari-lah kita pĕrgi ka-hotel.**
If like that, come we go to hotel. Wait at-here one eye-flick. I
In that case, let's go to the hotel.   Wait here a moment,

69   **Nanti-lah di-sini sa-kĕjap. Saya 'ndak mĕngambil**
going-to fetch car.
I'll get the car.

70   **kĕreta.**

71   Che' Mahmud sudah datang dĕngan kĕreta.
        Che' Mahmud has come with car.
        Che' Mahmud arrives with the car.

72 ZAH.   **Abah 'dah datang. Mari kita naik kĕreta.**
Father has come. Come we mount car.
Daddy has come.   Let's get in.

73 NOR.   **Rah mari dudok di-bĕlakang dĕngan ĕmak, biar Mr.**
Rah come-here sit at-back with mother, allow-that Mr. Martin
Come and sit in the back with me, Rah, so that Mr. Martin

74   **Martin dudok dĕpan.**
sit front.
can sit in the front.

75   Di-dalam kĕreta mĕnuju ka-hotel.   Mr. Martin mĕnunjok pokok
76   kĕlapa.
        In-interior of-car going-in-the-direction to-hotel. Mr. Martin points-to
        tree, coconut.
        In the car, on the way to the hotel.   Mr. Martin points to a coconut
        palm.

77 MAR.   **Itu-kah pokok kĕlapa?**
That (is) tree, coconut?
Is *that* a coconut palm?

78 NOR.   **Itu-lah dia. Ingat ta' lagi kita bĕrchakap fasal**
That, right enough, (is) it. Remember, (or) not still, we talk
Yes, that's a coconut palm.   Do you remember us talking

kĕlapa muda?
about coconuts, young?
about young coconuts?

MAR. **Ingat. Bila kita boleh makan kĕlapa muda?**
Remember. When we able eat coconuts, young?
Yes, I do. When can we have some to eat?

NOR. **Bila-bila pun boleh. Pĕtang ini pun boleh.**
When-when, can. Evening this, can.
Whenever you wish. This evening, if you like.

ZAH. **Kĕlapa muda sĕdap, ia mak?**
Coconut young, nice, yes, mother?
A young coconut is delicious, isn't it, mummy?

Mr. Martin mĕnunjok kapada sa-batang pokok pinang.
Mr. Martin points to one-trunk (of) tree, betel.
Mr. Martin points to a betel-nut palm.

MAR. **Pokok kĕlapa itu kĕchil pula.**
Tree, coconut, that, (is) small, strange-to-say.
That coconut palm is quite small.

ZAH. **Itu bukan kĕlapa. Pinang.**
That (is) not-coconut. Betel.
That's not a coconut. It's a betel-nut palm.

MAR. **Penang? Saya ingat Penang nama tĕmpat.**
Penang? I think Penang name of-place.
Penang? I thought Penang was the name of a place?

ZAH. **Itu bĕtul-lah, Pulau Pinang. Ini pokok pinang.**
That (is) correct, indeed. Island, Betel. This (is) tree, betel.
So it is. Betel-nut Island. This is the betel-nut tree.
Buah dia orang makan dĕngan sireh.
Fruit of-it people eat with sireh.
People eat the nut with the sireh-vine.

MAH. **Esok-lah baharu Rah chĕritakan itu sĕmua. Mana-**
To-morrow newly Rah relate that all. How Mr. Martin going-to
Wait till to-morrow to tell him all about that. How
lah Mr. Martin 'nak tahu hal sireh, pinang, gambir,
know affair of-sireh, betel, gambier, lime, all? To-morrow
should Mr. Martin know about sireh, and betel-nut, and

B

91　**kapor, sěmua?　Esok pagi di-rumah kita boleh-lah**
morning at-house of-us able Rah show to him things those.
gambier, and lime and all that?　To-morrow morning

92　**Rah tunjok kapada dia barang-barang itu.**
you can show him all those things, at home.

93　　　Sudah sampai ka-hotel.
　　　Has-been arrival to hotel.
　　　They arrive at the hotel.

94　**Ini-lah dia hotel-nya.　Biar saya sěmua balek.　Pagi**
This (is) it, (the) hotel in-the-case.　Allow-that we all go-back.
This is the hotel.　We'll go home now.　To-morrow

95　**esok saya datang jěmput Mr. Martin.**
Morning, to-morrow, I come invite-to-accompany Mr. Martin.
morning I'll come and call for you.

96　MAR.　**Baik-lah　Che' Mahmud.　Banyak-banyak těrima**
Good, Che' Mahmud.　Much-much received favour.
Very well, Che' Mahmud.　Thank you very much.

97　**kaseh.**

98　　　Ch' Mahmud anak-běranak pun balek ka-rumah.
　　　Che' Mahmud child-and-parent return to-house.
　　　Che' Mahmud and his wife and daughter go home.

SCENE I : NOTES

1 itu : note that in Malay the adjective follows the noun.　Demonstrative adjectives (*ini*, 'this'; *itu*, 'that' or 'the') come *after* any descriptive adjectives, *e.g. kělabu*, 'grey'; *topi*, 'hat'; *topi kělabu itu*, 'that grey hat'.　So, here, 'the Mr.-Martin-about-to-arrive day'.

Che' : short for *ěnche'*, which is the correct form of address to any Malay, man or woman, who has no distinctive title.

běrbual-bual : you will constantly be meeting the prefix *běr-*, which has many shades of meaning.　The root-word *bual* merely gives the idea of 'bubbling up'.　The *běr-* here gives it a definitely verbal force: 'They were chatting.'

　　The duplication of the root gives an impression of variety and repetition: 'They were chatting about this and that.'

anak-běranak : an idiomatic expression (*anak* = 'child') indicating the presence of the two generations; *tiga běranak* is the expression used for two parents and one child, or for one parent and two children, *ĕmpat bĕrchuchu* (*chuchu* = 'grandchild') might be one grandparent, two parents and one grandchild, or any other three-generation group of four. The context will always make clear the composition of the particular group in question.

3 Rah: short for *Zaharah*. When a Malay name is abbreviated it is usually the last syllable, not the first, that is retained.

ta': short for *tidak*, 'not'. This alternative-question form of sentence is very common in colloquial Malay. It does not imply impatience, as in the English, 'Do you remember, or do you not?' See Sentence Pattern 3.

4 abah: a word often used by children in addressing their father. The 3rd person word is *bapa* (or, more formally, *ayah*), e.g. *Bapa saya bĕlum balek*, 'My father hasn't come home yet.'

5 Kita dudok . . . : 'We stayed . . .' Note that the Malay verb does not change to indicate past tense. That must be gleaned from the context. Sometimes an adverbial phrase gives the clue. See Note 6 below (*hari itu*).

rumah dia: 'his house', *lit.* 'the house of him'. Similarly, *rumah Husain*, 'Husain's house'. When a noun or pronoun is placed after a noun it belongs to that noun, either indicating possession (*genitive*), as here, or defining or describing the first noun in some way, e.g. *pokok*, 'plant', 'tree'; *pinang*, 'betel-nut'; *pokok pinang*, 'betel-nut palm'.

6 masa kita di-London: for 'when', meaning 'during the time when', Malay uses a time-noun (*masa, hari,* etc.) followed by a descriptive noun-phrase. See Sentence Pattern 2.

hari itu: *lit.* 'that day'; sometimes to be translated 'the other day', 'recently', but often, as here, merely an indication of past time.

7 abah dĕngan ĕmak: between two closely associated words *dĕngan* ('with') is used, rather than *dan* ('and') e.g. *kalam dĕngan dawat*, 'pen and ink'.

abah: note the use of a noun of relationship instead of a personal pronoun. 1st and 2nd person pronouns are much less used in Malay than in English.

9 ingat: 'Yes, I remember.' The commonest way of answering a question in the affirmative is to repeat the relevant word. So, *Ahmad suka makan pisang?* 'Do you like bananas, Ahmad?'— *Suka*, 'Yes', or *Ta' suka*, 'No'. Note the omission of the subject pronoun when the context makes it unnecessary.

'tapi: short for *tĕtapi*.

Rah sakit hati: note that the child uses her own name and speaks of herself in the 3rd person in speaking to an adult. When she is playing with other children she will call herself *aku*, a 'familiar' 1st person pronoun.

Note, too, that there is no copula in Malay. A subject noun or pronoun is followed immediately by its predicative adjective or noun, without any intervening 'verb to-be'. With a 3rd person subject you are usually warned by the demonstrative adjective *itu* (or *ini*) separating subject from predicate: *Rumah itu běsar*; 'The house (is) big.' Remember that *rumah běsar itu* means 'that big house' and is *not* a statement.

sakit hati: usually 'annoyed', 'vexed', but neither word is quite suitable to this context, a sign that an English child would have expressed the same thought in some different fashion.

11 **Jangan-lah**: 'Don't.' The enclitic particle *-lah* sometimes adds emphasis, but after a command or a prohibition, as here, the effect is to moderate rather than to emphasize: it makes the 'order' sound less brusque.

bukan-kah: *-kah* is an interrogative particle. It is frequently omitted, as in line 1 above.

bukan: there are two negatives in Malay, *tidak* and *bukan*. They have different functions. *Tidak* (or *ta'*, and in writing sometimes *tiada*, in speech *ta'da*) is a straightforward negative merely stating that something is not so. *Bukan*, in a statement, has a hint of contradiction, a correction of some erroneous impression which is in the air, even if it has not actually been stated. But in a question, as here, it is equivalent to the English 'is it not?', *i.e.* it invites the hearer to agree.

Peter pun tinggal juga. Lagi pun: *pun* is a word of 'feeling' rather than of meaning. Hence it is often impossible to translate it by any one specific word. Its function is to light up the word that precedes it, usually in order to invite the hearer to turn his attention to it, and away from some earlier word, thus establishing a balance between them, as here between Zaharah and Peter. When the pattern is 'noun + *pun*' followed by 'verb (or adjective) + *juga*' the English translation is 'too', 'as well'. In *lagi pun*, 'moreover', *pun* implies that there is 'still' another point to catch your attention.

12 **bukan ta' tengok**: this is *bukan* with its contradictory sense (Note 11 above), cancelling the 'not-seeing' as an erroneous idea. When you come to Sentence Pattern V.2 you will find contrasting sentences illustrating the distinction between the two negatives. You will also find that there are occasions when either *bukan* or *tidak* may be used, not because there is no difference between them, but because the speaker's point of view is different.

Tengok dalam T.V.: Che' Normah brings these words to the beginning of the sentence in order to give them emphasis.

14 **Dapat tengok sĕmua:** note again the apparent omission of a subject pronoun. But it is more likely that, in such a sentence, a Malay has no specific 'viewer' in mind. Many Malay 'sentences' do not lend themselves to analysis on the lines of European grammatical structure; they consist rather of a sequence of noun-ideas set down side by side, as here, perhaps, 'There-was-the-possibility of-seeing-all.' Remember this as you go through the Scenes. It will help to fix for you the differences between Malay and English idiom.

15 **pĕrarakan:** 'procession'. This is a 'full-dress' noun, formed from the base-word *arak* by adding prefix *pĕ(r)-* and suffix *-an*. In this case the affixed form is much more common than the simple form, but in many words the simple form is sufficient, *e.g. kĕrja* or *pĕkĕrjaan*, 'work', *pĕrang* or *pĕpĕrangan*, 'warfare'.

The prefix *bĕr-* would turn the root into an intransitive verb *bĕrarak*, 'to go in procession'. See note on *bĕrbual* in line 1 above.

Malay affixes are of supreme importance in the study of the language. They do much of the work that is done in European languages by tense, voice and mood formations (none of which exist in Malay), as well as by prepositional phrases, but their uses cannot be reduced to hard-and-fast rules. The affixes will be dealt with as they occur in the text. To find a prefixed word in the vocabulary look up the root-word.

18 **'nak:** short for *hĕndak*.

20 **ka-sini-lah:** *-lah* often reassures, or confirms, rather than emphasizes, implying that something is turning out as you expected. Hence the 'Yes' in the translation. Cf. *Itu-lah dia* in lines 34 and 42 below.

26 **dĕngan ĕmak-nya:** *-nya* acts as the possessive (*genitive*) form of *dia*, and therefore can mean 'of him', 'of her', 'of it', 'of them'. But in this sentence the writer is using it in a more idiomatic way, meaning 'the mother of-the-case-in-question', 'the mother with whom you and I are concerned'. This use of *-nya* will become clearer to you as other examples occur. It is akin to the 'impersonal' use referred to in the note on *agak-nya* in line 34 below.

boleh kita pĕrgi . . .: *boleh*, 'able', 'can', is used thus in colloquial Malay to express a promised result in the immediate future, so that it is often the equivalent, in speech, of a formal purpose clause beginning with *supaya*, 'in order that we may . . .'. See Sentence Pattern 5.

kita: this is the commonest use of this pronoun, *i.e.* to mean 'we', including the hearer. When the hearer is not included, the pronoun is *kami*.

28 Mĕreka : 'they', used only in writing. In speech *dia* or, more often, *dia orang*, is used. (There are also dialect forms *depa* and *dema*, contractions of *dia apa* and *dia sĕmua*.) The use and the meaning of personal pronouns vary considerably from place to place.

pada pukul ĕmpat : 'at four o'clock'; *pada*, not *di-*, is the correct preposition to use before words which are not place-words, but *di-* is commonly used in newspaper Malay before time-words also.

29 nampak-lah : *lit.* 'there comes into sight'. This is the correct use of this verb (literary form *tampak*), *i.e.* as an intransitive verb of state meaning '*be* visible', but it is freely used also in modern Malay as a transitive verb meaning 'to see', as in line 43 below.

   -lah : this is another use of the particle *-lah*, to indicate the predicate word of a sentence.

sa-buah : *lit.* 'one fruit of . . .'. There are about twenty classifiers, or 'numeral coefficients' of this sort in Malay (cf. 'one piecee coat' in pidgin English); *buah* is the coefficient used for all large things, *e.g. dua buah meja*, 'two tables'; *tiga buah rumah*, 'three houses'.

30 bĕrkĕliling : this word usually means 'around', 'encircling' (*i.e.* prepositional, with the *bĕr-* implying 'being in a state of . . .'), but it has come to be the word used for an aircraft circling round an airfield preparatory to landing : thus *bĕr-*, here, makes an intransitive verb as in *bĕrbual* in line 1 above. The word used for an aircraft circling in the sky, as in a display, is *bĕrlegar*.

daripada mĕmandang : the base-word is *pandang*, with the prefix *mĕ-*. This prefix has many functions. Here it creates a verbal-noun, 'from looking-at'.

   When *mĕ-* comes before a word which begins with either of the lip-consonants *b* or *p*, the lip-nasal *m* is inserted between prefix and root, and the lighter (or *voiceless*) consonant, *p*, drops out, whereas the heavier (or *voiced*) consonant, *b*, is retained. Thus *bacha*, 'read', becomes *mĕmbacha*, but *pukul*, 'strike', becomes '*mĕmukul*'.

31 ia : this is the written form of *dia*, when it is nominative (*i.e.* when it is the subject of a verb).

bĕrasa : = *bĕr- -rasa*, 'feels', from *rasa*, 'feeling', 'perception'. The *bĕr-* prefix turns the word into an intransitive verb as in *bĕrbual* above. So, *chakap*, 'speech'; *bĕrchakap*, 'talk', 'speak'. But the simple base-word is itself often used verbally in colloquial style.

33 itu dia: *lit.* 'That (is) it', the usual equivalent of English 'There it is'. See Sentence Pattern 7.

kapal těrbang-nya: the same use of -*nya* as in *ěmak-nya* in line 26 above, *i.e.* 'the aircraft in-the-case', 'the one we are expecting'.

'dah turun: *'dah* is short for *sudah*.

34 agak-nya: 'by the guess of it', a very common expression, corresponding to 'I should think' in English. So also, *rupa-nya*, 'apparently', 'by the look of it', where English uses the same impersonal form.

itu-lah dia: for the -*lah* see Note 20 above.

35 běsar-nya kapal těrbang itu: *lit.* 'the bigness of it, of that plane', a very common idiom. Note that *běsar* in this sentence is a noun. The divisions between parts of speech are less clearly defined in Malay than in English.

40 Orang 'dah turun 'dah: note the idiomatic repetition of *sudah*. The underlying meaning of the word is accomplishment, completion, not 'past-ness'. Here, the second *'dah* announces the completion of *orang 'dah turun*, 'the passengers have alighted'. Hence the 'all' in the translation.

41 yang běrtopi kělabu itu: *lit.* 'that-one (*i.e. itu*) who (is) be-hatted grey'; *běr-*, here, shows possession, 'having a hat'.

42 Choba kita lambai, biar dia 'nampak: another colloquial equivalent of the written conjunction *supaya*, 'in order that'. See Note 26 above, but *biar* is more definitely purposive than *boleh*. Compare Sentence Patterns 5 and 6.

44 ta' měmandang dia: here the pronoun-subject comes after the verb, an arrangement which is always permissible when there is no stress on the subject, but it must not be *separated* from the verb by any word or words, except for a few adverbs such as *lagi* and *baharu*. This point is dealt with in Note VIII.66.

měmandang: the *mě-* prefix is usual, even in speech, when the doer of the action is in the 3rd person.

Jangan-jangan: here, the duplication weakens, 'Let it not be that . . .', a mere suggestion. So, *běsar-běsar* usually means 'fairly big', not 'very big'. Only context will determine whether a duplication strengthens or weakens.

jangan: note that the word can be used 'sideways', a wishful prohibition as it were, not merely as a 'don't' directed straight towards the listener as in English, *e.g. Jangan ta' sěmpat kita ini 'karang;* 'I hope we shan't be too late!' (*lit.* 'Let-it-not-be-that not-sufficient-time this-we presently').

45 těmpat měreka měnanti: 'the place where they are waiting', *lit.* 'the place of-them-waiting'. In a sentence of this sort there is no Malay word to correspond to the English word 'where'.

The use of *di-mana*, which means 'where?' (interrogative) is an anglicism to be avoided. You will come to a note on these very common descriptive noun-groups in Sc. II. line 46.

měnanti: the *mě-* derivative here is very near to the English present participle.

měnanti: the root-word is *nanti*. Before a root which begins with a nasal (*n, ng, ny, m*) there is no need of a nasal infix (as in *bacha*/*měmbacha*) to link the prefix to the root. In front of *m* words, indeed, the prefix is seldom used, *e.g. makan*, 'eat'; *minum*, 'drink', in which words prefix and root have fused.

47 Apa khabar Che' Mahmud?: this speaker habitually pronounces the Arabic *kh* sound with a strong scrape. Many speakers drop the Arabic sound and pronounce it merely as *k*.

49 Chakap Mělayu pula!: *pula* is another word which indicates feeling rather than fact (cf. *pun* in Note 11 above). The underlying idea in it is succession, or sequence. When the sequence is unexpected, as here, it indicates surprise: 'In England he didn't know any Malay, now he is talking it fluently!'

50 bělajar: 'learn', from the root *ajar*, 'teach', an irregular formation in which the usual *r* infix has become *l* because of the *r* in the root-word.

53 bětul-bětul: 'quite true', the duplication being used in this case to strengthen the statement.

bukan main-main: here the *bukan* cancels the mistaken impression which Che' Mahmud might have had.

main-main: duplication sometimes gives an idea of pretence, or resemblance; (*běr*)*main* means 'to play' (*e.g.* tennis), *main-main* means 'to play about', 'make a pretence'.

56 pun: to turn Mr. Martin's attention to Che' Normah.

58 těrima kaseh: if it were a Malay speaking he would not use *těrima kaseh* after *Khabar baik*. The phrase is much less used than is the conventional 'thank you' in English, though not through any lack of courtesy. When it is used, it more often means the 'No, thank you' of a polite refusal.

61 Bila saya dapat rumah: 'When I get a house'; in written Malay *bila* means only 'when?' (interrogative), but in spoken Malay it replaces the written form '*apabila*' as a subordinating conjunction of time meaning 'on the occasion or occasions when'.

dapat: implies 'getting as the result of seeking'. Its meaning is rather to bring off some project. It is never used of 'getting' something which you know to be there. Contrast line 69 below, 'I'll go and get the car', where *ambil* is used.

63 barang-barang Mr. Martin mana?: 'Where is your luggage?' *Mana* is here short for *di-mana?*, 'where?' Only context will determine whether *mana* means 'which?' (adjectival) as in *Peter mana?* 'Which Peter?', or 'which one?' (short for *yang mana?*) as in *Mana dia Mr. Martin?* 'Which is Mr. Martin?', or 'How?' (short for *macham mana?* or *bagaimana?*) as in *Mana-lah Mr. Martin tahu hal sireh?*; 'How should Mr. Martin know about sireh?', or 'Where?' (short for *di-mana?*) as in this example.

barang-barang: 'things'; the duplication here probably indicates variety, but out of this sort of use there has grown a tendency to regard reduplication merely as a sign of the plural. In newspaper Malay nearly all plurals are duplicated, but it remains true that the Malay word is singular or plural without change of form, *e.g. Saya hĕndak mĕngambil kĕreta;* 'I'll go and get the car'. And *Orang 'dah turun 'dah;* 'The people (passengers) have all disembarked.'

64 sudah saya suroh: this is the usual word-order, rather than *saya sudah suroh,* because the point to be made is not that *I* have given the order, but that the order has been given. Do not think of *suroh* in such a sentence as an auxiliary verb. It is itself the statement, and the noun-group *saya suroh,* 'me-ordering', is its subject.

66 kapal laut: *lit.* 'sea-ship', as opposed to *kapal tĕrbang,* 'flying ship'. But usually the word *kapal* alone is sufficient. The term *kapal api,* 'steamship' (*lit.* 'fire ship') is seldom used nowadays.

sadikit: *i.e. sa-dikit,* 'one small-amount', but in speech the word is always telescoped to *sikit.* It might have been spelt thus in the text, since *'dah* is used for *sudah* and *'nak* for *hĕndak,* but it is not desirable to multiply such contractions. Some few of them are becoming current coin in colloquial written style (*e.g.* in short stories) and may be compared with 'can't', 'won't', etc. in English, but most of them, as in English, are left to the reader's discretion.

67 dua tiga: 'two *or* three'. Malay frequently omits conjunctions between 'established' pairs, *e.g. siang malam,* 'day and night'; *ibu bapa,* 'father and mother'.

68 mari-lah kita pĕrgi: 'let's go', *lit.* 'come, we go'. This is more definite than *Choba kita lambai,* 'Let's wave', which is not much more than a suggestion that it might be a good idea; *mari kita . . .* implies that the speaker is about to suit the action to the word.

mari-lah: an imperative is nearly always followed by the enclitic *-lah.* See Note 11 above.

69 'ndak mĕngambil kĕreta: *mĕngambil* from *ambil.* When the root-word begins with a vowel, the *mĕ-* prefix is followed by the nasal infix *-ng, e.g. ambil | mĕngambil, ikat | mĕngikat* ('tie') *ukor | mĕngukor* ('measure').

měngambil: the *mě-* prefix is always used after *hěndak*. '*the* car': because of *ambil*. If it had not been his own car he would have said *měnchari kěreta*, 'to get (seek) *a* car'.

74 děpan: the spoken form of (*di-*) (*ha*)*dapan*. For the pronunciation of this word and of *Rah* (l. 73) see Introd., p. xiv, footnote 2.

75 měnuju: from *tuju*. Before the dental consonants *d* and *t* the prefix *mě-* takes the dental nasal *n*, and the lighter (or *voiceless*) consonant *t* drops out. Thus *děngar*, 'hear', becomes *měnděngar*, but *tulis*, 'write', becomes *měnulis*. Of all the *měn-* words that you will come across, the vast majority will be from *t* roots, since there are very few verb-roots that begin with *n*. Do not be tempted to look for a root-word beginning with the vowel *u*; that would require the infix *-ng-*. See Note 69 above.

měnunjok: from *tunjok*, 'point to', 'show'. There is also a cognate word *unjok*, 'to hold out', 'to offer', but the *mě-* derivative of this would be *měngunjok*. See Note 69 above.

77 Itu-kah pokok kělapa?: 'Is *that* a coconut palm?', implying 'I've been on the look-out for one'; but *Pokok kělapa-kah itu?* 'Is that tree *a coconut palm?* (or what?)'. The interrogative particle is attached to the word which requires answering, and since that word is the important word it is usually brought to the position of emphasis at the beginning of the sentence.

81 Bila-bila pun: 'whensoever'. There are several duplicated words corresponding to the English words ending in '-ever'. They are usually followed by *pun*, drawing the hearer's attention first to this possibility, then to that, then to some other, *e.g. di-mana-mana pun*, 'wheresoever'; *apa-apa pun*, 'whatsoever'.

Pětang ini pun: the *pun* here pinpoints 'this' evening, as opposed to to-morrow or any other evening. In a later note this use will be contrasted with *pětang 'karang*, 'this evening', meaning 'later on, not at the moment'.

82 sědap: listen to the double stress which the child gives to the word, for emphasis, 'de . . . licious!'

83 sa-batang pokok pinang: *lit.* 'one trunk of . . .', 'one shaft of . . .', another very common numeral coefficient used for all rod-like things such as telegraph poles, pencils, etc.

87 Ini pokok pinang: 'This (is) a betel-nut palm.' Note that when *ini* (or *itu*) comes *before* a noun it is a pronoun, not an adjective. 'This betel-nut palm' would be *pokok pinang ini*. See Note 1 above.

89 Esok-lah baharu Rah chěritakan: note this idiomatic use of *baharu*. It will recur. Here, the idea is that *to-morrow* will be time enough. When the emphasis is on the *baharu*, 'newly then', 'only then', 'not until then', the *-lah* is usually attached to *baharu*, *e.g. Uli těpong itu hari ini, esok baharu-lah boleh bakar;* 'If you make the dough to-day, you mustn't bake it until to-morrow.' See Sentence Pattern II.7.

chĕritakan: chĕrita, 'a story', 'an account'; *bĕrchĕrita,* the intransitive verb-form, 'to tell a story', *e.g. Diam-lah sĕmua, saya 'nak bĕrchĕrita,* 'Now stop talking, everybody, I'm going to tell you a story'; *chĕritakan,* 'to make something into a story', 'to relate (something)'. The suffix *-kan* creates a causative verb, *e.g. Nanti dahulu. Saya 'nak chĕritakan hal itu;* 'Wait. I'll tell you all about it.' There will be clearer examples in later scenes. The easiest are those which add *-kan* to an adjective to create causative verbs corresponding to the verbs in *-en* and *-fy* in English, *e.g. panjang,* 'long'; *panjangkan,* 'make long', 'lengthen'; *bĕsar,* 'large'; *bĕsarkan,* 'to make large', to magnify'.

Mana-lah: here short for *Bagaimana-lah?* or *Macham mana-lah?* 'How?' See Note 63 above.

94 hotel-nya: again the idiomatic use of *-nya,* the hotel that we are concerned with at the moment. See Note 26 above.

Biar saya sĕmua balek: a very common formula of leave-taking.

saya sĕmua: strictly speaking, *saya* (in common with all the other personal pronouns and pseudo-pronouns) is singular or plural according to context, but it is usual, in speech, to indicate the plural by adding *sĕmua,* 'all'. So, *dia sĕmua* (shortened to *dema*) is used for 'they' in Perak.

sĕmua: the word is used here to include wife and child. If Zaharah had not been there Che' Mahmud would probably have said merely, *Saya balek dahulu, ia?* So also a Malay will enquire after his friend's children only, it being understood that the enquiry includes the wife.

SCENE I: TAKING STOCK

In writing the scene which you have just been studying the author thought only of presenting everyday ideas in everyday language, with no consideration of 'ground covered'. Yet if you look through the Notes you will find that you have already had examples illustrating most of the points of Malay idiom which are discussed in grammar books. It will be useful to gather them together at this stage, but you must remember, of course, that they afford only first glimpses. Further examples in subsequent Scenes will throw different lights on the same points. Take nothing that you read in this book as fixed and rigid. That is advice that will hold good as long as you continue to study Malay.

Except in cases of special difficulty literal translations are not given here, since all the examples recorded have already occurred in the text and most of them have been discussed in the Notes.

The subdivisions of an entry do not necessarily appear in the order of their importance or frequency. Each point is noted when it first appears, and retains its original numbering throughout.

This is the picture up to date:

1. THE ADJECTIVE FOLLOWS THE NOUN:
    topi kĕlabu, 'a grey hat'.

2. THERE IS NO COPULA:
    Itu dia. 'That (is) it.'

3. INI and ITU

    i. As demonstrative adjectives they *follow* any other adjectives or adjective phrases used:
        topi kĕlabu itu, 'that grey hat'
        yang bĕrtopi kĕlabu itu, 'the one-with-a-grey-hat'.
    ii. If they *precede* the noun they are demonstrative pronouns:
        Itu pokok pinang. 'That (is) a betel palm.'

4. A NOUN OR PRONOUN WHICH FOLLOWS ANOTHER NOUN IS DEPENDENT ON THAT NOUN:

    either as a possessive genitive:
        rumah dia, 'the house of-him', 'his house'
    or   as a description:
        kapal laut, 'a ship of-the-sea', 'a sea-going vessel'.

5. NUMERAL COEFFICIENTS ARE USED:
    (a) *buah* ('fruit') for large things: *sa-buah kapal tĕrbang*, 'an aircraft'
    (b) *batang* ('rod') for stem-like things: *dua batang pokok pinang*, 'two betel palms'.

6. PRONOUNS

    (a) Personal Pronouns
        These are less used in Malay than in English. Those of the 1st and 2nd person are usually replaced by nouns of relationship or by names:
        Abah dĕngan ĕmak dapat tengok pĕrarakan sahaja.
        We didn't see anything except the procession.
        Rah sakit hati.
        I'm annoyed.
        Normah pun suka, bukan?
        You would like it too, wouldn't you, Normah?
        Rah hĕndak ta' pĕrgi sambut dia?
        Would you like to go and meet him?

Note. The pronouns and the meanings given below cover only the examples which have occurred in the text or the notes. Local usage when you listen, and literary convention when you read, will supply many other words which serve as pronouns. Even of those words listed as 'personal pronouns' many are, by origin, nouns, *e.g. sahaya* or *saya*, 'I', means 'slave', and *awak*, 'you', means 'body'.

The following personal pronouns have occurred in Scene I:

i. 1ST PERSON

Singular ('I')	Plural ('We')
saya (usual between Malays and non-Malays)	*saya sěmua*
	kita (includes the listener)
aku (familiar)	*kami* (excludes the listener)

ii. 2ND PERSON ('You')

None used.

iii. 3RD PERSON

Singular ('He', 'She', 'It')	Plural ('They')
dia	*dia sěmua*
ia (written form, when a subject)	*měreka* (written only)

iv. *-nya* used as a 3rd person genitive—

    a. specifically: *abah-nya*, 'his (*i.e.* Peter's) father'

    b. impersonally: *kapal těrbang-nya*, 'the plane in-the-case'

            agak-nya, 'the guess of-it'

(*b*) Interrogative Pronouns

i. *apa?* 'what?'

    Děngan apa dia datang?

    How (*lit.* with what) is he coming?

ii. *mana?* 'which?'

    a. which?

        Peter mana?

        Which Peter?

    b. where? (short for *di-(těmpat) mana?*)

        Barang-barang Mr. Martin mana?

        Where is your luggage, Mr. Martin?

    c. how? (short for *bagaimana?* 'which way?')

        Mana-lah Mr. Martin tahu hal sireh?

        How should Mr. Martin know about sireh?

(*c*) Relative Pronouns

    yang, 'who', 'which', always used to distinguish:

        yang běrtopi kělabu itu, 'the (one) who (is) grey-hatted'.

Note. For demonstrative pronouns, see No. 3 above.

7. WORDS ARE SOMETIMES DUPLICATED:

    i. to show variety and repetition—
        bĕrbual-bual.
        chatting about this and that.

    ii. to moderate—
        Jangan-jangan pĕning lagi.
        I hope he isn't still feeling giddy.

    iii. to emphasize—
        Ini bĕtul-bĕtul Che' Mahmud.
        I really mean it, Che' Mahmud.

    iv. to give an impression of imitation—
        Bukan main-main.
        I'm not joking.

    v. to indicate the plural—
        Barang-barang Mr. Martin mana?
        Where are your things, Mr. Martin?

Note. Duplication is sometimes indicated by an index figure: *barang²*, or *barang₂.*

8. The negatives TIDAK, BUKAN, JANGAN

    There are two negative adverbs, *tidak* and *bukan.*

    (*a*) *tidak* simply denies:
        Dia tidak dudok di-rumah kita.
        He will not be staying with us.

    (*b*) *bukan*

        i. corrects an erroneous impression:
            Rah bukan ta' tengok pĕrarakan itu.
            lit. You didn't not-see the procession.

        ii. in a question it means 'isn't it so?'
            Bukan-kah Peter pun tinggal juga?
            Peter stayed at home too, didn't he?

    The prohibitive negative *jangan* (unlike the English *Don't*) may be used either directly or indirectly.

    (*c*) *jangan*

        i. as a direct 2nd person prohibition:
            Jangan-lah bagitu.
            Don't talk like that.

        ii. as a 3rd person optative (*i.e.* expression of wish):
            Jangan pĕning lagi.
            lit. Let it not be that (he is) giddy still.
            I hope he isn't still feeling giddy.

9. THERE IS NO TENSE-FORMATION

    i. the time of the action is to be gathered from context only:

        'Tapi dia tidak dudok di-rumah kita.
        But he won't be staying with us.

    ii. the time is indicated by an adverbial word or phrase:

        Kita dudok di-rumah dia masa kita di-London hari itu.
        We stayed at his house when we were in London.
        Pagi esok saya datang.
        I'll come to-morrow morning.

10. PREFIXES and SUFFIXES play an important part in Malay syntax:

    (*a*) *bĕr-* (verbal prefix)

        i. possessive:

            bĕrtopi kĕlabu, 'having a grey hat', 'with a grey hat'

        ii. forming an intransitive verb:

            Mĕreka bĕrbual-bual, 'They were chatting.'
            Ia bĕrasa suka, 'She feels happy.'

    (*b*) *mĕ-* (verbal prefix)

        i. as a verbal noun

            a. after a preposition:

                daripada mĕmandang, 'from gazing at'

            b. after *hĕndak* (and other words) implying futurity:

                hĕndak mĕngambil kĕreta, 'to fetch the car' (*lit.* 'intending
                the getting').

    [Method of joining prefix to root. Brackets indicate
    that the letter is dropped.

    1. before *d* and (*t*) insert *n*:   *dĕngar* | *mĕndĕngar*
                                   tunjok | *mĕnunjok*

    2. before *b* and (*p*) insert *m*:   *bacha* | *mĕmbacha*
                                     pandang | *mĕmandang*

    3. before vowels insert *ng*:   *ambil* | *mĕngambil*
                                     unjok | *mĕngunjok*

    4. before *n* insert nothing: *nanti* | *mĕnanti*]

    (*c*) *pĕ-* . . . *-an* and *pĕr-* . . . *-an* (noun affixes)

        kĕrja or *pĕkĕrjaan*, 'undertaking', 'work'
        pĕrarakan, 'procession'

    (*d*) *-kan* (verbal suffix)

        i. causative

            Esok-lah boleh Rah chĕritakan itu sĕmua.
            To-morrow you can tell him all about that.

11. PUN

> A spotlight, that draws attention to the word or expression which precedes it, usually by balancing it against another word or idea. (Hence it is nearly always used with the subject when *juga* is used with the predicate. See No. 12.)
>
> *Bila-bila pun boleh. Pětang ini pun boleh.*
> You can have one at any time. This evening, if you like.

12. JUGA

> i. meaning 'too', 'also' (usually with *pun* attached to the subject)
>
> *Bukan-kah Peter pun tinggal juga?*
> Peter stayed at home too, didn't he?
> *Zaharah pun ada juga.*
> Zaharah's here too.

13. PULA

> i. indicating surprise:
>
> *Chakap Mělayu pula.*
> He's talking Malay!
> *Pokok kělapa itu kěchil pula.*
> That coconut palm is quite small!

14. -LAH

> A particle which may be added to any part of speech
>
> i. it emphasizes:
>
> > a. usually by confirming an impression already suggested:
> >
> > *Itu-lah dia*, 'Yes, that's the one.'
> > *Itu bětul-lah*, 'That's quite true.'
> > *Ka-sini-lah*, 'Yes, he's coming here.'
> >
> > b. by marking out the predicate word, and so, as a rule, confirming an action which the reader is already expecting:
> >
> > *Ta' běrapa lama lěpas itu nampak-lah sa-buah kapal těrbang.*
> > Soon, there came in sight an aircraft.
> >
> > c. by singling out a word from others in the same category:
> >
> > *Esok-lah baharu Rah chěritakan itu sěmua.*
> > To-morrow will be time enough to tell him all about that.
> > *Kita nanti-lah;* 'We wait here.' (*i.e. That's* what we do.)
> > *Esok di-rumah kita boleh-lah Rah tunjok barang² itu.*
> > To-morrow, at home, you can show all those things.
>
> ii. it is habitually used after a direct imperative, to make it less brusque:
>
> *Jangan-lah macham itu.*
> Don't talk like that.
> *Rah siap-lah děngan ěmak-nya.*
> You get ready with your mother.
> *Mari-lah kita pěrgi ka-hotel.*
> Let us go to the hotel (*lit.* Come, we go . . .).

15. PREPOSITIONS

    (a) the locative preposition *di-* ('at' or 'in') is frequently omitted in speech

        Barang² Mr. Martin mana? (= *di-mana*)
        Where is your luggage, Mr. Martin?

    (b) *pada* is the correct preposition for 'at' or 'in' before words which are not place words

        pada pukul ĕmpat pĕtang, 'at 4 p.m.'

16. CONJUNCTIONS

    i. a co-ordinating conjunction is often omitted between established pairs:

        dua tiga minggu lagi, 'in two or three weeks time'
        Ingat ta' lagi? 'Do you remember or not?'

17. Translation of 'WHEN'

    (a) as an interrogative adverb, *bila*:

        Peter pun hĕndak datang juga? Bila?
        Peter's coming too? When?

    (b) as a subordinating conjunction meaning 'during the time when', by *masa, hari,* etc., followed by a descriptive noun-phrase. See No. 22:

        Kita dudok di-rumah dia tiga hari masa kita di-London hari itu.
        We stayed with him three days when we were in London.

18. BOLEH and BIAR

    Both words act as colloquial equivalents of the written conjunction *supaya* 'in order that'.

    (a) *boleh* (*lit.* 'can', 'able') indicates a promised result in the immediate future:

        Rah siap-lah boleh kita pĕrgi ka-kapal tĕrbang.
        You get ready so that we can go to the airport. (*Or* 'and we'll go'.)

    (b) *biar* (*lit.* 'allow') more definitely expresses purpose:

        Choba kita lambai biar dia nampak.
        Let's wave, so that he'll see us.

19. BAHARU

    This word (*lit.* 'new', 'newly') is commonly used where English requires 'until' or 'before':

        Esok-lah baharu Rah chĕritakan itu sĕmua.
        Wait until to-morrow to tell him about all that.

20. Translation of 'YES'

    i. in affirmative answer is usually given by repeating the relevant word of the sentence:

> *Rah ingat ta' Peter?—Ingat.*
> Do you remember Peter?—Yes.
> *Rah hĕndak ta' pĕrgi sambut dia?—Hĕndak.*
> Would you like to go and meet him?—Yes, I would.

    ii. the confirming particle *-lah* is often equivalent to a 'yes' in English.

> *Ka-sini-lah.*
> Yes, he's coming here.

SCENE I: SENTENCE PATTERNS

Note. The translations given are free translations. They give the colloquial English that would be likely to be used in similar circumstances. All new words will be found in the Vocabulary, and the notes on constructions which have occurred, or will occur, should enable you to make out the literal meaning of the Malay sentences.

1. ' Its easier if . . . '

a. **Tengok dalam T.V. lagi sĕronok.**
   It was more fun seeing it on television.

b. Goreng dĕngan minyak kĕlapa lagi sĕdap.
   It's tastier if you fry it in coconut-oil.

c. Jahit dĕngan bĕnang hijau lagi chantek.
   It will look prettier if you sew it with green thread.

d. Makan dĕngan tangan lagi sĕnang.
   It's easier to eat with your hand.

e. Masak dalam kuali lagi chĕpat.
   It's quicker to cook it in a frying-pan.

2. *Masa* for 'time during which'

a. **Rah tinggal dĕngan dia masa abah pĕrgi ka-London.**
   You stayed with him while I went to London.

b. Saya kĕnal dia masa saya dudok di-Raub dahulu.
   I knew him when I lived at Raub.

c. Saya dĕngar orang mĕmanggil masa mĕmbacha surat khabar tadi.
   I heard somebody calling while I was reading the newspaper.

d. Dia singgah di-sini masa dia hĕndak ka-Singapura hari itu.
   He called here when he was on his way to Singapore.

e. Dawat itu tĕrtumpah masa saya mĕnchuchi meja tadi.
   The ink was spilt when I was polishing the table.

3. *-kah* (often with *tidak*) for indirect question

a. **Měngapa abah tanya Rah ingat-kah tidak Peter itu?**
Why do you ask whether I remember Peter?

b. Měngapa tanya saya pandai-kah tidak chakap China?
Why do you ask whether I can speak Chinese?

c. Měngapa dia tanya 'dah makan-kah bělum?
Why did he ask whether we had had dinner?

d. Měngapa tanya dia ada-kah tidak di-rumah?
Why do you ask whether he is at home?

e. Měngapa dia tanya saya nak pěrgi-kah tidak ka-Sěrěmban?
Why did he ask whether I was going to Seremban?

4. *Hěndak* for futurity

a. **Abah dia 'nak tiba hari ini.**
His father will be arriving to-day.

b. Adek dia 'nak masok sěkolah esok.
His younger brother is going to begin school to-morrow.

c. Kakak Ahmad 'nak měmběli baju baharu di-kědai.
Ahmad's elder sister is going to buy a new baju at the shop.

d. Abang awak 'tu 'nak měngajak awak balek.
Your big brother is coming to ask you to go home.

e. Esok bapa hěndak měnuai padi.
My father is going to cut his padi to-morrow.

5. *Boleh* (colloquially) for promised result

a. **Pukul tiga siap-lah boleh kita pěrgi ka-padang kapal těrbang.**
You get ready at three o'clock and we'll go to the airport.

b. Datang-lah bila lapang boleh kita běrbual-bual.
Come when you have time, and we'll have a chat.

c. Nanti-lah di-kědai kopi itu pagi-pagi boleh kita pěrgi sama.
You wait for me at the coffee-shop in the morning and we'll go together.

d. Běli-lah buku boleh saya ajar měmbacha.
You buy the book, and I'll teach you to read.

e. Mari kita sudahkan kěrja ini boleh kita buat kěrja lain pula.
Let's get this finished, then we can get to work on something else.

6. *Biar* (colloquially) for purpose

a. **Choba kita lambai biar dia nampak kita.**
Let's wave, so that he'll see us.

b. Jangan tutup tingkap itu biar angin masok.
Leave the window open, so that we can get some air.

c. Kuat-lah sadikit běrchakap biar sěmua orang děngar.
Speak a bit louder, so that everybody can hear you.

d. Běli-lah buku biar saya ajar měmbacha.
Buy the book, so that I can teach you to read.

e. Mari kita sudahkan kěrja ini biar dapat měmbuat kěrja lain pula.
Let's get this finished, so that we can get to work on something else.

7. 'Here it is!'

a. **Itu dia agak-nya kapal tĕrbang-nya.—Itu-lah dia.**
There's the plane, I think.—Yes, that's it.

b. Ini dia budak yang kita nanti-nanti tadi.—Ini-lah dia budak-nya.
Here's the child that we have been waiting for so long.—Yes, this is the one.

c. Ini dia makalah yang kita chari-chari sa-lama ini.—Ini-lah dia-nya.
Here's the article (newspaper) that we have been trying to find all this time.—Yes, this is it.

d. Ini dia buku yang awak chari tadi.—Itu-lah dia buku-nya.
Here's the book that you were looking for.—Yes, that's it.

e. Itu dia agak-nya Bukit Ara.—Itu-lah dia-nya.
That will be Bukit Ara, I think.—Yes, that's it all right.

8. 'What a big one!'

a. **O bĕsar-nya kapal terbang itu.**
What a big plane!

b. Lĕbat-nya hujan ini.
What heavy rain!

c. Gĕlap-nya malam ini.   Tapak tangan pun ta' nampak.
How dark it is!   You can't even see your hand.

d. Nakal-nya budak 'ni.   Sa-kĕjap pun ta' mahu diam.
What a naughty child!   He won't keep still for a single second.

e. Sakit-nya gigi ini.   Kalau budak, mahu mĕnangis.
Oh, my tooth does ache!   For two pins, I could cry.

SCENE II

DI-RUMAH

AT HOME

1 Che' Mahmud pĕrgi mĕnjĕmput Mr. Martin ka-hotel-nya. Hari ini ia
2 hĕndak mĕnunjokkan kapada Mr. Martin pĕrkara yang bĕrkĕnaan dĕngan
3 rumah tangga-nya sĕrta hĕndak mĕnjamu-nya makan chara Mĕlayu. Rumah
4 Che' Mahmud itu kira-kira tiga batu dari bandar Kuala Lumpur.
5 Dalam pukul sa-bĕlas ia pun balek mĕmbawa Mr. Martin. Che' Normah
6 bĕrdiri di-muka pintu hadapan.

Che' Mahmud goes inviting Mr. Martin, to-(the) hotel-of-him. This-day, he
intends showing to Mr. Martin things which connected with house-and-ladder-of-him
together-with intending inviting him eat Malay-style. The house of Che' Mahmud
(is) about three-mile-stones from town Kuala Lumpur.

Within strike eleven he returns bringing Mr. Martin. Che' Normah stands at-face
of-door front.

Che' Mahmud goes to call for Mr. Martin at his hotel. To-day he is going
to show him everything in connection with his house and family, and is going
to invite him to a meal in Malay style. Che' Mahmud's house is about three
miles from Kuala Lumpur.

About eleven o'clock he returns with Mr. Martin. Che' Normah is standing
at the front door.

7 Mr. Martin sudah sampai ka-kaki tangga.

Mr. Martin has reached the foot of the entrance-steps.

8 NOR. **Sila-lah naik Mr. Martin.**

Be-pleased come up Mr. Martin.

Come up, Mr. Martin.

9 MAR. **Baik, Che' Normah. Mana dia Zaharah?**

Good, Che' Normah. Where (is) she, Zaharah?

Thank you, Che' Normah. Where is Zaharah?

10 NOR. **Ada. Dia ta' pĕrasan barangkali. Zaharah! Ini**

Is-here. She not perceiving, perhaps. Zaharah! This (is) Mr.

She's here. She hasn't realized that you have come I

11 **Mr. Martin 'dah sampai.**

Martin has arrived.

expect. Zaharah! Mr. Martin is here.

12 Zaharah bĕrlari datang ka-anjong. Mr. Martin hĕndak mĕmbuka kasut
13 kĕrana mĕlihat Che' Mahmud mĕmbuka kasut.

27

Zaharah runs coming to-porch-room. Mr. Martin intending undo shoes because seeing Che' Mahmud undoing shoes.

Zaharah comes running into the room. Mr. Martin is about to take off his shoes because he sees Che' Mahmud taking his off.

14 MAH. **Ta' usah buka kasut.**
Not-need undo shoes.
Don't take your shoes off.

15 MAR. **Tĕtapi Che' Mahmud buka kasut?**
But Che' Mahmud undoes shoes?
But you are taking yours off?

16 MAH. **O. Jangan ikut saya.**
O. Don't follow me.
Oh, don't take any notice of what I do.

17 Mr. Martin naik dĕngan tiada mĕmbuka kasut. Che' Normah mĕnunjok
18 kapada sa-buah kĕrusi.
Mr. Martin goes up with not undoing shoes. Che' Normah points to one-unit (of) chair.
Mr. Martin goes up without taking off his shoes. Che' Normah points to a chair.

19 NOR. **Sila dudok. Buat-lah macham rumah sĕndiri. Ini-**
Be pleased, sit. Just-do like house of-self. This (is) style of-
Sit down, won't you? Make yourself at home. This is
20 **lah chara rumah Mĕlayu. Tengok-lah, tingkap**
Malay house. Look, shutter-windows all opened.
what a Malay house is like. You see, all the windows
21 **sĕmua tĕrbuka.**
are open.

22 Mr. Martin dudok sĕrta mĕmandang-mandang. Kĕmudian ia bangkit lalu
23 pĕrgi ka-tingkap sĕrta mĕnjĕngok ka-luar.
Mr. Martin sits with looking-about-him. Then he rises, afterwards goes to-window together-with peeping to-outside.
Mr. Martin sits down and looks round about him. Then he gets up and goes to the window and looks out.

24 MAR. **Bagus bĕtul pokok-pokok ini. Ha! Pokok saya**
Fine truly these-trees. Ah. Tree I point-out yesterday is-
You've some fine trees here. Ah. You've got that tree
25 **tunjok sa-malam pun ada.**
present.
that I pointed out yesterday.

Ia mĕmandang kapada Zaharah sĕrta tĕrsĕnyum sadikit.
He looks to Zaharah together-with smiling a little.
He looks at Zaharah with a twinkle in his eye.

MAR. **Apa nama-nya Zaharah? . . . Penang?**
What (is) name of-it, Zaharah? . . . Penang?
What's it called, Zaharah? . . . Penang?

Pĕrkataan itu di-bunyikan-nya chara Inggĕris.   Zaharah tiada pĕrasan Mr.
Martin mĕnyakat-nya.
The word is-sounded-by-him English-style.   Zaharah not conscious Mr. Martin teasing-her.
He pronounces the word in the English way.   Zaharah does not realize that
he is teasing her.

ZAH. **Bukan 'Penang' . . . pi-nang.**
Not 'Penang' . . . 'pi-nang'.

MAR. **Pinang.   Bĕtul?**
Pinang.   Is that right?

ZAH. **Nanti Rah pĕrgi ambil sa-biji buah pinang tunjok**
Wait Rah go get one-unit fruit betel, show Mr. Martin.
I'll go and get a betel-nut and show it to you.
Mr. Martin.

NOR. **Rah ambil-lah tĕmpat sireh sa-kali, boleh kita tunjok**
Rah fetch receptacle of-sireh one-time, able we show to him.
Bring the sireh set at the same time, Rah, so that we can
pada dia.
show it to him.

Zaharah pĕrgi mĕngambil tĕmpat sireh.   Di-tunjokkan-nya kapada Mr.
Martin sa-biji pinang bĕlum bĕrkupas dĕngan sa-biji yang sudah bĕrkupas.
Zaharah goes fetching receptacle of-sireh.   There-is-a-showing-by-her to Mr. Martin one-unit betel nut not-yet skinned with one-unit which has-been skinned.
Zaharah goes and fetches the sireh set.   She shows Mr. Martin a betel-nut
that has not been peeled and one that has been peeled.

ZAH. **Ini dia buah pinang.   Ini isi dia bila sudah kita**
This (is) it, fruit of-the-betel.   This (is) flesh of-it when has-been
Here's a betel-nut.   This is the inside, when you have
kupas.
we skin.
peeled it.

40 NOR. **Pinang ini kita makan děngan sireh. Ini dia daun**
This betel we eat with betel-vine. This (is) it, leaf of betel-vine.
You eat it with sireh. This is sireh leaf. Look, I'm going

41 **sireh. Tengok saya makan. Mr. Martin hěndak**
See, I eat. Mr. Martin wishes try?
to chew it. Would you like to try it?

42 **choba-kah?**

43 MAR. **Mahu juga. Sědap-kah?**
Wish to-a-certain-extent. Pleasant?
Mm, yes. Is it nice?

44 MAH. **Ta' usah-lah. Pědas sangat.**
Not-need. Hot very.
Don't you do it! It's very hot.

45 NOR. **Dudok-dudok-lah dahulu, biar saya ka-dapor.**
Just sit first, allow-that I to-kitchen.
You sit down for a bit, I'll go and see to the meal.

46 MAH. **Mari kita tengok-tengok sadikit rumah ini. Těmpat**
Come we see-see a little the-house. This-place of-us-sitting we
Let's have a look round the house. This place where we

47 **kita dudok ini kita panggil anjong. Sa-bělah dalam**
call 'anjong'. On-the-side-of inside, 'sěrambi' in-its-turn the name
are sitting is called the *anjong*. And that room through

48 **itu, sěrambi pula nama-nya.**
of-it.
there is the *sěrambi*.

49 Che' Mahmud měnunjok ka-sěrambi sambil běrjalan ka-situ.
Che' Mahmud points to-'sěrambi' together-with walking to-there.
Che' Mahmud points to the *sěrambi* and walks towards it as he does so.

50 MAH. **Di-sěrambi ini tidak pakai kěrusi meja. Di-atas**
This being-on-a-sěrambi, not (is) a-using (of) chairs, table. On
Here, in the *sěrambi*, we don't have table and chairs.

51 **lantai di-běntang tikar. Di-atas tikar itu-lah dudok.**
floor there-is-a-laying (of) mats. On the mats, (it is), one-sits.
Mats are spread on the floor, and that's what we sit on.

52 **Dudok-nya běrsila macham ini.**
The sitting-in-the-case (is) cross-legged, like this.
Cross-legged, like this.

53   Che' Mahmud dudok měnunjokkan bagaimana dudok běrsila itu.
    Che' Mahmud sits showing what-like (is) that cross-legged sitting.
    Che' Mahmud sits down, showing what he means by sitting cross-legged.

54 MAH. **Mari-lah masok ka-sini.**
    Come, enter to-here.
    Let's go inside.

55 MAR. **Nanti saya buka kasut dahulu.**
    Wait I unfasten shoes first.
    I'll take off my shoes.

56   Lěpas měmbuka kasut Mr. Martin pun masok ka-sěrambi.
    After he has taken off his shoes Mr. Martin goes into the sěrambi.

57 MAH. **Di-sěrambi ini těmpat orang laki-laki. Orang**
    In the sěrambi, this, place of persons male. Persons female, in-the
    Here in the sěrambi is where the men sit. The women sit
58   **pěrěmpuan di-dalam ini pula těmpat-nya.**
    inside, this, in-turn, place-of-them.
    in this inner room.

59   Ia měmbawa Mr. Martin masok ka-těngah rumah.
    He conducts Mr. Martin entering to-middle of-house.
    He takes Mr. Martin into the living-room.

60 MAH. **Nama těmpat ini těngah rumah. Di-sini juga těm-**
    Name of this place, mid-house. At-here, exactly, place of eating.
    This is called the *těngah rumah.* This is where we eat.
61   **pat makan.**

62   Mr. Martin těrpandang kapada dua bilah kěris těrgantong pada dinding.
    Mr. Martin finds-himself-looking at two-lath of kris, hung on wall.
    Mr. Martin notices two krises hanging on the wall.

63 MAR. **Ini-kah kěris, Che' Mahmud? Těrgantong pada**
    These, krises, Che' Mahmud? Hung on wall, these.
    Are those krises, Che' Mahmud, hanging on the wall
64   **dinding ini.**
    there?

65 MAH. **Ia. Itu-lah dia kěris. Kěris panjang ini kěris**
    Yes. Those (are) they, krises. This long kris (is) inherited
    Yes. Those are krises. This long one is an heirloom.

66   **pĕsaka. Kĕris pendek ini kĕris saya sĕndiri.**
creese. This short kris (is) kris of-me myself. Come we go-
This shorter one is my own kris.   Let us go down into

67   **Mari kita turun ka-dapor pula.   Rumah dapor ini**
down to-kitchen next.   This kitchen-building we make separate
the kitchen now.   We make the kitchen a separate build-

68   **kami buat rumah asing, fasal ta' mahu bagi asap**
building, because not wish cause smoke enter to mother-part of-
ing, so that the smoke won't get into the main part of the

69   **masok ka-ibu rumah.   Dapor kami ta' ada pakai**
house.   Kitchens of-us, there-is-not using funnels for-smoke.
house.   We don't have chimneys in our kitchens.

70   **chorong asap.**

71   NOR.   **Tengok-lah Mr. Martin.   Kami mĕmasak pakai**
See, Mr. Martin.   We cooking, there-is-using wood for-fire.
You see, Mr. Martin.   We use firewood for cooking.

72   **kayu api.**

73   MAH.   **Mari kita tengok-tengok ka-luar pula.   Boleh pakai**
Come we look-look to-outside next.   Able use these clogs.
Let's have a look-round outside now.   You can put on

74   **tĕrompah ini.**
these clogs.

75   Che' Mahmud mĕmbĕri Mr. Martin pakai sa-pasang tĕrompah.
Che' Mahmud gives Mr. Martin the-wearing one-pair clogs.
Che' Mahmud gives Mr. Martin a pair of wooden sandals to put on.

76   MAR.   **Susah pula pakai tĕrompah ini.   Rasa macham 'nak**
Difficult, surprisingly, wear these clogs.   The feeling like going-to
Hm!   It's not easy to wear them.   You feel you are going

77   **jatoh.**
fall.
to fall.

78   MAH.   **Memang bĕtul.   'Nak pakai banyak kali baharu**
By-the-nature-of-it, true.   There-is-required wearing many times
Yes, that's true.   It takes practice to get used to them.

79   **biasa.**
newly accustomed.

80   Che' Mahmud mĕnunjok kapada rĕban ayam.
Che' Mahmud points to the fowl-house.

MAH. **Rumah kĕchil itu rĕban ayam.**
Building small that, coop for-chickens.
That small shed is a chicken coop.

MAR. **Ayam ini ta' ada-kah bĕrkĕpong dĕngan apa-apa?**
Chickens these, not there-is, shut-in with anything at-all?
You don't keep your chickens shut in in any way?

MAH. **Ta' ada. Ayam kami pakai lĕpaskan bagitu sahaja.**
Not is. Fowls of-us, the-usage (is) let-loose thus only. Day-
No. We just let them loose, like this. As soon as it's light
Siang-siang pĕrgi-lah dia ka-dalam kĕbun di-bĕla-
light-daylight go they into the garden at-the-back. See in the
off they go into the plantation at the back there. You
kang itu. Tengok-lah dalam kĕbun itu saya tanam
plantation I plant tuberous-roots wooden, bananas, sweet potatoes.
see, I have planted tapioca and bananas and sweet potatoes
ubi kayu, pisang, kĕledek. Sayor pun ada juga sadi-
Vegetables there-are also a-little. At the back over-there is fruit-
in the garden. There are a few vegetables, too. Behind
kit. Di-bĕlakang sana ada dusun, ada kĕbun gĕtah.
plantation, is plantation of rubber. Behind the rubber plantation
the garden, over there, there is an orchard, and a rubber
Di-bĕlakang kĕbun gĕtah itu hutan. Mari-lah kita
(is) jungle. Come we go-up to-house back. Gone-by, eating rice
plantation. Behind the rubber it is jungle. Let's go back
naik ka-rumah balek. Lĕpas makan nasi 'karang
presently, able in-continuation we walk-about into the orchard.
into the house. After we have had our meal we can
boleh pula kita bĕrjalan-jalan ka-dalam dusun itu.
come out again and take a stroll in the orchard.

Mĕreka kĕdua pun naik ka-rumah. Di-tĕngah rumah sudah tĕrhidang
makanan di-atas safrah.
The two of them go up into the house. In the living-room the meal is
set-out on a cloth.

NOR. **Kita buat chara Mĕlayu bĕtul, dudok bĕrsila.**
We do style Malay correct, sit cross-legged. Eat, too, with hand,
We are having it in true Malay style, sitting on the floor.
Makan pun dĕngan tangan, ia? Basoh-lah tangan.
yes? Wash hand.
And we'll eat with our hands, shall we? Wash your hand.

95 Che' Normah měnyorongkan ayer basoh tangan di-dalam sa-buah batil
96 perak.

97   Mr. Martin měmbasoh tangan kanan-nya. Sambil itu ia měmandang
98 makanan yang těrhidang běrbagai-bagai jěnis-nya.

Che' Normah holds forward water wash-hands in one-unit bowl silver.

Mr. Martin washes the-hand right of-him. At the same-time-with that, he looks at food which ready-set-out being-of-all-kinds the varieties-of-it.

Che' Normah holds out towards him a silver bowl with water in it.

Mr. Martin washes his right hand. As he does so, he surveys the variety of dishes set out.

99 MAR. **Wah, banyak barang makanan ini.**

Oh. Much stuff for food this.

My word! What a lot of food!

100 NOR. **Mana-lah banyak-nya, kita makan běrěmpat.**

How, the muchness in-the-case, we eating being-four.

Oh, no, it isn't much, seeing there are four of us to eat it.

101 MAH. **Barang-barang ini kita tidak makan satu-satu.**

Things these we not eat one-by-one. We eat all-mixed.

We don't eat all these dishes separately. We combine

102   **Kita makan běrchampor-champor.**

them.

103 Sambil běrchakap itu Che' Mahmud měnyěndok nasi ka-dalam pinggan.

As he talks Che' Mahmud spoons some rice into a plate.

104 MAH. **Mula-mula kita sěndok nasi ka-dalam pinggan.**

Begin-begin we spoon cooked-rice into plate. That-being-gone-

First of all you ladle some rice into your plate. After that,

105   **Lěpas itu ambil-lah lauk.**

by take meat, etc.

take something from the other dishes.

106   Mr. Martin makan děngan měnurut chara yang di-lakukan oleh Che'
107 Mahmud.

Mr. Martin eats with-following fashion which there-is-a-carrying-out by Che' Mahmud.

Mr. Martin begins to eat, following Che' Mahmud's example.

108   **Kuah gulai rěmpah děngan sambal ini barangkali**

This sauce, curried (with) spices, with salad-side-dishes perhaps

This curry and the dishes that go with it you may find

Mr. Martin rasa pĕdas sadikit. Ada pakai chili.
Mr. Martin taste hot a little. There-is using chillies.
rather hot. There are chillies in it.

ZAH. **Sambal ini yang nombor satu sa-kali pĕdas. Rah**
Dish this (is the one) which number-one most-of-all hot. I, even,
This is the hottest dish of all. Even I can't manage it.

pun ta' lalʻı 'nak makan.
not getting-by, intending to eat.

NOR. **Bukan pĕdas sangat. Emak sĕngaja tidak buat**
Not hot exceedingly. Mother purposely not make hot, allow-that
It's not very hot. I purposely didn't make it very hot, so

pĕdas, biar Mr. Martin dapat rasa.
Mr. Martin able taste.
that Mr. Martin could taste it.

Sĕmua lauk yang ada sudah bĕlaka di-rasa oleh Mr. Martin.
All dishes which there-are-present, has-been, one-and-all, there-being-a-tasting by Mr. Martin.
Mr. Martin has tasted all the dishes.

MAR. **Saya suka daging hitam ini.**
I like meat dark this.
I like this dark meat.

NOR. **Daging itu masak kichap, tidak ada pakai chili.**
Meat that, cooked, soya-sauce, not there-is use chillies. Using
That's cooked with soya sauce, and no chillies. Just a

Pakai sadikit lada hitam sahaja.
(of) a little pepper black only.
little black pepper only.

Lĕpas makan mĕreka pĕrgi dudok-dudok sa-bĕntar ka-anjong.
After the meal they go and sit in the porch verandah for a little while.

SCENE II: NOTES

1 **pĕrgi mĕnjĕmput:** *lit.* 'goes, inviting'. The free translation is
'goes to call for', but the *mĕ-* derivative does not, in itself, indicate
purpose. (For that, *hĕndak* is necessary.)

jĕmput: in this context the word implies that he has already
invited him to do something or other. 'An invitation to tea' is
surat jemputan 'nak minum teh; 'a tea-party' is usually *jamuan teh*.

ka-hotel-nya: note how the feeling of 'motion towards' persists through the participial *mĕ-* derivative, 'goes (inviting) to . . .'

2 **hĕndak mĕnunjokkan:** always the *mĕ-* prefix after *hĕndak*, whether it implies intention, as here, or mere futurity. (*Warning:* Beware of taking the word 'always' too literally when you are considering Malay syntax.)

    -kan: not the causative suffix here (the base-word *tunjok*, 'show', is itself transitive), but a remnant of the preposition *akan*, 'towards', 'for', for the benefit of (in this case, 'Mr. Martin' understood).

bĕrkĕnaan: the base-word is *kĕna*, 'come in contact with'. The prefix and suffix *bĕr-...-an*, used together, imply inter-connection. When the connection is close, or repetitive, the base-word is duplicated and the suffix is not always used, *e.g.* *bĕrchampor-champoran*, 'all mixed up together'; *bĕratus-ratus*, 'hundreds upon hundreds'.

3 **sĕrta:** *lit.* 'together with'; one of the words for 'and' in written Malay.

mĕnjamu-nya: here the pronoun *-nya* is used in place of the object-pronoun *dia*. This is usual after *mĕ-*, when there is no emphasis on the pronoun. In this example it can still be felt as a genitive if you think of the *mĕ-* form here as a verbal-noun: 'intending the-inviting of-him.'

bandar Kuala Lumpur: *lit.* 'the town Kuala Lumpur'. It is common in Malay idiom to put a class-word (*generic*) in front of a particular word, as in English 'the boy David'. So, *buah pisang*, 'the fruit, banana'; *bunga mĕlati*, 'the flower, jasmin'.

5 **dalam pukul sa-bĕlas:** *pada* is used for 'at a (definite) time'; *dalam* makes the time a little indefinite.

8 **Sila-lah:** the usual formula in Kuala Lumpur and the north of the Peninsula to invite a guest to enter, or to eat, or to drink. In the south, *jĕmput* is the word used.

10 **pĕrasan:** a shortened form of *pĕ-rasa-an*, an affixed noun formed from the base-word *rasa*, 'feel', 'perceive'. (See Note I.15.) This shortened form is usual for the adjectival meaning 'aware of', the longer form for the noun meaning 'opinion', 'feeling'.

Ini Mr. Martin 'dah sampai: the word *ini* often refers not to one definite person or thing but to a whole situation. In this sentence, *ini* is the subject, and the remaining noun-group is the predicate. It is not 'This (is) Mr. Martin' but ' This (is) Mr. Martin-having-arrived'. See Sentence Pattern 2.

    Note the slight difference in meaning in these three sentences: *Ini dia Mr. Martin;* 'Here's Mr. Martin (coming along)'. *Ini-lah dia Mr. Martin;* '*This* is Mr. Martin' (this one, not that one). *Ini Mr. Martin 'dah sampai;* 'Ah! Mr. Martin has arrived!'

12 anjong: a room which 'juts out', forming a covered verandah; cf. *tanjong*, 'a headland'.

mĕmbuka kasut: cf. *buka baju*, 'to take off one's coat'; *buka topi*, 'to take off one's hat'.

14 Ta' usah: *lit.* 'There is no need'. This is a more courteous prohibition than *jangan*. Sometimes the *ta'* is omitted, so that *Usah-lah!* comes to mean 'Don't!'

21 tĕrbuka: the prefix *tĕr-* does not present much difficulty. It implies that a process or action is complete, as here, 'all the windows are in-a-state-of-having-been-opened'. Sometimes this completeness comes about suddenly, and then the *tĕr-* gives a feeling of unexpectedness, *e.g. bakar* or *mĕmbakar*, 'burn', 'set on fire'; *rumah tĕrbakar*, 'house on fire'.

22 sĕrta: the verb-word which follows *sĕrta* will usually begin with *mĕ-*. You can think of *mĕmandang* here as a verbal-noun. (Remember that the 'stage-directions' are in *written* style.)

mĕmandang-mandang: the duplication of the base-word shows that it was not just one look that he gave, he kept on looking about him. Notice that the nasal sound (here *m*) which is inserted between the prefix and the base-word is picked up again in the repetition when the initial consonant of the base-word has been dropped: *e.g. mĕmukul-mukul*, 'hammering away', but *mĕmbacha-bacha*, 'reading on and on'.

ia: this, not *dia*, is the usual written form of the 3rd person pronoun when it is the subject of a verb. Cf. Note I.31.

bangkit: note that although this is 'written style' and the subject is in the 3rd person, the verb has no *mĕ-* prefix. When *mĕ-* is used with a subject, it relates the action closely to the actor. There is a group of what may be called, for brevity, 'coming and going' verbs which never take *mĕ-*. They are all intransitive verbs of movement, expressing simple actions which the doer performs without giving them much conscious thought. The commonest of them are: *pĕrgi*, 'go'; *datang*, 'come'; *naik*, 'go up'; *turun*, 'go down'; *bangun* and *bangkit*, 'rise up'; *dudok*, 'sit down'; *tĕrbang*, 'fly'. (*Note.* This applies only when they are intransitive verbs. When they become transitive verbs by the addition of the causative suffix *-kan*, they do take the prefix *mĕ-*, *e.g. mĕndatangkan*, 'make to come', *i.e.* 'cause'; *mĕnaikkan*, 'make to go up', *i.e.* 'raise'.)

lalu: *lit.* 'passing by', another word for 'and'; *sĕrta* is used to connect two actions when the 2nd follows smoothly on the 1st, almost merging into it (*dudok sĕrta mĕmandang-mandang*), *lalu* is used when the second action is clearly separated from the first.

25 pun: here the particle lights up not the immediately preceding word *sa-malam*, but the noun *pokok*, complete with its description: 'the I-showed-you-yesterday tree'.

26 tĕrsĕnyum: *sĕnyum* usually takes *tĕr-* because a smile as a rule comes of its own accord, with no volition behind it. See Note 21.

28 di-bunyikan-nya: the causative suffix *-kan; bunyi*, 'a sound'; *bunyikan*, 'make to sound'. A clearer example is: *tinggal* (intransitive) 'be left', 'remain'; *tinggalkan* (transitive) 'make to be left', 'leave behind'.

di-: up to the present you have seen only the place-preposition *di-* (*di-hadapan*, 'in front'; *di-padang kapal tĕrbang*, 'at the airfield'). The *di-* in *di-bunyikan* is best thought of as a verbal prefix (though it is possibly the same word in origin as the preposition *di-*). In this example it is simplest to think of *di-bunyikan* as a sort of passive, 'the word is sounded'. This explanation will not always fit the construction, but it will serve for the time being until other instances occur.

-nya: following a *di-* + *unprefixed verb* construction *-nya* indicates the agent (*i.e.* the person who carries out the action of the verb), and can therefore be translated 'by him', 'by her', 'by them'. Contrast the use of *-nya* in the next line where, after a *mĕ-* derivative, it is the *object* of the verb (*i.e.* not the doer of the action but the receiver of the action).

29 mĕnyakat-nya: from *sakat*. The nasal that is inserted before *s* is *ny*, and *s*, being a voiceless consonant (like *p* and *t*), drops out (*e.g. simpan, mĕnyimpan*, 'keep', 'put away').

There is no Malay word that is the exact equivalent of 'tease' in its happier sense; *mĕngejek* has a flavour of 'taunting', 'ridiculing', and *mĕngusek* implies 'bothering', 'interfering with'. Even *mĕnyakat* has a tinge of malice in it, *e.g. Budak-budak sĕlalu mĕnyakat adek-nya;* 'Children always tease (almost 'take it out of') their younger brothers and sisters.'

-nya: replacing *dia* as an object pronoun (*i.e.* meaning 'him', 'her', 'them') after a *mĕ-* derivative. See Note 3 above.

32 Nanti Rah pĕrgi ambil: *i.e.*, 'Wait, I go, I get'. Similarly for the imperative *Pĕrgi ambil!* 'Go, get'. Contrast, 3rd person written style *pĕrgi mĕngambil, lit.* 'goes, fetching' ('goes and gets') as in line 36 below. When purpose is implied *hĕndak* is used, *pĕrgi hĕndak mĕngambil*, 'goes to get'. Note that English idiom, unlike Malay, does not necessarily distinguish between the accomplished act and the intended act. 'Zah. goes and gets

. . .' exists side by side with 'Zah. goes to get . . .', where the context alone makes it clear that she really did get it. This point is illustrated in Sentence Pattern V.1.

Nanti: there are no tense-forms in Malay. This is one of the expressions used to indicate futurity, *lit.* 'Wait, I go.'

sa-biji: *lit.* 'one seed of . . .' This is the classifier or numeral coefficient for small, usually roundish, things, *e.g. dua biji tĕlor*, 'two eggs'; *tiga biji jam tangan*, 'three wrist-watches'.

buah pinang: *lit.* 'betel fruit'; *buah* here is not a numerical coefficient. See Note 3 above.

34 ambil-lah . . . boleh kita: *lit.* 'bring. . . , we shall be able . . .' See Note I.26. Malay speech constantly makes use of this side-by-side arrangement of two ideas, where English would make one of the ideas the main statement (here 'bring'), and would make the other idea subordinate to it (here 'so that we can . . .').

35 pada dia: short for *kapada dia*. If she had not been speaking to a child she would probably have said *(ka)pada-nya*; *-nya* is the usual pronoun after compound prepositions, *e.g. di-atas-nya*, 'on it' (*lit.* 'on-the-top of-it').

36 Di-tunjokkan-nya kapada Mr. Martin sa-biji pinang: 'She shows Mr. Martin a betel-nut'. In line 28 above, this *di-* + *simple verb* construction came immediately after a word that was apparently the subject, and it was easy to think of it as a parallel to the English passive verb: 'the word is-sounded by him'. In the present example (which is more typical) the thing that is 'shown' comes *after* the verb. Moreover, it is separated from the verb by the phrase *kapada Mr. Martin*. Now a subject, in Malay (if we discount descriptive groups such as *orang yang-bĕrtopi-kĕlabu-ita*), may not be separated from its verb except by certain adverbs of time (*lagi, bĕlum, baharu,* etc.); it must come immediately before it, or immediately after it. It therefore fits the construction better to take *sa-biji pinang* as the object, not the subject, of *di-tunjokkan-nya*. The verb-phrase must then be thought of as an impersonal active statement, followed by the agent: 'there-was-a-showing by-her to Mr. Martin (of) a betel-nut'. In English the most natural translation of the construction is usually an active, personal statement: 'She showed Mr. Martin a betel-nut.'

If this attempt to explain the *di-* + *simple verb* construction does not help you, forget it for the time being and continue to think of the construction as a passive form. But remember always, if you are European, that Malay syntax is very different from Indo-European syntax and that you must not expect to be

C

able to fit it neatly into the pigeon-holes which you are accustomed to use for your own language. If you are Asian, you will probably not need some of the explanations given in these notes, because the shape of things in your own language may sometimes give you the clue to the build of a Malay sentence.

37 bĕlum bĕrkupas: 'not yet peeled'. This is a more difficult use of the prefix *bĕr-*. *Buah pinang yang tĕrkupas* would mean 'peeled betel-nuts', and the speaker would be thinking merely of the finished state in which the nuts were found, with no conscious thought of the person who did the peeling. *Buah pinang yang bĕrkupas* means rather 'nuts which have been peeled by somebody'. When the *bĕr-* prefix is used thus, as the equivalent of an English perfect participle, the speaker or writer is to a certain extent conscious of an agent, an actor, a doer, in the background.

38 isi dia: this might have been *isi-nya*, but a child seldom uses *-nya*.

bila sudah kita kupas: *bila* (spoken) for *apabila* (written), as in I.61. In written Malay *bila* is always interrogative; *apabila* means 'on the occasion or occasions when', *masa* usually means 'during the period when'.

> *kita:* this is a common use of the pronoun *kita*, which is often best translated by the indefinite 'you' of English proverbs, *e.g.* 'You can't eat your cake and have it.'
> *sudah kita kupas:* for the word-order cf. I.64.

43 juga: the *juga* shows that he is not too sure that he does want to try it. This is another word to add to the *-lah, pun, pula* group, that is to say, it is a word which gives a particular shade of meaning to other words, rather than has meaning of its own. Its usual function is, as here, to put the brake on. Hence its translation will often be 'nevertheless', 'all the same'; at other times it will best be rendered by intonation only. In lines I.11 and I.48 it occurred with *pun*, in which case its translation is 'too', 'also'.

45 dudok-dudok-lah dahulu: the duplication weakens the imperative here, 'You just sit down for a bit (before you do anything else).' *Dahulu* is commonly used in such phrases, cf. *Nanti dahulu;* 'Wait a bit'. It makes the 'command' less peremptory.

biar saya ka-dapor: 'I'll go . . . ,' *lit.* 'allow-that I to the kitchen'. The 'going' verb is frequently omitted when *ka-* is present to give the idea of 'motion towards'; *biar*, in speech, is often the equivalent of an English 'immediate' future.

46 tengok-tengok: the duplication gives variety, 'see this, that, and the other'. This is the essential function of duplication.

tĕmpat kita dudok ini: *lit.* 'the place of we-sitting'. The position of *ini* shows that the noun-group *kita dudok* is used as a description of *tĕmpat*, just as in *rumah tukang*, 'the house of the workman', the second noun defines the first noun. When 'where' means 'in which', or 'when' means 'on which', 'during which', Malay idiom uses this descriptive (or defining) noun-group. Cf. Scene I. line 6, *masa kita di-London*, 'time of us-(being)-in-London', for '(the time) when . . .'; line 1, *hari Mr. Martin akan tiba*, 'day of Mr. Martin-about-to-arrive' for 'the day on which . . .', line 45, *tĕmpat mĕreka mĕnanti*, 'the place of-them-waiting' for 'the place where . . .'

47 sa-bĕlah dalam: *lit.* 'on-the-side-of-the-inside'. So, also, *sa-bĕlah luar*, 'outside'; *sa-bĕlah utara*, 'on the north'; *sa-bĕlah sana*, 'over there'. In speech *sa-bĕlah* is often reduced to *bĕlah*.

sĕrambi pula: *lit.* 'the *sĕrambi* in its turn'. This feeling of sequence, the extension of an idea that is already in train, is inherent in *pula*. See Note I.49.

sĕrambi: a long, narrow verandah-room that runs across the front of the house. Sometimes the *tangga* (entrance steps or staircase) gives direct access to it; sometimes, as here, the *tangga* leads into the *anjong*, from which one passes into the *sĕrambi*.

49 sambil bĕrjalan: *lit.* 'together with walking'. *Sambil*, used only in written Malay, is followed by the *mĕ-* derivative, when such a derivative exists. But in this word the verbal form is *bĕrjalan*.

bĕrjalan: this is the commonest function of the *bĕr-* prefix, to create a verb, usually intransitive, and often from another part of speech: *jalan*, 'a way', 'movement'; *bĕrjalan*, 'move', 'walk'. The *mĕ-* form of this verb, *mĕnjalankan*, is transitive and causative, 'make to go', 'cause to work', *e.g. mĕnjalankan kĕreta*, 'drive a car'. (*Note*. In spoken Malay the prefixes *bĕr-* and *mĕ-* are sometimes omitted.)

50 di-sĕrambi ini: not specifically 'on *this* verandah', but the circumstance of its being a verandah, the idea that on a *sĕrambi*, wherever it might be, you would (probably) not find furniture. Cf. *di-dalam ini* in line 58 below, and Sentence Pattern 2.

tidak pakai: you may feel tempted to say that the subject is 'left out'. It is not that it is left out, but rather that it does not exist, in the sense in which the word is used in English grammar. The real 'subject' of the sentence is the word *pakai* itself, which is as much a noun as it is a verb: 'there-(is)-not using-furniture'.

kĕrusi meja: 'chairs, tables', *i.e.* 'furniture'. See Note I.67.

di-bĕntang tikar: see Note 36 above; *tikar* in this sentence corresponds to *sa-biji pinang* in that sentence: 'there-is-a-spreading (of) mats', *i.e.* 'mats are spread' or 'we spread mats'. If you find it difficult to 'feel' *tikar* as object of *bĕntang*, then continue to think of it as a subject, with *di-bĕntang* as a parallel of the English passive. In any case do not at this stage allow yourself to feel frustrated because you 'haven't really got to the bottom of this *di-* construction'. You cannot by-pass it, since, as you see, it is used freely in everyday conversation, but you can take it for granted while you are waiting for other examples to turn up.

51 di-atas tikar itu-lah dudok: the *-lah* belongs to the whole phrase, not to *itu* alone. It is not 'on *those* mats (and not any others)', but, 'that's where we sit, on these mats (not on chairs, as in the *anjong*)'. The function of *-lah* in such a sentence as this is to proclaim the predicate: '*Here* lies the statement, *this* is what I am telling you.'

dudok: see note on *pakai* line 50 above.

52 dudok-nya: *lit.* 'the sitting of-it', 'the sitting that we are concerned with'. For this impersonal use of *-nya*, implying a common interest between speaker and hearer, cf. I.26.

53 dudok běrsila itu: the literal translation tells you that *itu* here qualifies the whole noun-group 'to sit, being cross-legged'.

56 lěpas měmbuka kasut, Mr. Martin pun masok: the subject of a main statement which follows a subordinate time-statement is always followed by *pun*. (Further examples are given in Sentence Pattern VII.3.ii.)

57 Orang pěrěmpuan / di-dalam ini pula těmpat-nya: listen for the pause after *pěrěmpuan*. This is a very common sentence-pattern, *lit.* 'The women, here inside, in its turn, the place of them.' *Orang pěrěmpuan* is brought to the beginning of the sentence as being the 'topic thought'. After that has been 'declared', then the statement is made. So it often happens that the first word or phrase of a Malay sentence will not have any definable grammatical relationship with the rest of the sentence, that it is, in fact, not an integral part of the sentence at all, but a sign-post standing in front of it.

pula: another clear example of the primary function of *pula*, to indicate sequence, or extension, of an idea already presented.

59 Ia měmbawa Mr. Martin masok: 'He takes Mr. Martin into . . .', *lit.* 'He takes him, entering.' This use of a verb-form where English uses a preposition, after a verb of movement or conveyance, is a common idiom. (Further examples are given in Sentence Pattern V.1.iii.)

těngah rumah: the living-room. Sometimes this stretches right across the house, between the front verandah (*sěrambi*) and the kitchen, which is a few steps below the level of the *těngah rumah*, with a floor of split bamboo. But the writer here has in mind a type of house which is common in and around Kuala Lumpur.

Mr. Martin has already come through the *anjong* into the *sĕrambi*, and from there (through a curtained doorway) into the *tĕngah rumah*. This occupies the right half of the remainder of the rectangle (if the projecting *anjong* is on the right of the *sĕrambi*). The left half is partitioned off to make two bedrooms. From the back wall of the *tĕngah rumah* a covered staircase leads down to the kitchen (*rumah dapor*), which is on ground level with a concrete floor.

60 di-sini juga: a slightly different use of *juga*. Here it has a limiting rather than a 'braking' function. (See Note 43 above.) It closes in on the word or the idea, to the exclusion of other possibilities. 'This, not any other place, is where we have our meals.' So, *baharu-baharu ini juga*, 'just a moment ago' or 'quite recently'; *hari ini juga*, 'this very day'.

62 tĕrpandang: the *tĕr-* shows that his attention has suddenly been caught by the krises. See Note 21 above and contrast line 26, *Ia mĕmandang kapada Zaharah*, where the *mĕ-* prefix deliberately connects action and actor.

dua bilah kĕris: *lit.* 'two lath of kris', another common numerical coefficient, used for knives, etc.

tĕrgantong pada dinding ini: *tĕr-* here shows completed state. There were the krises, hung on the wall.

pada: the preposition for 'in' or 'at' before a place-word is *di-*. Before time-words it is replaced by *pada* (but see Note I.28), as in *Pada masa itu;* 'At that time.' Here, however, *pada* is short for *kapada;* in Malay a thing is hung *to* a wall.

ini: belonging not to *dinding* but to *kĕris*, 'this hung-on-the-wall-kris'.

65 itu-lah dia kĕris: *-lah* for confirmation, implying 'as you (correctly) thought'.

kĕris . . . kĕris . . . kĕris . . . kĕris: note that Malay idiom is not intolerant of repetition.

69 Dapor kami / ta' ada pakai chorong: see Note 57 above. Here, *Dapor kami*, as the pause on the record tells you, is the 'declaration of topic'. Then follows the statement, *lit.* 'There is not a using of chimneys.'

kami: note the 'exclusive' 1st person pronoun, 'we Malays'. See Note I.26.

71 Kami mĕmasak / pakai kayu api: again the pause warns you that the first two words declare the topic, *lit.* 'we cooking, there is use (of) firewood'. There is no subject of *pakai*. Cf. Note 69 above. The English equivalent of such a sentence is 'When we cook . . .' As a result of this side-by-side arrangement of ideas presented in their logical sequence, Malay uses fewer subordinating conjunctions (*e.g.* 'if', 'when', 'although') than English does.

73 tengok-tengok ka-luar: the preposition *ka-*, indicating 'motion towards', is sufficient indication of direction without any verb of movement, *e.g. Dudok ka-sini*, 'Come and sit here.' Cf. Note 45 above.

75 mĕmbĕri pakai: the English is 'gives him clogs *to* wear', but the Malay sentence does not imply purpose. Cf. *Ayam itu di-bĕri-nya makan padi;* 'He gives the fowls padi to eat.' In such sentences *pakai* and *makan* are probably nearer to being nouns than verbs: 'He gives to the fowls padi as food.' 'He gives to him clogs as (foot)wear.'

76 Susah pula: *pula* indicating surprise.

78 'Nak pakai: another verbal idea with no personal subject attached: 'There-is-required a wearing.' Cf. Note 50 above.

baharu biasa: *lit.* 'newly accustomed', *i.e.* 'not until then will you feel at ease in them'. See Note I.89 and Sentence Pattern 7.

82 ta' ada-kah bĕrkĕpong?: the *bĕr-* here gives a passive sense, 'Are they not shut in (by somebody)?' See Note 37 above.

83 ayam kami / pakai lĕpaskan: an idiomatic use of *pakai*, very common in colloquial Malay, *e.g. Budak-budak 'ni baju kotor pakai champak sahaja; lit.* 'These children, dirty clothes, the practice is, just throw them down.'

lĕpaskan: the suffix *-kan* is here causative: *lĕpas* means 'free', 'loose'; *lĕpaskan*, 'make to be free', 'let go'.

84 pĕrgi-lah dia: in written Malay *Pĕrgi-lah dia* (or *ia*) would usually mean 'off they went'; in a context of this sort, where there is no question of past time, the *-lah* gives the same feeling of assurance, of things happening as you would expect them to happen, thrown into the future: 'In the mornings, off they'll go, you'll find.' When the subject follows the verb, instead of preceding it, it is a sign that the action is of more importance than the actor. Cf. Note I.44.

86 ubi kayu, pisang, kĕledek: note that there is no *dan* ('and') at the end of the catalogue. Neither are the separate items spot-lighted by *pun*, because the speaker is merely emumerating things which might be expected to be found together. But when he wants to draw attention to something different (*sayor*, 'green-stuffs'), then he does use *pun*.

89 'karang: short for *sĕkarang*, 'presently' or 'now'. *Karang* means 'arrange'; *sĕkarang = sa-karang*, 'arranged all-in-one with the time in question'. So it is used for 'this evening' in such a sentence as *Masa ini ta' sĕmpat. Pĕtang 'karang boleh saya chĕritakan;* 'There isn't time now. I'll tell you about it this

evening.' But in line I.81, *pĕtang ini* is used because a demonstrative is required, '*this* evening' not to-morrow evening.

In the present sentence '*karang* is a time-indicator, 'when we
(shall) have had our meal.'

91 naik: note that there is no *mĕ-* prefix in spite of the 3rd person
subject because *naik* is one of the verbs of motion referred to in
Note 22 above.

sudah tĕrhidang: *sudah* and *tĕr-* both indicate completion, *lit.*
'have come into the state of having been served', *i.e.* 'are set
out'.

92 makanan: the suffix *-an* has many shades of meaning. Most
-an derivatives are nouns. The base-word *makan* may mean
'eat' as a verb, or 'food' (sustenance) as a noun, *e.g. makan pakai*,
'food and clothing', but *makanan* is the word used of the food
itself.

93 chara Mĕlayu: the speaker slurs the first *a* of *chara*.

dudok bĕrsila: the pronunciation *bĕrsela* is a common variant.
There are many words in which the vowel varies, according to
the speaker, between *e* and *i* (though one or the other spelling
has been officially adopted for the written word), *e.g. sihat* and
sehat, *hitong* and *hetong*. The same applies to *o* and *u*.

95 mĕnyorongkan: from *sorong*, 'to push forward' or, as here, 'to
hold out in front of one'. Note that in the 'stage-directions',
which are in written style, the writer consistently uses *mĕ-* for a
verb which has a 3rd person subject.

-kan: the suffix here represents the preposition *akan*; she
holds out the bowl *for* him, she proffers it *to* him.

97 tangan kanan: only the right hand is used in eating.

100 Mana-lah?: for *Macham mana-lah?* 'How?'. The shortened
pronunciation of *-lah* as *lĕ* is widespread, as is also *-kĕ* for *-kah*.

kita makan bĕrĕmpat: the speaker's falling intonation tells you
that this noun-group stands on its own, giving the 'circumstances' in which the statement is set. It may be compared
with such 'absolute' (*i.e.* unattached) English phrases as 'that
being so', 'other things being equal'.

bĕrĕmpat: very near to the verbal use of *bĕr-* in *bĕrjalan*, etc.

102 bĕrchampor-champor: *bĕr-* with duplication indicating interconnection of one thing with another.

104 kita sĕndok nasi: 'you ladle some rice'; for this general use of
kita see Note 38 above.

110 Rah pun: the *pun* draws the hearer's attention away from Mr.
Martin to Zaharah. '*I* can't manage it (let alone *you*).' It is
because *pun* so often does this that it is sometimes called a
'balance particle'.

111 ta' lalu 'nak makan: a colloquial use of *lalu*, *lit.* 'not getting past, intending to eat'.

112 bukan pĕdas sangat: the contradictory negative.

113 dapat rasa: *dapat*, when it means 'be able', implies that some external difficulty has to be overcome. Cf. Note I.61.

SCENE II: TAKING STOCK

An analysis of the Notes shows that the picture has been filled in to the extent indicated below. Points already dealt with in Scene I are referred to by their original numbers and subsections. Simple constructions which are constantly recurring, *e.g.* Numbers 1 and 2 (Position of Adjective and Absence of Copula), are not given further notice.

3. INI and ITU

    i. as a demonstrative adjective, either word may belong to a complete noun-group, not merely to one noun:

        Dia mĕnunjokkan bagaimana dudok bĕrsila itu.
        He shows what he means by sitting cross-legged.
        Di-sĕrambi ini tidak pakai kĕrusi meja.
        Here in the *sĕrambi* we don't have furniture.
        (*lit.* this circumstance of being on the *sĕrambi*.)
        Orang pĕrĕmpuan di-dalam ini pula tĕmpat-nya.
        Here, inside, is where the women sit.

    ii. As a demonstrative pronoun, either word may be a subject, with a noun-group for complement:

        Ini Mr. Martin 'dah sampai.
        Mr. Martin has come! (*lit.* This (is) Mr. Martin-having-come.)

5. NUMERAL COEFFICIENTS

    (*c*) *biji* for small (roundish) things:

        sa-biji buah pinang, 'a betel-nut'.

    (*d*) *bilah* for lath-like things:

        dua bilah kĕris, 'two krises'.

6. PRONOUNS

    (*a*) Personal

        i. *kita* is often used in general statements, corresponding to the 'you' of English proverbial expressions such as 'You can't eat your cake and have it':

           Ini isi dia bila kita sudah kupas.
           This is the inside of it when you have peeled it.

kami excludes the listener:

> *Kami mĕmasak pakai kayu api.*
> When we (Malays) cook, we use firewood.

iv. *-nya*

b. impersonally:

> *Dudok-nya bĕrsila, macham ini.*
> We (or You, or They) sit cross-legged like this.

c. as an object pronoun (*i.e.* meaning 'him', 'her', 'it', 'them'), instead of *dia*, after a *mĕ-* derivative:

> *Ia hĕndak mĕnjamu-nya makan chara Mĕlayu.*
> He is going to invite him to a Malay meal.
> *Zaharah tiada pĕrasan Mr. Martin mĕnyakat-nya.*
> Zaharah doesn't realize that Mr. Martin is teasing her.

d. after a *di-* + *simple verb* construction, *-nya* indicates the doer of the action, the agent:

> *Pĕrkataan itu di-bunyikan-nya chara Inggĕris.*
> He pronounces the word in the English way.
> (*lit.* The word, there-is-a-pronouncing by-him . . .)
> *Di-tunjokkan-nya kapada Mr. Martin sa-biji buah pinang.*
> She shows Mr. Martin a betel-nut.
> (*lit.* There is a showing by her to Mr. Martin a betel-nut.)

(*b*) Interrogative

ii. *c. mana* for 'how?':

> *Mana-lah banyak-nya?*
> How can you say that it's a lot?

7. DUPLICATION

i. Variety and repetition:

> *Dia dudok sĕrta mĕmandang-mandang.*
> He sits down and looks round about him.
> *Mari kita tengok-tengok sadikit.*
> Let's have a look round.

ii. moderation:

> *Dudok-dudok-lah dahulu.*
> Just sit down for a bit.

8. TIDAK and BUKAN

(*a*) *tidak* or *tiada* or *ta'* merely denies:

> *Zaharah tiada pĕrasan dia mĕnyakat-nya.*
> Zaharah does not realize that he is teasing her.

(*b*) *bukan*

i. Correcting an erroneous impression:

> *Bukan pĕdas sangat.*
> No, it isn't very hot.

9. INDICATION OF TIME

  ii. by adverbial word or phrase:
    Lĕpas makan nasi 'karang boleh pula kita bĕrjalan-jalan.
    After we've had our meal we'll go for another little walk.

10. AFFIXES

  (*a*) *bĕr-*

    ii. forming an intransitive verb of 'doing' or of 'being':
      Dia mĕnunjok ka-sĕrambi sambil bĕrjalan ka-situ.
      He points to the *sĕrambi* and goes towards it.
      Kita makan bĕrĕmpat.
      There are four of us to eat it.
      (*lit*. We eat, being four.)

    iii. as the equivalent of an English perfect participle passive:
      Di-tunjokkan-nya sa-biji pinang bĕlum bĕrkupas.
      She shows him an unpeeled betel-nut.
      Ayam ini tidak ada-kah bĕrkĕpong dĕngan apa-apa?
      The chickens are not shut in in any way?

    iv. implying interconnection (usually in combination with
      duplication and/or the suffix *-an*):
      Kita makan bĕrchampor-champor.
      We eat them together (*lit*. mixed).
      *Dia hĕndak mĕmunjokkan pĕrkara yang bĕrkĕnaan dĕngan rumah
      tangga.*
      He is going to show him things connected with the home.

  (*b*) *mĕ-*

   i. as verbal noun

    a. after a preposition:
      Dia makan dĕngan mĕnurut chara Mĕlayu.
      He eats Malay fashion (*lit*. with following Malay style).
      Dia naik dĕngan tiada mĕmbuka kasut.
      He goes up without taking off his shoes (*lit*. with not-
      unfastening).
      Dia dudok sĕrta mĕmandang-mandang.
      He sits down and looks about him. (*lit*. together with
      looking).
      Ia pĕrgi ka-tingkap sĕrta mĕnjĕngok ka-luar.
      He goes to the window and looks out.

    b. after *hĕndak* implying purpose or futurity:
      Ia hĕndak mĕmunjokkan . . .
      He is going to show . . .
      Ia hĕndak mĕnjamu-nya . . .
      He is going to invite him . . .
      Ia hĕndak mĕmbuka kasut.
      He is about to take off his shoes.

ii. as a finite verb after a 3rd person subject:

> *Che' Normah měnunjok kapada sa-buah kěrusi.*
> Che' Normah points to a chair.
> *Ia měmandang kapada Zaharah.*
> He looks towards Zaharah.
> *Che' Mahmud měnyěndok nasi ka-dalam pinggan.*
> Che' Mahmud ladles some rice into a plate.

iii. participial, following a verb of movement, to indicate a second action which is almost simultaneous with the first:

> *Dia pěrgi měngambil těmpat sireh.*
> She goes and gets (*lit.* goes, getting) the sireh set.
> *Ia pun balek měmbawa Mr. Martin.*
> He comes back with (*lit.* bringing) Mr. Martin.
> *Dia dudok měnunjokkan bagaimana dudok běrsila itu.*
> He sits down and shows what he means by *dudok běrsila.*

[Method of joining prefix *mě-* to root:

1. before *ch* or *j* insert *n*:   *chari* / *měnchari*
                              jadi / *měnjadi*

5. before (*s*) insert *ny*:   *sakat* / *měnyakat*

Note 1. When an initial consonant is dropped and the root is duplicated, the nasal infix is repeated before the root:

> *pandang* / *měmandang*   *měmandang-mandang*
> *sakat* / *měnyakat*   *měnyakat-nyakat*]

2. Verbs of movement, such as *pěrgi* 'go', *datang* 'come', do not take the *mě-* prefix.

3. An imperative is not followed by a *mě-* derivative: *Pěrgi ambil*, 'Go and fetch' (*lit.* 'Go, get').

(*c*) *pěr-* . . . *-an*, noun affixes

> *kata*, 'say', 'saying', 'utterance'; *pěrkataan*, 'word'

(*d*) *-kan*

i. a suffix which creates a causative verb:

> *bunyi*, 'sound'; *bunyikan pěrkataan*, 'make-to-sound (*i.e.* pronounce) a word'; *lěpas*, 'freed', 'loose'; *lěpaskan ayam*, 'let-loose the fowls'

ii. an apparent suffix which is really the remnant of a preposition *akan*, with the meaning 'to', 'towards', and therefore implying 'for somebody's benefit':

> *Dia hěndak měnunjokkan kapada Mr. Martin pěrkara yang běrkěnaan děngan rumah tangga.*
> He is going to show Mr. Martin everything connected with the house.
> *Dia měnyorongkan ayer basoh tangan.*
> She holds out to him water for him to wash his hands.

(*e*) *tĕr-*

A prefix which implies completion

i. in a completed state:

> *Tingkap sĕmua tĕrbuka.*
> All the windows are open.
> . . *dua bilah kĕris tĕrgantong kapada dinding.*
> . . two krises, hung on the wall.
> *Di-tĕngah rumah sĕdang tĕrhidang makanan di-atas safrah.*
> In the living-room the meal was set out on the cloth.

ii. of involuntary completion, often implying suddenness:

> . . *sĕrta tĕrsĕnyum sadikit.*
> . . with a little smile.
> *Ia tĕrpandang kapada dua bilah kĕris.*
> He notices (*lit.* finds himself looking at) two krises.

(*f*) *di-*

A verbal prefix used before the simple (*i.e.* unaffixed) form of the verb.

In this construction the action is of more importance than the actor (or agent), as the order of words shows. In many sentences, as in the second example below, no agent is specified. In others, the word *orang* ('person', 'persons', 'somebody or other') stands for the agent in the background. (See VI.10 f.)

If the doer of the action (*i.e.* the agent) and the result of the action (*i.e.* the object) are both mentioned after the verb, they follow the *di-* construction *in that order*, *i.e.* agent before object, as in the first example:

> *Di-tunjokkan-nya kapada Mr. Martin sa-biji pinang.*
> She shows Mr. Martin a betel-nut.
> *Di-atas lantai di-bĕntang tikar.*
> Mats are spread on the floor (*lit.* There is a spreading (of) mats).

Note: -*nya* indicating agent, after a *di-* verb, is sometimes preceded by *oleh.*

(*g*) *-an*

A suffix which usually creates a noun. The resultant derivatives have many shades of meaning.

i. a noun which suggests a passive meaning:
> *makanan,* 'that which is eaten', 'food'.

11. PUN

i. to draw attention to a new idea:
> *Sayor pun ada juga sadikit.*
> There are a few vegetables, too.

ii. to draw attention to the subject of a main statement which follows a subordinate time-statement (written style):

> *Lĕpas mĕmbuka kasut dia pun masok.*
> After taking off his shoes, he went inside.

12. JUGA

ii. to indicate reservation or moderation:

> *Mr. Martin hĕndak choba-kah?—Hĕndak juga.*
> Will you try it?—Ye-es, I think I will.

iii. to limit, by excluding alternatives:

> *hari ini juga,* 'this very day'
> *Di-sini juga tĕmpat makan,* 'This is where we have our meals.'

13. PULA

i. showing surprise:

> *Susah pula pakai tĕrompah ini.*
> Hm. It's not so easy as I thought, getting about on these clogs.

ii. the basic significance of *pula* is recurrence, repetition, sequence, extension:

> *Sa-bĕlah dalam itu sĕrambi pula nama-nya.*
> Now that room inside there, that's called the *sĕrambi.*
> *Orang pĕrĕmpuan di-dalam ini pula tĕmpat-nya.*
> The women, they sit here, inside.
> *Mari kita turun ka-dapor pula.*
> Let's go down to the kitchen now.
> *Lĕpas makan nasi 'karang boleh kita pula bĕrjalan-jalan.*
> After dinner we can take another walk.

14. -LAH

i. for emphasis:

a. by confirming an impression already gained—

> *Ia. Itu-lah dia kĕris.*
> Yes, that's a krise (as you thought).

b. by marking out the predicative word—

> *Siang-siang pĕrgi-lah dia ka-dalam kĕbun.*
> Early morning, off they go (you'll find) into the plantation.

c. by singling out one word or phrase—

> *Di-atas tikar itu-lah dudok.*
> That's what we sit on, mats.

ii. after an imperative, to moderate it:

> *Dudok-dudok-lah dahulu.*
> Just sit down for a bit.
> *Ambil-lah tĕmpat sireh sa-kali.*
> Get the sireh set at the same time.

> *Ta' usah-lah.*
> Don't (take off your shoes).
> *Sila-lah naik.*
> Do come up, please.

15. PREPOSITIONS

    (c) *ka-* 'towards'

        i. frequently used alone, without a verb of movement, to convey the idea of 'motion towards':

> *Saya ka-dapor.*
> I (am going) to the kitchen.
> *Mari kita tengok-tengok ka-luar pula.*
> Let's go and have a look outside now.

        ii. frequently used where the corresponding English preposition would be 'at' rather than 'to'.

> *Ia pĕrgi mĕnjĕmput Mr. Martin ka-hotel-nya.*
> He goes and calls for Mr. Martin at his hotel.

16. CONJUNCTIONS

        ii. Subordinating conjunctions are fewer than in English, because of the frequent use of the 'free' noun-group to declare the attendant circumstances. (See No. 22.iii):

> *Kami mĕmasak, pakai kayu api.*
> When we cook, we use firewood.

17. Translation of 'WHEN'

    (c) In writing, *apabila* is used for the subordinating conjunction 'when', but in speech this is invariably shortened to *bila*:

> *Bila sudah kita kupas . . .*
> When you have peeled it . . .

18. BOLEH and BIAR

    (a) *boleh* for promised result:

> *Rah ambil-lah tĕmpat sireh boleh kita tunjok pada dia.*
> Fetch the sireh set, Rah, and we'll show it to him.

19. BAHARU

        i. for 'not until', 'then and only then'
        Hĕndak pakai banyak kali baharu biasa.
        You won't feel at home in them until you've worn them many times.
        (*or* You'll have to wear them a good many times before . . .)

20. AFFIRMATIVE ANSWER

        i. given by repetition of the relevant word:
        Hĕndak choba-kah?—Hĕndak.
        Would you like to try it?—Yes, I should.

ii. given by the confirming particle *-lah*:

> *Itu-lah dia kĕris*, 'Yes, that's a kris.'

21. THE USE OF A CLASS TERM (GENERIC) BEFORE A SPECIFIC TERM IS COMMON IN MALAY:

> *bandar Kuala Lumpur*, *lit.* 'the town, Kuala Lumpur.'

22. THE NOUN-GROUP

The interpretation of many Malay sentences depends on an understanding of the part played by some particular noun or noun-group.

i. a noun-group may be attached to a noun of place or time as a description which, in English, would be expressed by 'where' meaning 'in which', or 'when' meaning 'on which':

> *tĕmpat mĕreka mĕnanti*
> (*lit.* the place of-them-waiting)
> the place where they were waiting
> *tĕmpat kita dudok ini*
> (*lit.* this place of we-sitting)
> the place where we are sitting
> *masa kita di-London*
> (*lit.* time of we-(being)-in-London)
> when we were in London
> *hari Mr. Martin akan tiba*
> (*lit.* day of Mr.-Martin-about-to-arrive)
> the day on which Mr. Martin was to arrive

ii. a noun or noun-with-adjunct may stand, unattached, at the beginning of a sentence to 'declare the topic', *i.e.* it is the subject of the *thought* (the logical subject), but not the grammatical subject of any verb:

> *Orang pĕrĕmpuan | di-dalam ini pula tĕmpat-nya.*
> The women, it is here, inside, that they sit.
> *Dapor kami | ta' ada pakai chorong.*
> Our kitchens, we don't have chimneys in them.
> *Ayam kami | pakai lĕpaskan sahaja.*
> Our fowls, we just let them loose.

iii. a noun-group may stand, unattached, at the beginning of a sentence to declare the circumstances attending the main statement. In such sentences English uses a subordinate clause beginning with a conjunction (*e.g.* 'if', 'when', 'because', 'although'):

> *Kami mĕmasak | pakai kayu api.*
> When we cook, we use firewood.

iv. a noun-group may form a complement (or a subject, or an object):

Ini | Mr. Martin 'dah sampai.
Mr. Martin has arrived.
(*lit.* This (is) Mr. Martin-having-arrived.)

v. a verb, usually unprefixed, may itself be the subject of a sentence (*i.e.* a noun), as with *pakai* and *dudok* below.

Di-sĕrambi ini tidak pakai kĕrusi meja.
Here in the *sĕrambi* we don't have furniture.
(*lit.* using furniture (is) not)
Di-atas tikar itu-lah dudok.
It's on the mats that we sit.
(*lit.* Sitting (is) on the mats.)
Dudok-nya bĕrsila macham ini.
We sit with our legs crossed, like this.
(*lit.* The-sitting in-the-case (is) sitting-cross-legged like this.)
Dapor kami ta'ada pakai chorong.
We don't have chimneys in our kitchens.
(*lit.* Our kitchens, using chimneys does not exist.)
Kami mĕmasak pakai kayu api.
We use firewood when we cook.
(*lit.* We-cooking, using fire-wood (exists).)

SCENE II: SENTENCE PATTERNS

1. 'Please . . . will you?'

a. **Sila-lah naik Mr. Martin.**
Do come up, Mr. Martin.

b. Silakan-lah. Jangan malu-malu.
Do please begin (i.e. to eat, or drink). Don't be shy.

c. Choba chĕpat sadikit bĕrbaju.
Now hurry up and get dressed, please!

d. Tolong saya mĕngangkat meja ini.
Lend me a hand with this table, will you?

e. Choba tolong dia bĕrkĕmas itu.
Help him with the clearing up, will you?

2. *Ini*, as subject, sets the scene

a. **Ini Mr. Martin 'dah sampai.**
Mr. Martin's here!

b. Jangan gadoh. Ini 'nak pĕrgi 'dah.
Don't fuss! I'm just going.

c. Ini mĕngapa mĕnangis pula. Pagi hari raya patut-nya suka hati.
What's all this! Crying? On a holiday morning when you ought to be gay.

d. Kalau nantikan tukang boleh di-buat-nya bĕtul-bĕtul. Ini ta' sabar lagi
   mĕnanti.
   *If you had waited for the carpenter he would have done it properly. But you hadn't
   the patience to wait (sc. and now look at the result!).*

e. Ini 'dah rosak, baharu tahu.
   Now that it's spoilt, you realize what you've done.

3. Jangan

a. **Jangan-jangan pĕning lagi.**
   I hope he isn't still feeling dizzy.

b. Jangan bising sangat.
   Don't make such a noise!

c. Bagi tahu sa-kali lagi nombor rumah kita, jangan dia sĕsat ka-tĕmpat lain.
   Tell him the number again, to make sure that he doesn't go to the wrong house.

d. Ta' bĕrlampu pun ta' mĕngapa. Lampu jalan ada. Jangan nampak
   mata-mata sudah-lah.
   *Never mind about not having a light. There are the street lights. As long as the
   policeman doesn't see us it's all right!*

e. 'Dah ada kĕreta api. Jangan ta' sĕmpat kita ini.
   The train's in! I hope we'll be in time!

4. 'in which', 'with whom', etc.

a. **Tĕmpat kita dudok ini kita panggil anjong.**
   The place that we are sitting in is called the ' anjong'.

b. Pen saya pakai mĕnuliskan-nya hari itu ta' bĕrapa baik.
   The pen that I wrote it with wasn't a very good one.

c. Kawan dia pĕrgi ka-nĕgĕri Pĕranchis hari itu pandai bĕrchakap Pĕranchis.
   The friend with whom he went to France could speak French.

d. Pĕrkara itu sudah ada kĕluar dalam surat khabar. Surat khabar itu sudah
   tutup sĕkarang.
   The paper in which it appeared is no longer in circulation.

e. Pintu itu bĕrkunchi dĕngan kunchi mangga. Kunchi mangga itu 'dah di-
   pĕchah orang.
   The padlock with which the door was fastened had been wrenched open.

5. Diri, sĕndiri

a. **Kĕris pendek ini kĕris saya sĕndiri.**
   This short kris is my own.

b. Sa-malam ada dua orang pĕngganas mĕnyĕrah diri.
   Two terrorists gave themselves up yesterday.

c. Anak-nya tinggal sa-orang diri di-rumah.
   Her child stayed at home, all alone.

d. Bĕrunding sama sĕndiri dahulu, 'dah putus baharu kita bagi tahu kĕtua.
   *We'll discuss it among ourselves first of all, and when we have come to a decision
   we'll let the headman know.*

e. Hěndak-lah jaga diri-sěndiri, jangan běrgantong kapada orang lain sa-mata-mata.
You must look after yourself. Don't rely entirely on other people.

6. A 'free' statement, for an English subordinate clause

a. **Kami měmasak, pakai kayu api.**
When we cook we use firewood.

b. Hěndak sampai chěpat, orang naik kapal těrbang.
If you want to get there quickly you go by air.

c. Dia měmbuat rumah di-Batu Gajah, di-situ kampong dia yang asal.
The reason why he is building a house at Batu Gajah is that that is where he came from originally. (Or *He is building . . . because . . .*).

d. Kami pěrgi hari itu, naik kěreta api.
When we went there, we went by train.

e. 'Nak makan buah itu, kupas dahulu. 'Dah kupas, baharu makan.
When you are going to eat that fruit peel it first. Don't eat it without peeling it.

7. *Baharu* and *baharu-lah*

a. **Hěndak pakai banyak kali baharu biasa.**
You'll have to wear them many times before you will feel at home in them.

b. Lambat lagi baharu kita sampai ka-Kuala Lumpur, kěreta api ini baharu běrtolak dari Rawang.
We shan't get to Kuala Lumpur for a long time yet, the train has only just left Rawang.

c. 'Dah saya suroh banyak kali baharu-lah di-buat-nya.
Not until I had told him over and over again did he do it.

d. Ta' kan dia tahu lorong-lorong di-pěkan ini. Dia baharu datang sa-malam.
He isn't likely to know the streets of this town. He only arrived yesterday.

e. Baharu sa-kali ini-kah dia datang ka-sini?
Is this the first time that he has been here?

8. 'Behind, beyond, beside . . .'

a. **Di-bělakang sana ada kěbun gětah.**
At the back there, there's a rubber plantation.

b. Di-sa-balek sana rumah itu ada padang.
Beyond that house there's an open space.

c. Di-sěbělah bawah-nya tidak běrsapu chat.
It isn't painted underneath.

d. Di-sěbělah měnyěbělah rumah itu di-tanam pokok bunga.
On each side of the house they have planted flowers.

e. Di-sěběrang sana sungai itu maseh hutan lagi.
On the other side of the river it is still jungle.

SCENE III

DI-DUSUN BUAH BUAHAN

IN THE ORCHARD

1 Lĕpas makan nasi Che' Mahmud mĕmbawa Mr. Martin pĕrgi bĕrjalan-
2 jalan ka-bĕlakang rumah-nya ia-itu dari kampong-nya lalu masok ka-dusun.
3 Che' Normah dĕngan Zaharah pun pĕrgi sama. Bĕrbĕtulan pula masa itu
4 tĕrjatoh pada musim buah-buahan di-dusun itu tĕngah mĕnjadi-jadi.

After eat cooked-rice Che' Mahmud conducts Mr. Martin going walking-about to-back of-the-house-of-him, that-is-to-say from land-round-his-house passing-on entering into-orchard.

Che' Normah with Zaharah go together. With-exactitude, strange-to-say, that-period happens-to-fall at a time of the-various-fruits-in-the-orchard in-the-middle-of-being-abundant.

After their meal Che' Mahmud takes Mr. Martin for a walk at the back of the house, through the garden into the orchard.

Che' Normah and Zaharah go with them. It happens to be just the very time when the fruit is ripening in abundance.

5 Che' Mahmud bĕrchakap sambil mĕnunjok kapada buah pisang.
Che' Mahmud speaks together-with pointing towards banana-fruit.
Che' Mahmud points to some bananas as he speaks.

6 MAH. **Choba tengok pisang itu, lain sadikit daripada yang**
Please look-at those bananas, different a-little from (the ones)
Look at these bananas, they are rather different from

7 **itu, bukan-kah?**
which (are) those, is-it-not-so?
those, aren't they?

8 MAR. **Ia. Lain sangat.**
Yes. Different very-much.
Yes, quite different.

9 MAH. **Pisang memang banyak bangsa-nya.**
Bananas by-nature many (are) the-kinds-of-them.
There are many different sorts of bananas, you know.

10 NOR. **Bangsa-nya itu sudah-lah macham-macham, guna-**
The kinds of-them are-already various, uses-of-them, in addition,
To begin with, there are many different kinds, and then

11 **nya pula bĕrlain-lain. Ada pisang yang sĕdap di-**
varying. There are bananas which (are) delicious there-being-an-
there are different ways of using them too. There are

57

12   **makan mĕntah sahaja, macham pisang ĕmbun yang**
eating raw only, like the dew-bananas which, in-large-numbers,
some which are nice only if you eat them raw, like the

13   **banyak sampai ka-England itu. Ada pisang yang**
reach to England. There-are bananas which (are) excellent fried
'dew' bananas that get to England in large quantities,

14   **elok di-goreng sahaja. Ada pula pisang yang elok**
only. There are, in-their-turn, bananas which are excellent curried
and there are some that are only good for frying. And then

15   **di-gulai sahaja.**
only.
again there are others which are only good if they are
curried.

16   Mĕreka sudah sampai ka-dalam dusun.
They have-completed arriving into the orchard.
They come into the orchard.

17 MAH.   **Ini-lah dia dusun. Pokok-pokok-nya sĕmua pokok**
This (is) it, the orchard. The various trees of-it all fruit-trees.
Now this is the orchard. The trees in it are all fruit trees.

18   **buah-buah. Pokok kĕlapa, pokok pinang, pokok**
Trees coconut, trees betel, trees banana not exist at-here. If there-
There are no coconut palms, or betel-palms or bananas

19   **pisang tidak ada di-sini. Kalau ada pokok-pokok**
are those trees—sort near house just now—not we give-name
here. When there are trees of that sort—like those round

20   **itu—macham dĕkat rumah tadi—tidak kita nam-**
'dusun', we give name 'kampong' only.
the house just now—you don't call it *dusun*, you just call

21   **akan dusun. Kita namakan kampong sahaja.**
it your *kampong* land.

22 NOR.   **Pokok-pokok dalam dusun ini bĕrchampor-champor**
Trees in this orchard mingled, just. Moreover, not there-is,
The trees in this orchard are mixed up, anyhow. And

23   **sahaja. Lagi pun ta' ada bĕrbaris.**
being-in-line.
they are not in rows, either.

24 MAH.   **Orang tua-tua dahulu ta' kira sangat tĕntang baris**
People of-varying-generations, before, did not take-into account very
In days gone by people didn't bother overmuch about

atau atoran. Dia kira asal pěnoh tanah-nya děngan
much concerning lines or arrangement. They reckoned, provided-
lines or arrangement. They thought that as long as their
pokok sudah-lah.
that full (was) their-land with trees, there-was-completion.
land was covered with trees, that was all that mattered.

MAR. **Sudah lama-kah dusun ini?**
Has-become old this orchard?
Is it old, this orchard?

MAH. **Lama. Tětapi pokok-nya tidak sa-kali tanam**
Old. But trees-of-it not one-time planting only.
Yes. But the trees in it were not all planted at the same
sahaja.
time.

Che' Normah měnunjok kapada sa-buah pondok kěchil.
Che' Normah points to a little hut.

NOR. **Mari kita pěrgi ka-pondok itu, boleh kita suroh**
Come, we go to-the-hut, able we ask Pa' Awang get fruit a little.
Let's go to the hut and ask Pa' Awang to get some fruit.
Pa' Awang měngambil buah sadikit.

MAR. **Pa' Awang dudok di-sini-kah?**
Pa' Awang lives here?
Is this where Pa' Awang lives?

NOR. **Bukan. Dia dudok di-pondok ini dalam musim**
No. This he-living-in-hut, in this fruit-season only.
Oh, no. He only lives in the hut now during the fruit
buah ini sahaja.
season.

Che' Mahmud měnunjok ka-bawah pondok.
Che' Mahmud points underneath the hut.

MAH. **Tengok, di-bawah pondok itu buah durian. Mr.**
Look, under the hut, durian fruit. Mr. Martin surely there-has-
Look, there underneath the hut, they are durians. You
Martin těntu sudah ada měmbacha hal durian?
been reading the affair of durians?
have surely read about durians?

39 MAR. **Ada.**
There has been.
Yes, I have.

40 Che' Mahmud mĕngambil sa-biji durian lalu di-dĕkatkan-nya kapada
41 hidong Mr. Martin.
Che' Mahmud picks up one-unit durian, then there-is-a-bringing-near by him (it) to the
nose of Mr. Martin.
Che' Mahmud picks up a durian and holds it near Mr. Martin's nose.

42 MAH. **Tahan-kah tidak mĕnchium bau-nya? Banyak**
Bear-or-not, sniffing the smell of it? Many people not bear.
Can you bear the smell of it? Many people can't.

43 **orang ta' tahan.**

44 MAR. **Pada saya ta' ada apa-apa.**
To me, there-is-not anything.
I don't mind it, particularly.

45 MAH. **Kalau tahan mĕnchium bau-nya tĕntu suka makan**
If endure sniffing the smell of it, assuredly like eating the flesh of it.
If you can bear the smell of it, you'll surely like the taste

46 **isi-nya. Biar saya bĕlah sa-biji. Rah pinjam**
Allow that I split one-unit. Rah, borrow wood-knife to Pa'
of it. I'll split one. Go and borrow a *parang* from Pa'

47 **parang pada Pa' Awang.**
Awang.
Awang, Rah.

48 Zaharah naik ka-pondok kĕmudian turun balek.
Zaharah goes up to-the hut then comes down, back.
Zaharah goes into the hut and then comes out again.

49 ZAH. **Pa' Awang ta' ada.**
Pa' Awang not is-there.
Pa' Awang isn't in.

50 NOR. **Bĕtul kata Rah 'tu, ta' ada dia. Ĕntah ka-mana**
Correct the saying of Rah, there-is-not-present he. Not-any-idea
She's quite right. He isn't there. I wonder where he

51 **agak-nya. Kalau ada dia, ta' kan-lah dia bĕrdiam**
to-where, the guess of it. If present he, not likely he keeping-quiet
can be. If he had been in, it isn't likely that he would

52 **diri sahaja dalam pondok mĕnengok kita datang.**
himself only in the hut seeing us coming.
just have stayed quietly in the hut when he saw us coming.

53 MAH. **Choba tengok dalam pondok 'tu kalau ada parang-**
Please look in hut if is-present 'parang' of-him. Not having-a-
See if his *parang* is in the hut, will you? How are we going

54 **nya. Ta' bĕrparang macham mana pula 'nak**
'parang', method which (I ask you!) going-to split this durian.
to split this durian if we haven't got a *parang*?

55 **mĕmbĕlah durian ini.**

56 Che' Normah masok ka-dalam pondok mĕnchari parang.
Che' Normah goes into the hut and looks for the *parang*.

57 NOR. **Ada parang-nya. Rah mari ambil parang ini.**
Is-present the 'parang'-of-him. Rah come get this parang.
Yes, his *parang* is here. Come and get it, Rah.

58 Zaharah pĕrgi mĕngambil parang itu lalu di-bĕri-nya kapada Che' Mahmud.
Zaharah goes getting the 'parang', then there-is-a-giving-by-her to Che' Mahmud.
Zaharah goes and gets the *parang* and gives it to Che' Mahmud.

59 MAH. **Tengok saya mĕmbĕlah durian ini. Sĕnang sahaja**
See I split this durian. Easy, merely, if coincide opposite section
Watch me split this durian. It is quite easy if you get the

60 **kalau kĕna tĕntang pangsa-nya.**
of-it.
knife exactly on the dividing line of a section.

61 Che' Mahmud mĕmbĕlah durian. Dĕngan dua tiga tuil sahaja sudah
62 tĕrkopak. Masing-masing mĕngambil sa-ulas lalu makan.
*Che' Mahmud splits durian. With two three lifting-of-edge only, has-become opened-
out. Each-separately takes one pip then eats.*
Che' Mahmud splits the durian. He just prises up the rind in two or three
places, and there it is, spread open. They each take a 'pip' and eat it.

63 NOR. **Macham mana rasa-nya Mr. Martin?**
Sort which, the taste of it?
How do you like it, Mr. Martin?

64 MAR. **Saya suka juga.**
I like on-the-whole.
I rather like it.

65 ZAH. **Biji dia jangan makan. Ta' sĕdap.**
Stone of it do-not eat. Not pleasant.
Don't eat the stone. That isn't nice.

66 Tĕngah mĕreka makan durian itu ada sa-biji durian gugor.
Middle-of they eating durian, there-is (this), one unit of durian falls.
While they are eating, a durian drops from a tree.

67 NOR. **Itu durian gugor. Pĕrgi ambil Rah.**
That (is) a durian falling. Go get, Rah.
There's a durian fallen. Go and get it, Rah.

68 Zaharah pĕrgi mĕngambil durian itu.
Zaharah goes and gets the durian.

69 ZAH. **Durian ini bagus 'bah. Durian tapak gajah.**
This durian (is) fine, father. Durian sole-of-foot of-elephant.
This is a nice one, daddy. It's an elephant's-foot durian.

70 MAH. **Durian tapak gajah itu bĕsar sahaja. Isi-nya bukan**
Durian sole-of-elephant big only. Flesh-of-it not so-much
An elephant's foot durian is big, that's all. Its flesh hasn't

71 **bĕrapa sĕdap.**
pleasant-to-eat.
much taste.

72 ZAH. **Ta' bĕrapa sĕdap 'tu ta' mĕngapa. Rah suka fasal**
That not-(being)-very-nice, (is) not being-something. Rah likes
That doesn't matter. I like it because the pips are yellow,

73 **isi dia kuning, lagi pun tĕbal.**
because flesh of-it yellow, moreover thick.
and big.

74 MAH. **Ia-lah. Bawa ka-sini biar abah bĕlah.**
Yes, indeed. Bring to-here, allow that father split.
Yes, that's true. Bring it here for me to open it.

75 Che' Mahmud mĕmbĕlah durian itu.
Che' Mahmud splits the durian.

76 MAR. **Bĕsar isi yang ini. Dua sahaja satu tĕmpat.**
Large, pips which (are) these. Two only, one place.
What big pips this one has! Only two in each compartment.

MAH. **Itu-lah sĕbab-nya Zaharah suka. Tĕmpat isi-nya**
That (is) the reason-of it Zaharah likes. These receptacles of-
That's why Zaharah likes it. We call these sections
ini kita namakan ruang pangsa. Choba-lah rasa.
flesh-of-it we name spaces of-sections. Please taste.
ruang pangsa. Taste one.

Di-hulorkan-nya durian itu kapada Mr. Martin.
There-is-a holding-out by-him the durian to Mr. Martin.
He holds out the durian to Mr. Martin.

MAR. **Rasa-nya ta' bĕrapa sĕdap macham tadi.**
Taste-of it not how-much pleasant like just-now.
It's not as nice as the other one.

NOR. **Macham mana kita ini? 'Nak tunggu sampai Pa'**
How this-we? Intending wait until Pa' Awang return home (or)
What shall we do? Are we going to wait until Pa' Awang
Awang balek-kah, pĕrgi bĕrjalan dahulu?
go walking first?
comes back, or shall we walk round a bit first?

MAH. **Bĕrjalan-jalan-lah dahulu. Kita tunjokkan buah**
Walk about first. We show fruit other to Mr. Martin. When
We'll stroll round a bit. We'll show Mr. Martin some
lain kapada Mr. Martin. Bila ada Pa' Awang balek
it-is-that Pa' Awang returns, able we tell him get fruit.
other fruit. When Pa' Awang comes back we can ask him
boleh kita suroh dia mĕngambil buah.
to get some fruit for us.

Mĕreka pun bĕrjalan arah kapada sa-pokok manggis.
They walk in-the-direction to one-tree mangosteen.
They go towards a mangosteen tree.

NOR. **Buah itu buah manggis, Mr. Martin. Yang muda-**
That-fruit (is) mangosteen fruit. (Those) which (are) young, of-
Those are mangosteens, Mr. Martin. The young ones are
nya kuning, yang masak-nya hitam. Biar saya jolok
them, (are) yellow, (those) which (are) ripe, of-them, (are) dark-in-
yellow, and the ripe ones are black. Let me knock one
sa-biji.
colour. Allow that I knock down one-unit.
down for you.

90 Děngan měnggunakan galah Che' Normah dapat měnjolok dua tiga biji
91 manggis. Manggis itu di-chěkah-nya dan di-běri-nya kapada Mr. Martin.

92 Manggis itu tidak těrus di-makan oleh Mr. Martin kěrana ia hairan
93 měnengok buah itu sudah těrkupas děngan sa-kali těkan. Di-buang-nya sa-
94 bělah daripada kulit-nya.

With using (a) pole Che' Normah manages the-knocking-down two, three, units of mango-steen. The mangosteen is-split-open-by-pressure by-her and is-given by-her to Mr. Martin.

The mangosteen is not straightway eaten by Mr. Martin because he (is) amazed seeing (that) the fruit has-become peeled with one-time pressure. There is a throwing-away by-him one-half from the skin of it.

Che' Normah uses a pole and manages to knock down two or three mango-steens. She squeezes one open and gives it to Mr. Martin.

He does not eat it immediately because he was so surprised to see it 'peeled' with one pressure of the hand. He throws away one half of the skin.

95 MAR. **Chantek macham bunga isi manggis ini.   Chukup**
Pretty like flower, flesh of this mangosteen.   Enough white.
It's lovely, the inside of it, like a flower.   How white!
96 **puteh.**

97 ZAH. **Tengok.   Pada kulit-nya ada tanda běrapa isi-nya.**
Look.   On skin-of it there-is indication how-many the-contents of-
Look.   You can tell how many pips it has, from the rind.
98 **Manggis ini tadi isi-nya ěnam.   Tengok kulit-nya**
it.   This mangosteen just now contents of it six.   Look-at skin-
This one had six.   Look at the rind, and you know at
99 **'dah tahu isi-nya ěnam.**
of-it, it-has-become known contents of-it six.
once that there are six pips.

100 MAR. **Wah.   Pandai Zaharah.**
Oh.   Clever (is) Zaharah.
My word!   You are clever!

101 ZAH. **Bukan pandai.   Manggis 'dah memang macham itu.**
Not clever.   Mangosteens, already-exists-the-fact, by-the-nature-of
No, I'm not.   Mangosteens are always like that.
things, (are) like that.

102 MAH. **Mari kita běrjalan ka-sana pula.   Buah langsat,**
Come we walk to-there, further.   Fruits langsat, rambutan,
Let's go on a bit further.   There are langsats and ram-
103 **rambutan, pulasan, banyak yang rěndah di-sa-bělah**
pulasan, many which (are) low at-over-there.   Here all of them
butans and pulasan and lots of low-growing things over

sana. Di-sini sěmua-nya tinggi, ta' dapat kita
(are) high, not succeed we getting-them.
there. Everything here is too high for us to get.
měngambil-nya.

SCENE III: NOTES

3 pun: belonging to both names.

běrbětulan: the affixes *běr-* and *-an* show interconnection between their visit and the ripeness of the fruit. Cf. *Kami jarang běrjumpa sěbab rumah běrjauhan;* 'We seldom meet because we live a long way from each other' (*lit.* 'our houses are distant one from the other'). See Note II.2.

pula: used here with an air of pleasurable surprise, they happened to arrive just at the right time! Cf. *Saya singgah di-kampong Che' Harun, kěna pula ada orang kahwin;* 'I called at Che' Harun's house, and I found that there was a wedding on if you please!'

4 těrjatoh: *těr-* for a chance coincidence.

buah-buahan . . . měnjadi-jadi: the whole of this phrase describes *musim,* 'the season of fruits-being-in-abundance', *i.e.* 'just at the time when the trees were loaded with fruit'. Cf. II.46 *těmpat kita dudok,* 'the place of us sitting', *i.e.* 'the place in which (or where) we are sitting'.

měnjadi-jadi: for this use of *jadi* cf. *Ta' měnjadi padi tahun ini,* 'There wasn't a very good harvest this year.' *Měnjadi sangat durian tahun lalu,* 'There was a fine crop of durians last year.'

buah-buahan: when duplication is used to show variety it is frequently reinforced by the suffix *-an,* which itself expresses variety.

5 sambil měnunjok: *lit.* 'together-with showing', as in *sěrta měmandang* in II.22; always the *mě-* derivative after a preposition, provided it exists. See Note II.49.

6 yang itu: 'those (ones)'. The pronoun *yang* means 'who' or 'which', but it is not exactly parallel with the English relative pronouns as you will see in later notes. For this use, with no antecedent, cf. *yang merah,* 'the red one (*or* ones)', *lit.* '(the one) which (is) red', in answer to *Yang mana?* 'Which?', *lit.* '(the one) which (is) which?'

9 memang: a word which cannot always be translated, though it is very common in conversation. The underlying idea is 'that's how things *are*', *e.g. Budak itu memang běrtanya pěrkara yang bukan-bukan,* 'That child is always asking foolish questions!'

10 sudah-lah macham-macham : *sudah* is a word to be watched. Here, the idea of completion in it signifies that that state of affairs is already in existence and has to be accepted, before the next point comes in question. Cf. *Baju-nya sudah merah, pakai pula sĕlendang merah;* 'She was wearing a pink head-scarf with a pink *baju,* if you please.' Compare the English use of 'to begin with'.

11 bĕrlain-lain : duplication for variety. A very common *bĕr*-derivative, verbal in feeling, 'being different'.

Ada pisang yang sĕdap di-makan mĕntah : *ada* expresses existence, 'There do exist bananas which . . .'

di-makan : in this sentence it is easy to think of this as a passive, meaning 'eaten', but, as you have already seen, there are many sentences which will reveal their meaning to you more readily if you begin from an 'impersonal' translation for the *di-* + *simple verb* construction, *e.g. Jangan di-usek bĕnda ini; lit.* 'Let there not be a disturbing (of) these things'; *i.e.* 'Do not touch.'

17 Ini-lah dia dusun : *-lah* for confirmation. 'You were expecting to see the orchard. Well, here it is.' Note again the idiom of the personal pronoun followed immediately by the word which it 'replaces'. Cf. *Itu-lah dia kĕris* in II.65.

20 kita : see Note II.38.

23 lagi pun : 'moreover'. The basic idea in *lagi* is 'still'; here, 'there is still this to be considered'.

ada bĕrbaris : *ada* indicates that this is the existent state of affairs. The construction (*ada* + *bĕr*) is discussed in Note V.14. For the present, take it for granted.

25 atoran : the suffix *-an* creating an abstract noun; *ator,* 'arrange'; *atoran,* 'arrangement'.

27 sudah lama : an adjective such as *lama,* indicating a state which has come about, will usually be preceded by *sudah* when it is a predicate (*i.e.* when it makes a statement). So, *Kain ini sudah koyak* for 'This cloth *is* torn.'

28 Lama : repetition of relevant word for answer. See Note I.9.

31 boleh kita suroh : see Note I.26.

34 dia dudok di-pondok ini / dalam musim buah ini sahaja : the speaker's intonation tells you that the Malay sentence is different in structure from the English sentence given in the free translation. There is a definite break after *ini,* showing that all that precedes it is a noun-group, in this case the subject about which the statement is made: 'This his-living-in-the-hut (is) only during the fruit season', a statement which is parallel with such a statement as *Buku itu / di-dalam lachi;* 'The book (is) in the drawer.'

In modern written Malay a lengthy subject is often gathered together and re-stated as a pronoun + enclitic particle (*ia-lah*) before the predicate is added, *e.g. Dia dudok di-dalam pondok 'ini ia-lah dalam musim buah ini sahaja, lit.* 'His-living-in-this-hut, it (is) only during . . .'

dalam musim buah ini: the 'circumstantial' *ini*; not 'this (particular) fruit season', but 'it being the fruit season', *i.e.* 'now when the fruit is ripe'. Cf. Note II.50.

36 měnunjok ka-bawah pondok: *lit.* 'to underneath'. The idea of 'motion towards' is often expressed in Malay where it is not necessary to express it in English.

38 sudah ada měmbacha: *i.e.* 'at some time or other there has existed you-reading . . .' The different shades of meaning expressed by *sudah* and *ada*, separately and in combination, are very fine. If you are interested study the translations given in Sentence Pattern 3.i–v.

durian: the speaker says *děrian*, a common pronunciation in Pahang, and also in some other parts of the Peninsula.

39 Ada: repetition of relevant word for answer.

40 Che' Mahmud měngambil sa-biji durian lalu di-děkatkan-nya: in written Malay this is a very common sentence pattern, used when the actor performs two actions in succession on the same object, *e.g. Dia měngambil surat lalu di-buka-nya;* 'He took the letter and opened it.' (But, *Dia dudok lalu měmbuka surat itu;* 'He sat down and opened the letter.')

46 pinjam parang pada Pa' A.: *pada* here is short for *kapada* 'to'. Cf. *minta kapada*, where English uses 'ask-for (something) *from*', and *tanya kapada*, for English 'ask (somebody)'.

50 Bětul kata Rah 'tu: the speaker slurs the first *a* of *kata*.

Ěntah ka-mana: for *ěntah* see Sentence Pattern 4. Note the *ka-* again, 'whither' for English 'where'.

51 ta' kan: = *ta' 'kan* = *ta' akan*.

54 ta' běrparang: *běr-* showing possession.

57 mari ambil: no *mě-* for the verb which follows an imperative, because it is itself an imperative, *lit.* 'come, get'. See Note II.32.

58 pěrgi měngambil lalu di-běri-nya: see Note 40 above.

61 sudah těrkopak: *sudah* to indicate that a 'state' has come about, *těr-* to emphasize the completion of that state. With the rind falling back from it in sections the fruit will now look like a big, opened flower.

63 Macham mana rasa-nya?: *lit.* 'How, the taste of it?' *i.e.* 'How do you like it?' Malay constantly uses impersonal phrases of this sort where English would ask for a personal judgement, *e.g.*

'Did you enjoy the concert last night?' *Bagus-kah wayang sa-malam 'tu?*

64 Saya suka juga: *juga* for mental reservation, 'I rather like it.' But a Malay would more likely have given an impersonal answer; *Sĕdap* ('It's good') or *Ta' sĕdap*. Note the omission of the pronoun object ('it').

65 biji dia: 'the seeds of-it'. Children seldom use *-nya*.

70 Isi-nya bukan bĕrapa sĕdap: *bukan*, not *tidak*, because he feels that Zaharah thinks that it *is* very nice.

72 Ta' bĕrapa sĕdap 'tu / ta' mĕngapa: *tidak* (*ta'*), because it is purely a factual statement, 'the fact that-it-is-not-very-nice'.

itu: binding together the whole noun-group subject, before the predicate is added, 'That fact / does not matter.' Cf. *Dia dudok di-pondok ini* in Note 34 above.

74 biar abah bĕlah: see Note I.42.

81 'Nak tunggu-kah / pĕrgi bĕrjalan dahulu?: 'Are we going to wait? Or shall we take a walk?' No word for *or* is used in such sentences. The interrogative particle *-kah?* is some-times repeated in the second half of the sentence.

88 Biar saya jolok sa-biji: 'Let me knock one down' or 'I'll knock one down'. Note that the coefficient is used in sentences of this sort, where English uses only the numeral, *e.g. Bĕrapa biji tĕlor?—Tiga biji,* 'How many eggs?—Three.'

90 Dĕngan mĕnggunakan: *mĕ-* for a verbal-noun after a preposi-tion, *lit.* 'with using'.

mĕ-: before a base which begins with *g*, the prefix *mĕ-* takes *ng* as the connecting nasal. Similarly, *ng* is used before the corre-sponding lighter (or *voiceless*) consonant *k*, which is then dropped, *e.g. kachau*, 'stir', becomes *mĕngachau*. When the base itself begins with *ng* (there are very few such words) there is no need of a connecting nasal, *e.g. nganga, mĕnganga,* 'gaping open'.

dapat mĕnjolok: *mĕ-* for a verbal-noun after a transitive verb, *lit.* 'manages the knocking down (of)'.

dua tiga: 'two or three'. Note the absence of a conjunction. Cf. *kĕrusi meja* in line II.50.

92 hairan mĕnengok: *lit.* 'surprised, seeing'. The *mĕ-* derivative is always used after a word such as *hairan* which expresses a feeling, *e.g. jĕmu mĕndĕngar,* 'sick of hearing' (*lit.* 'sated, hearing').

95 Chukup puteh: 'quite white', a colloquial use of *chukup* ('enough').

98 Tengok kulit-nya / sudah tahu: two side-by-side sentences, *lit.* 'Look at the rind of it, it-has-become-known'. In English, either (colloquially) the two statements are joined by 'and':

'Look at the rind, and you know at once . . .' or else the first
half is made into a subordinate clause: 'If you look at the rind
you know at once.'

101 Manggis 'dah memang macham itu: for this use of *sudah*
cf. Note 10 above. That bananas are of different sorts, that
you can tell how many pips a mangosteen has by counting the
marks on the rind, these are already existent facts before you
begin thinking about them.

104 ta' dapat kita mĕngambil-nya: when *ta' dapat* means 'not able
to' there is the implication that something outside your own
control is preventing you from carrying out your purpose. Cf.
Note I.61. For the word-order cf. Note I.64, *sudah saya suroh.*
The statement (*i.e.* the predicate) here is *ta' dapat*, and the rest
of the sentence (the noun-group 'we-getting-them') is the
subject, the performance which 'does not come off'.

-nya: as usual, instead of *dia*, for the pronoun object of a
mĕ derivative.

SCENE III: TAKING STOCK

3. INI and ITU

    i. with a noun-group

        Ta' bĕrapa sĕdap 'tu ta' mĕngapa.
        The fact of its not being very tasty doesn't matter.
        Dia dudok di-pondok ini, dalam musim buah ini sahaja.
        He lives in the hut only when the fruit season is on.

    ii. as subject, with noun-group for complement:

        Itu durian gugor.
        There's a durian down! (*lit.* That (is) a-durian-falls.)

6. PRONOUNS

    (*c*). the relative *yang* (always a *distinguishing* pronoun)

        i. meaning 'who' or 'which':

            Ada pisang yang sĕdap di-makan mĕntah.
            There are some bananas which are good if you eat them raw.

        ii. with *itu*, the translation is 'the one', 'the ones', 'those':

            . . . *lain sadikit daripada yang itu.*
            . . . a bit different from those.

7. DUPLICATION

    i. variety (often with the suffix *-an*)

        Buah-buahan di-dusun itu tĕngah mĕnjadi-jadi.
        All the various fruits in the orchard were ripening in abundance.
        (*or* All the various trees were loaded with fruit.)

10. AFFIXES

(a) *bĕr-*

i. showing possession:

> *Ta' bĕrparang macham mana pula 'nak mĕmbĕlah durian ini?*
> How am I to split this durian without a chopping-knife?

iv. interconnection, with duplication and/or the suffix *-an:*

> *Bĕrbĕtulan pula masa itu tĕrjatoh pada musim buah-buahan.*
> The time happened to coincide exactly with the fruit season.

(b) *mĕ-*

i. as a verbal noun:

    a. after a preposition:

> *Dia bĕrchakap sambil mĕnunjok kapada buah pisang.*
> As he speaks, he points to some bananas.
> *Dĕngan mĕnggunakan galah Che' Normah dapat mĕnjolok dua tiga biji.*
> Che' Normah manages to knock a few down with a pole.

    c. after a transitive verb:

> *Tahan-kah tidak mĕnchium bau-nya?*
> Can you stand the smell of it? (*lit.* smelling it.)

iii. corresponding to an English present participle:

    a. after a verb of movement, indicating a second action which is almost simultaneous with the first:

> *Che' Normah masok ka-dalam pondok mĕnchari parang.*
> Che' Normah goes into the hut and looks for the knife. (*lit.* enters, seeking.)
> *Zaharah pĕrgi mĕngambil parang itu.*
> Zaharah goes and gets the knife. (*lit.* goes, getting.)

    b. after a word which expresses feelings:

> *Dia hairan mĕnengok buah itu sudah tĕrkupas dĕngan ea-kali tĕkan.*
> He is surprised to see the fruit stripped of its peel with one pressure of the hand. (*lit.* surprised, seeing.)

[Method of joining prefix to root:

6. before *g* and (*k*) insert *ng*:   *guna* / *mĕnggunakan*
                                  karang / *mĕngarang*]

(e) *tĕr-*

ii. of unexpected chance:

> *Masa itu tĕrjatoh pada musim buah-buahan.*
> The time happened to coincide with the fruit season.

(f) di-

i. for a particular action, with agent specified. This construction is very common in written Malay:

Di-hulorkan-nya durian itu kapada Mr. Martin.
He holds out the durian to Mr. Martin.
Manggis itu di-chěkah-nya.
She splits open the mangosteen.
Manggis itu tidak těrus di-makan oleh Mr. Martin.
Mr. Martin does not eat the mangosteen immediately.
Di-buang-nya sa-bělah daripada kulit-nya.
He throws away one half of the rind.

Note. When a previous action precedes the *di-* action, and has the same object, the joining word is *lalu*:

Zaharah pěrgi měngambil parang lalu di-běri-nya kapada bapa-nya.
Zaharah goes and gets the *parang* and then gives it to her father.
Ia měngambil sa-biji durian lalu di-děkatkan-nya kapada hidong Mr. Martin.
He picks up a durian and holds it to Mr. Martin's nose.

ii. for action with no particular agent specified; often to be translated by an English perfect participle:

Ada pisang yang elok di-goreng sahaja.
There are some bananas which are only nice if they are fried.

(g) -an

ii. creating an abstract noun:

ator, 'arrange'; *atoran*, 'arrangement'

12. JUGA

ii. for reservation:

Saya suka juga, 'I rather like it.'

13. PULA

i. showing surprise, or protest:

Běrbětulan pula masa itu těrjatoh pada musim buah.
The time of their visit just exactly coincided with the fruit season.
Ta' běrparang macham mana pula 'nak měmbělah durian ini?
How am I going to split the durian if I haven't got a knife?

ii. denoting sequence:

Bangsa-nya sudah-lah macham-macham, guna-nya pula běrlain-lain.
To begin with, there are many different species, and then in addition they can be used in different ways.

D

14. -LAH

    i. *a.* for confirmation:

        Ini-lah dia dusun.
        Now *this* is the orchard (which I said I would show you).

15. PREPOSITIONS

    (*c*) *ka-* 'towards'

        ii. used *whenever* 'motion towards' is implied:

            Dia měnunjok ka-bawah pondok.
            He points under the hut.
            Ěntah ka-mana agak-nya.
            I wonder where he is?

    (*d*) *kapada* (often shortened to *pada*) 'to' (a person)

        i. used after words of 'asking', 'borrowing', etc., which in English
            are followed by 'from':

            Rah pinjam parang pada (= *kapada*) *Pa' Awang.*
            Go and borrow a chopper from Pa' Awang, Rah.

    Note. *ka-* is used for 'to' before place-words only. Otherwise use *kapada*;
            Tunjok kapada dia (or-*mya*).
            Show (to) him.

16. CONJUNCTIONS

    i. omission of co-ordinating conjunction between words, or between
        balanced statements:

        dua tiga biji manggis
        two or three mangosteens
        Hěndak tunggu-kah, pěrgi běrjalan dahulu?
        Are we going to wait for him, or shall we walk round?
        Tengok kulit-nya sudah tahu.
        Look at the rind, and you know at once.

18. BOLEH and BIAR

    (*a*) *boleh* for predicted result:

        Mari kita ka-pondok itu boleh kita suroh Pa' Awang měngambil bush
            sadikit.
        Let's go to the hut and ask Pa' Awang to get us some fruit.

22. THE NOUN-GROUP

    iv. as subject:

        Dia dudok di-pondok ini | dalam musim buah ini sahaja.
        It is only during the fruit season that he lives in this hut.
        Ta' běrapa sědap 'tu | ta' měngapa.
        It doesn't matter that it hasn't much taste.

23. SUDAH

This word expresses completion, a state of affairs that has come about. It is not a time-word.

i. equivalent to 'has', *i.e.* stressing 'completion':

Abah 'dah datang.
Daddy has come.
Bag satu lagi sudah saya hantar ka-hotel.
I've sent my other case to the hotel.

ii. equivalent to 'is', or 'has become', *i.e.* stressing the state of affairs that has come about:

Bangsa-nya sudah-lah macham-macham, guna-nya pula bĕrlain-lain.
To begin with, there are many different sorts, and then, in addition, there are different ways of using them.
Tengok kulit-nya, sudah tahu.
Simply look at the rind, and you know the answer.
Sudah lama-kah dusun ini?
Is the orchard old?
Manggis sudah memang macham itu.
That's how mangosteens are.
Dia hairan mĕnengok buah itu sudah tĕrkupas dĕngan sa-kali tĕkan.
He was surprised to see that the fruit was stripped of its peel with one pressure of the hand.

(For *sudah* with *ada*, see Sentence Pattern No. 3.)

24. ADA

This word denotes existence. It is not a copula (*i.e.* it means 'there is', 'there are' not 'is', 'are').

Ada pisang yang sĕdap di-goreng.
There are some bananas which are good fried.
Pokok ini tidak ada bĕrbaris.
There's no methodical arrangement of these trees.

(For *ada* with *sudah*, see Sentence Patterns No. 3.)

25. IMPERSONAL EXPRESSIONS are very common in Malay:

i. with -*nya*

Entah ka-mana agak-nya, 'I wonder where he is.'
Macham mana rasa-nya? 'How do you like it?'

SCENE III: SENTENCE PATTERNS

1. 'Some are nice to eat'

a. **Ada pisang yang sĕdap di-makan mĕntah, ada pula yang elok di-gulai sahaja.**
Some bananas are nice to eat raw, others are only good for cooking.

b. Ada kain yang elok di-buat baju, ada kain yang elok di-buat sĕlendang.
Some materials are suitable for making dresses, others for head-scarves.

c. Ada kayu yang elok di-buat kĕrusi meja, ta' elok di-buat rumah.
Some woods are suitable for making furniture but are no good for house-building.

d. Ada barang pĕrmainan yang patut di-bĕri kapada budak laki-laki sahaja.
There are some toys which will only do for giving to boys.

e. Ada tulisan yang sĕnang di-bacha, ada pula yang nampak chantek sahaja,
ta' dapat di-bacha.
*Some people's handwriting is easy to read, other people's is beautiful to look at but
unreadable.*

2. *Sahaja* for 'just', 'simply', 'all . . .'

a. **Pokok-pokok dalam dusun ini bĕrchampor-champor sahaja.**
The trees in this orchard are not planted regularly, they are just anyhow.

b. Agak-nya ta' bĕrpakai jalan ini.   Bĕrumput sahaja.
This path evidently isn't used very much.   It's all grown over with grass.

c. Ta' bĕrsapu-kah bilek ini tadi?   Barang-barang bĕrsepah sahaja.
Wasn't this room done?   The things are all over the place.

d. Mĕngantok sangat.   Bila tĕrlĕtak sahaja kĕpala, saya pun tĕrus tidor.
*I was very tired.   No sooner had I laid my head down than I went straight off to
sleep.*

e. Kalau 'nak maju kĕna rajin sadikit, ta' boleh bĕrsĕrah sahaja.
If you want to get on you must make an effort.   You can't just let things slide.

3. i. *sudah ada*; ii. *ada*; iii. *sudah*; iv. *'dah sudah*

i. *sudah ada*

a. **Mr. Martin tĕntu sudah ada mĕmbacha hal durian.**
I'm sure you have read about durians, Mr. Martin?

b. Saya 'dah ada bĕlajar di-maktab itu.
I was at that college, once.

c. 'Dah ada pĕnuntut kita sampai ka-North Cape.
Some of our students have actually been as far as the North Cape.

d. Saya 'dah ada pĕrgi ka-Sarawak, 'tapi ka-Tanah Jawa bĕlum.
I have been to Sarawak, but I've never been to Java.

e. Budak-budak ini sĕmua-nya sudah ada bĕrchachar.
These children have all been vaccinated.

ii. *ada*

a. Abbas ada mĕnyalin rengkasan ini, orang lain ta' ada.
Abbas has copied down these notes, but the other boys haven't.

b. Anak saudara saya ada bĕlajar di-maktab itu, anak saya sĕndiri ta' ada.
I have a nephew studying at that college, but not a son.

c. Surat-nya ada sampai, 'tapi duit-nya ta' di-sĕmatkan-nya sa-kali.
His letter has arrived all right, but he hasn't enclosed the money with it.

d. Ayah saya ada pĕrgi ka-Pulau Selan, saya ta' pĕrnah.
My father has been to Ceylon, but I haven't.

e. Budak-budak ini ada bĕrchachar, 'tapi ta' ada bĕrchuchok B.C.G.
These young people have been vaccinated, but they haven't had their anti-tuberculin injections.

iii. *sudah*

a. Sudah tahu, bĕrtanya pula.
You know, and yet you ask.

b. Anak saya yang kĕchil itu 'dah bĕrsĕkolah.
My youngest child goes to school now.

c. Ta' usah gadoh. Kami 'dah makan.
Don't bother to get anything. We have had our meal.

d. Anak-nya 'dah pĕrgi ka-England.
His son has gone to England.

e. Awak 'dah bĕrchachar, apa 'nak di-takutkan lagi?
You've been vaccinated. What have you got to be afraid of?

iv. *'dah sudah*

a. Ahmad 'dah sudah mĕnyalin rengkasan ini.
Ahmad has finished copying the notes.

b. 'Dah sudah makan ini kita pĕrgi ka-rumah Ma' Chik.
When we have finished our meal we'll go to Ma' Chik's house.

c. 'Dah sudah putus bichara-nya, dia pun naik ka-Makkah.
He waited till his case was decided, and then he went to Mecca.

d. 'Nak pĕrgi mĕnengok wayang sarkis? 'Dah sudah pĕrgi sa-kali hari itu jadi-lah.
You want to go to the circus, do you? You've been once. That's enough.

e. 'Dah sudah bĕrchachar boleh-lah bĕlayar.
When you've been vaccinated you'll be ready to sail.

v. Neither *sudah* nor *ada*

a. Saya membacha buku itu dalam kapal.
I read that book on the boat.

b. Anak saudara saya bĕlajar di-maktab itu.
My nephew is at that college.

c. Saya sampai pagi tadi.
I arrived this morning.

d. Sa-malam Salim pĕrgi ka-rumah atok-nya.
Salim went to his grandmother's house yesterday.

e. Tĕrus kami mĕmbawa budak itu bĕrchachar.
We took the child to be vaccinated, straight away.

4. ĕntah

a. **Ĕntah ka-mana agak-nya.**
   I wonder where he is?

b. Ĕntah bĕrapa harga-nya saya pun ta' tahu.
   I've no idea how much it cost.

c. Dia sĕndiri pun ĕntah tahu ĕntah tidak di-mana rumah orang itu.
   I doubt if he himself knows where the man's house is.

d. Ka-mana 'nak di-bawa-nya pasu bunga itu pun ĕntah-lah.
   Where he was taking the flower-pot, I really don't know.

e. Payah sadikit kita 'nak tahu dia mahu-kah tidak. Bila kita tanya di-ĕntah-ĕntahkan-nya sahaja.
   It's difficult to know whether he is willing or not. When you ask him he just shrugs his shoulders.

SCENE IV

DI-TĔMPAT KĔRETA BĔRLANGGAR

A STREET ACCIDENT

Pada suatu pĕtang Che' Mahmud dĕngan Mr. Martin dudok bĕrbual-bual di-anjong rumah Che' Mahmud. Che' Normah tiada di-rumah. Zaharah kĕlihatan bĕrlari-lari balek dari mĕngaji Kor'an. Muka-nya nampak puchat. Sĕrta sampai sahaja ia ka-rumah Che' Mahmud pun bĕrtanya kapada-nya.

On one evening Che' Mahmud with Mr. Martin sits chatting on porch-verandah of house of Che' Mahmud. Che' Normah is-not at-home. Zaharah is-to-be-seen running back from studying Kor'an. The face of-her appears pale. Together-with merely arrives she to-house, Che' Mahmud puts-questions to-her.

Che' Mahmud and Mr. Martin are sitting chatting one evening on the verandah of Che' Mahmud's house. Che' Normah is not at home. Suddenly they see Zaharah come running home from Koran school. She looks pale. The moment she reaches the house Che' Mahmud questions her.

MAH. **Mĕngapa Rah bĕrlari balek? Gopoh sahaja nam-**
Being-what, Rah runs back? Haste, just-nothing-but, the appear-
Why did you run home? You seem to be in a tremendous
pak-nya.
ance-of-it.
hurry.

ZAH. **Dahshat, abah. Becha roda tiga kĕna langgar dĕkat**
Fearful, father. Rickshaw, wheels three, incur colliding near jati-
Oh, daddy, it's dreadful! A trishaw. Something ran into
pokok jati pada sĕlekoh itu.
tree at the-bend.
it near the rain-tree at the bend there.

MAH. **Kĕna langgar? Apa mĕlanggar-nya?**
Incurred colliding? What ran-into it?
Ran into it? What ran into it?

ZAH. **Kĕreta kĕchil.**
Car small.
A car.

MAH. **Ada orang mati?**
Is-there person dead?
Was anybody killed?

77

12 ZAH. **Ĕntah-lah. Rah ta' sĕmpat 'nak pĕrgi mĕnengok.**
Not-knowing. Rah, not-time-enough, wishing go see. Pa' Abu
I don't know. I didn't have time to go and see. Pa' Abu

13 **Pa' Abu suroh Rah balek chĕpat bĕri tahu abah.**
bid Rah return quickly give-to-know father.
told me to come home quickly and tell you.

14 MAH. **Biar abah pĕrgi tengok. Mr. Martin 'nak pĕrgi-kah?**
Allow-that father go see. Mr. Martin want go?
I'll go and see. Are you coming, Mr. Martin?

15 MAR. **'Ndak juga. Jauh-kah?**
Want, fairly. Far?
Yes, I think I will. Is it far?

16 MAH. **Tidak. Di-sa-balek itu sahaja. Rah tinggal-lah di-**
Not. At-the-reverse-side, only. Rah remain at-house.
No. Just over there. You stay in the house, Rah. Your

17 **rumah. Ĕmak-nya pun ta' ada di-rumah.**
Mother-in-question not-is-present at-house.
mother isn't in.

18 ZAH. **Rah hĕndak-lah pĕrgi mĕnengok.**
Rah want go-seeing.
But I want to go and see.

19 MAH. **Ta' ada apa guna-nya. Mĕmbuat tĕrkĕjut sahaja.**
There-is-not any use-of-it. Making startled only. No-knowing,
There's no use in your coming. It would only make you

20 **Ĕntah ada orang luka, ĕntah ada orang apa di-situ.**
exists person wounded, no-knowing, exists person anything, at-there.
frightened. There may be somebody injured there, or
goodness knows what.

21 MAR. **Ia. Lĕbeh baik tinggal di-rumah, Zaharah.**
Yes. More good remain at-house, Zaharah.
Yes. It will be better for you to stay at home, Zaharah.

22   Mĕreka pun sampai lalu hampir mĕndapatkan sa-orang muda yang ada
23 di-antara orang ramai itu.
They arrive, then approach coming-up-to one-person young who is-present in-between people, in-numbers, those.
They arrive, and go up to a young man in the crowd.

24 MAH. **Ada-kah siapa-siapa luka Din?**
Is-it-that anybody (is) wounded, Din?
Was anybody injured, Din?

25 DIN **Ta' ada Pa' Chik. 'Tapi orang becha roda tiga itu**
    Not-is, Pa' Chik. But person of the rickshaw-wheels-three hurled
    No, Pa' Chik. But the trishaw man was thrown into the

26   **tĕrchampak ka-dalam parit. Dĕrebar kĕreta itu**
    into ditch. Driver of-the-car hurt, also, a little. Sudden-blow,
    ditch. The driver of the car was hurt a bit, too. He feels

27   **sakit juga sadikit. Sĕnak tĕrhimpit kapada**
    jammed to steering-wheel.
    sore where he was thrown against the wheel.

28   **sĕtereng.**

29 MAH. **Ada-kah siapa-siapa mĕnolong orang becha itu?**
    Is-it-that anybody helped the rickshaw man?
    Has anybody done anything for the trishaw man?

30 DIN **Sudah kami kĕluarkan dari dalam parit itu. Itu dia**
    There-has-happened we-getting-out (him) from in the ditch. That
    We got him out of the ditch. There he is, on the grass by

31   **di-atas rumput tĕpi jalan itu. Diam sahaja ta' bĕr-**
    (is) he on-top (of) grass, edge of-the-road. Quiet, only, not move-
    the roadside there. He's quite still. He hasn't moved at all.

32   **gĕrak-gĕrak dari tadi.**
    moving from just-now.

33 MAH. **Nafas-nya ada?**
    Breathing-of-him exists?
    Is he breathing?

34 DIN **Ada. Nadi-nya pun ada. 'Tapi pĕrlahan bĕnar.**
    Exists. Pulse of him, too, is. But slow truly.
    Yes. And his pulse is all right, but very slow.

35 MAH. **Pengsan sahaja-lah sadikit itu. Otak-nya barang-**
    Fainting, merely, the-small-occurrence. Brain-of-him perhaps
    Just unconscious, not dead. Concussion perhaps, when

36   **kali bĕrgonchang pada masa kĕpala-nya tĕrhĕmpas**
    shaken at time head of-him dashed-down just now.
    his head struck the ground.

37   **tadi.**

38 Che' Mahmud dĕngan Mr. Martin pĕrgi rapat kapada orang sakit itu.
39 Susah mĕreka hĕndak rapat itu kĕrana orang ramai bĕnar bĕrkĕrumun.
    Che' Mahmud with Mr. Martin go close-up to the-sick-person.
    Difficult this they-intending-close-up, because people (are) in-large-numbers, truly, crowding round.

Che' Mahmud and Mr. Martin go towards the injured man.
They find it difficult to get near to him because there is a large crowd of people round him.

40 MAH.   **Tolong jauh sadikit, biar orang sakit ini dapat**
Help, distant a-little, allow-that the-sick-person manage-to-get air
Move back a bit, please, so that he can get some fresh air.

41   **udara bĕrseh. Din, bawa tilam becha dĕngan kain**
clean. Din, bring mattress of rickshaw with cloth covering-of-it
Din, bring the mattress from the trishaw, and the cloth

42   **alas-nya ka-sini.**
to-here.
that goes over it.

43   Din datang mĕmbawa tilam sĕrta kain yang ada di-dalam becha itu.
Din comes bringing mattress together-with cloth which is in the-rickshaw.
Din comes with the mattress and the cloth from the trishaw.

44 DIN   **Ka-mana 'nak lĕtak tilam ini?**
To where intending place the-mattress?
Where am I to put the mattress?

45 MAH.   **Mari kita lĕtak di-bawah orang ini.**
Come, we place (it) underneath the-person.
Let's put it under him.

46 DIN   **Alas dia dĕngan tilam? Ia juga. Tĕtapi tilam ini**
'Line' him with mattress? Yes, exactly. But this-mattress (is)
Put the mattress under him? Yes, of course. But it's too

47   **pendek.**
short.
short.

48 MAH.   **Ta' apa. Dapat kita alas kĕpala dĕngan badan dia**
Not-anything. Manage we-put-under head with body-of-him, it-
It doesn't matter. As long as we get it under his head and

49   **sudah-lah. Kain ini kita sĕlimutkan kaki dĕngan**
is-completed. This cloth we make-into-a-rug-for feet with legs
body, that will do. We'll wrap the cloth round his feet

50   **bĕtis-nya.**
of-him.
and legs.

51   Mr. Martin dĕngan Din bĕkĕrja mĕngalas dan mĕnyĕlimutkan orang sakit
52   itu. Kĕpala-nya di-palingkan ka-sĕbĕlah. Tali pinggang-nya di-bukakan.

Mr. Martin with Din work getting-something-underneath and wrapping the sick man. The head-of-him, there-is-a-turning to one-side. Cord of-waist of-him, unfastening-is-done.

Mr. Martin and Din set to work getting the injured man on to the mattress, and wrapping him up. They turn his head sideways, and unfasten his belt.

MAH. **'Dah ada-kah orang pĕrgi mĕmanggil kĕreta sakit?**
Completed, there-being-this, person go summoning car for-the-sick?
Has somebody gone for the ambulance?

DIN **'Dah ada. Tadi lagi Pa' Abu pĕrgi ka-balai naik**
It-has-been. Just-now, still, Pa' Abu go to police-station
Yes. Pa' Abu went to the police-station on his bicycle,
bĕsikal.
mounting bicycle.
some time ago.

Sa-kĕtika lĕpas itu tiba-lah sa-orang sergeant dĕngan sa-orang mata-mata dari balai.
One moment after that, there-arrive one-person sergeant with one person policeman from police-station.
A moment later a sergeant and a policeman arrive, from the police-station.

MAH. **'Dah ada panggil kĕreta sakit, to' sarjan?**
Has-come-to-pass summoning car for-the-sick, Sergeant?
Has somebody asked for the ambulance, Sergeant?

SGT. **Sudah ĕnche'. Sa-kĕjap lagi sampai-lah. Tĕrok-**
Completed, ĕnche'. One-flick-of-eye-lid more, will-arrive. Serious,
Yes, ĕnche'. It will be here in a minute. Is he badly hurt?
kah orang itu?
this-person?

MAH. **Tĕrok juga. Pengsan ta' sĕdar-sĕdar dari tadi.**
Serious, fairly. Faint, not-any-consciousness from just-now. But
Pretty badly. He hasn't recovered consciousness yet.
'Tapi luka, patah ta' ada.
wound, fracture, not is-present.
But there's no sign of injury, and there are no bones broken.

SGT. **Dĕrebar kĕreta itu ka-mana?**
Driver of-the-car, whither?
Where's the driver of the car?

MAH. **Ada. Baring dalam kĕreta itu.**
Is-present. Lying in car.
He's here. He's lying in the car there.

65 SGT.   **Biar saya pĕrgi tengok dia.**
Allow-that I go see him.
I'll go and have a look at him.

66   Ia pĕrgi ka-kĕreta itu lalu bĕrchakap kapada dĕrebar kĕreta itu.   Dĕrebar
67 itu sa-orang China pĕranakan.
He goes to-the-car then talks to the driver of-car.   The-driver (is) one-person Chinese son-of-the-country.
He goes to the car and speaks to the driver, who is a Malayan-born Chinese.

68 SGT.   **Apa macham baba?   Sakit lagi?**
What like, baba?   Hurt, still?
How do you feel, baba?   Does it still hurt?

69 DĔR.   **Eh.   Sakit dato'.**
Eh!   Hurt, dato'.
Yes, dato', it does.

70 SGT.   **Macham mana bĕrlanggar tadi?**
Which-way colliding just-now?
How did the collision happen?

71 DĔR.   **Saya hĕndak balek ka-Kuala Lumpur.   Bila saya**
I intending return to-Kuala Lumpur.   When I turn the-bend this
I was on my way back to Kuala Lumpur.   When I was

72   **belok sĕlekoh itu becha roda tiga ini tiba-tiba masok**
rickshaw-wheels-three suddenly enter to-middle of-road.
coming round the bend, the trishaw suddenly came out

73   **ka-tĕngah jalan.**
into the middle of the road.

74 SGT.   **Dari mana dia masok?**
From where it enter?
Where did it come out from?

75 DĔR.   **Dari kanan.   Dia 'ndak bĕrpusing balek ka-Kuala**
From right.   He intending turn, back to-Kuala Lumpur.
From the right.   He was going to turn round and go back

76   **Lumpur.**
to Kuala Lumpur.

77 SGT.   **Bĕlakang dia-lah kĕna langgar?**
Back of-him incurred collision.
It was his back that caught it?

78 DĔR.   **Bĕlakang becha-dia.   Orang becha itu tĕrchampak**
Back of rickshaw-of-him.   The person of rickshaw hurled into
The back of his side-car.   He was thrown into the ditch.

ka-dalam parit. Kĕreta saya tĕrbelok ka-sini.
ditch. Car of-me suddenly-became-turned to-here.
My car swung round like this.

SGT. **Baba lari kuat sangat, tidak?**
Baba running strong very, not?
You were going fast, weren't you?

DĔR. **Tidak, dato'. Mahu belok sĕlekoh macham mana**
Not, dato'. Wishing turn corner, how, I ask you, run strong!
No, dato'. When I was taking a bend, I wouldn't be
pula lari kuat!
going fast, would I?

SGT. **Siapa di-antara tuan-tuan di-sini yang nampak**
Who among all-of-you at-here who see this car collide just now?
Who among you here saw the collision?
kĕreta ini bĕrlanggar tadi?

DIN **Pa' Abu, dato'.**
Pa' Abu, dato'.

SGT. **Pa'Abu sa-orang. Saya 'dah tahu. Lain daripada**
Pa' Abu (was) one-person. I have-come-to know. Other than
Pa' Abu for one, I know. Was there anybody else, besides
dia ada ta' lagi?
him, was-present (or) not, more?
him?

DIN **Saya pun nampak juga, 'tapi saya jauh sadikit.**
I saw also, but I (was) distant a-little. I in-the-middle-of standing
I saw it too, but I wasn't very near. I was standing at the
Saya tĕngah bĕrdiri dĕkat kaki tangga surau sana.
near foot of steps of-chapel yonder.
foot of the steps of the chapel over there.

SGT. **Tolong bagi nama dĕngan alamat awak kapada**
Help, give name with address-of-you to the-policeman, allow-that
Give your name and address to the constable, please, so
mata-mata itu biar di-tuliskan-nya.
there-be-a-writing by-him.
that he can write it down.

DIN **Saya kĕna mĕnjadi saksi-kah, dato'?**
I incur becoming witness, dato'?
Shall I have to be a witness, dato'?

93 SGT. **Kalau pĕrkara ini sampai ka-mahkamah kĕna-lah.**
If this affair arrives to-court, incur, right-enough.
If the case comes to court, yes, you will have to.

94 DIN **Kachau-lah saya, dato'. Saya ta' biasa bichara.**
In a-flutter, I, dato'. I not experienced, law-suit.
Oh, dear! What a bother! I've never had anything to
do with a court-case.

95 SGT. **Tolong bĕri card pĕngĕnalan, baba. Saya 'nak**
Help, give card making-known, baba. I going-to write name with
Give me your identity card, please, baba. I want to write

96 **tuliskan nama dĕngan alamat. Lesen pun 'nak**
address. Licence want also, I going-to take number of it.
your name and address. I want your licence too, to take

97 **juga, saya 'nak ambil nombor-nya.**
the number of it.

98 Pada kĕtika itu tiba-lah kĕreta sakit. Orang becha roda tiga itu pun di-
99 naikkan orang ka-dalam-nya sĕrta tĕrus di-bawa ka-rumah sakit. Baba
100 dĕrebar kĕreta tadi pun pĕrgi juga naik kĕreta sakit itu.

At moment this, arrives car for-the-sick. The person of the bicycle-rickshaw, there-is-a raising by-people to-inside-of-it, together with straightway there-is-conveying to house for-the-sick. The baba Chinese car-driver goes also, mounting the car for-the-sick.

At this point the ambulance arrives. The trishaw man is lifted into it and taken straight to hospital. The Chinese car-driver goes in the ambulance, too.

SCENE IV: NOTES

Title: di-tĕmpat kĕreta bĕrlanggar: *lit.* 'at the place of-car-colliding.'
For this use of a noun-phrase where English would use 'where' or
'at which', cf. Note II.46, *tĕmpat kita dudok ini.*

3 kĕlihatan: 'is to be seen'. The affixes *kĕ- . . -an* often create
an abstract noun, *e.g. jahat*, 'wicked'; *kĕjahatan*, 'wickedness'.
But sometimes, as here, the derivative formed is very near to the
English adjective ending in '-able' or '-ible'. At other times the
idea of 'incurring', of 'running into' some unfortunate situation
is present. See Sentence Pattern 1. *d.* and *e.* The *kĕ- . . -an*
words have much greater variety of function than the *pĕ- . . -an*
words, but they are not common in speech.

dari mĕngaji Kor'an: *lit.* 'from studying the Kor'an', *i.e.* the *mĕ-*
derivative after a preposition. Since this is of very common
occurrence, no further note will be taken of it.

4 sĕrta sampai sahaja: 'no sooner does she arrive than . . .'
Sahaja has a greater variety of shading than has 'only' in English,
but a preliminary translation with 'just' or 'nothing but' will
usually help you to feel its significance. Cf. line 5 below,
Gopoh sahaja nampak-nya, and see Sentence Pattern III.2.

bĕrtanya kapada-nya: see Note II.35. *-nya* is used, instead of
dia, for the pronoun-object after all compound prepositions, *di-
bawah-nya*, 'underneath it'.

8 pokok jati: the 'rain tree', known in the north of the Peninsula as
pokok pukul lima, 'the five-o'clock tree', because its leaves fold
themselves together at 5 p.m. Note, however, that *kayu jati* is
ebony.

9 Kĕna langgar. Apa mĕlanggar-nya?: note the use of the simple
form of the verb as long as the idea is general ('incurred being
bumped into'), but the *mĕ-* prefix appears as soon as the action is
linked with a definite subject: 'What was it that did the bump-
ing?'

Kĕreta kĕchil: an expression used commonly in Kuala Lumpur for
a car, as opposed to a bus or a truck. But the word *motorcar* (never
car) is current everywhere.

12 Ĕntah: see Sentence Pattern III.4.

Rah ta' sĕmpat 'nak pĕrgi mĕnengok: note the *hĕndak*, because,
in this sentence, intention (and therefore futurity) is implicit in
the word *sĕmpat*. Cf. *harap hĕndak*, 'hope to'; *bĕrjanji hĕndak*,
'promise to'; *pĕluang hĕndak*, 'opportunity to'; and line II.111,
ta' lalu 'nak makan. See Sentence Pattern 2.

16 di-sa-balek: the use of *balek* ('reverse side of') implies that though
the spot is quite near, it is not visible, because something or other
intervenes.

18 hĕndak-lah: note the stress that the child puts on *hĕndak*.

22 Mĕreka pun sampai: here, in spite of the 3rd person subject,
lit up by a *pun*, the verb has no *mĕ-* prefix because *sampai* is one
of the group of words expressing movement which never take *mĕ-*,
because such actions as 'coming' and 'going' are not the result of
considered decisions on the part of the actor. So also, *sampai*
after *sĕrta* in Note 4 above.

lalu hampir mĕndapatkan: *lit.* 'draw near', 'coming up to'.
The verb-word here is *hampir*, with *mĕndapatkan* used participally.
For this use of *dapat* see Sentence Pattern VIII.2.ii. For *lalu* see
Note III.40.

24 siapa-siapa: duplication indicating indefiniteness, 'anybody, by
chance'. There is no *pun* because he does not mean 'anybody at
all, whosoever he may be', inviting attention to one possibility after
another, as in Note 1.81, *bila-bila pun*, where the duplication is

deliberately comprehensive. So also (in contrast to the sentence in the text): *Ta' ada siapa-siapa pun luka;* 'Nobody was hurt (not this one, nor that one, nor the other one).'

25 Pa' Chik: *Pa'* short for *bapa* (in speech usually *bapak*), 'father'; *Chik* short for *kĕchil* (always pronounced *kĕchik*), 'small'. *Pa' Chik* is a title given to an uncle who is younger than one's father. The young man uses it here as a respectful mode of address to a man who is somewhat older than himself. Nouns of relationship are frequently used in this way instead of 2nd person pronouns.

becha roda tiga: for bicycle and side-car, plying for hire. In many places in the Peninsula the word used is *taxi*.

26 tĕrchampak: 'was thrown out', the *tĕr-* prefix showing that it was sudden and unexpected.

30 sudah kami kĕluarkan: for the word-order cf. Notes I.64 and II.38; also line 48 below, *Dapat kita alas . . .*

    kami: for 'we', not including the listener.

    -kan: causative suffix.

31 tĕpi jalan: short for *di-tĕpi*. Prepositions are frequently omitted in colloquial speech. Cf. *Pĕrgi pĕkan . . .,* 'Go to the village . . .'

34 bĕnar: *lit.* 'truly'. There is no special way of forming adverbs in Malay. When appropriate, the adjective can be used equally well as an adverb, and often as a noun too; *bĕnar* can mean 'true' or 'truly' or (usually with *-nya*) 'truth'. There are no rigid barriers between parts of speech in Malay.

    bĕnar: this is a useful word to remember for 'very'. So also are *bĕtul,* 'correct', and *sunggoh,* 'genuine'. (All three words may be used also for 'Yes' meaning: 'What you say is quite right.') Do not fall into the habit of using *banyak* for 'very'. It is a word of quantity ('much', 'many'), not of degree.

36 tĕrhĕmpas: *tĕr-* again denoting a sudden and unexpected occurrence.

39 susah / mĕreka hĕndak rapat itu: *hĕndak* is used because the 'getting near' is necessarily in the future. See Note 12 above.

    itu: binding the whole phrase together, 'their-desire-to-go-near' or 'they-wanting-to-be-near'. It is this noun-group that is the subject of the sentence, with *susah* as predicate.

kĕrana orang ramai bĕnar bĕrkĕrumun: the literal translation shows you the structure of the sentence, 'because the people (are) in large numbers, truly, crowding round', *i.e. ramai* is used predicatively; *bĕnar* is adverbial, belonging to *ramai;* *bĕrkĕrumun* is participial. For *ramai* (and *banyak*), used both predicatively and attributively, see Sentence Pattern 4.

40 Tolong: *lit.* 'help'. In the same way *choba,* 'try', is also used as the equivalent of the English word 'please', though it sometimes has a somewhat sharper note in it than 'tolong'. *Sila* (*lit.* 'be pleased to') is in the nature of an invitation. See Sentence Pattern II.1.

42 kain alas-nya : *alas* is usually used of something put *under,* as a support or a lining, as in lines 46 and 48 below.

46 Ia juga : 'Yes, of course', *lit.* 'yes, and nothing but yes'; the limiting function of *juga* as in II.60. See Sentence Pattern VI.3.*a* and *b*.

47 pendek : 'too short'. In the same way comparatives and superlatives are frequently to be gathered from context only. See See Note VIII.90.

48 Dapat kita alas kěpala / sudah-lah : two side-by-side statements, where English would use a subordinate clause, followed by a main statement, 'If we . . ., it will be all right.' See Sentence Pattern II.6.

53 'Dah ada-kah . . .? : 'It is an accomplished fact that . . .?' See Sentence Pattern III.3.i.

54 Tadi lagi : *lagi* gives the idea that it was 'still' *tadi* ('as early as that') when he went.

56 tiba-lah sa-orang sergeant : *-lah* for confirmation. We were expecting this arrival. (But note that when the reader's attention is already focused on the *actor,* rather than the action, the subject *precedes* the verb, and is lit up by a *pun,* as in *Měreka pun sampai-lah,* 'They arrived'.)

sa-orang sergeant : orang is the numerical coefficient for human beings.

58 to' sarjan : *to'* is short for *dato',* a title given in deference to his rank.

59 Sa-kějap lagi sampai-lah : *-lah* again for confirmation, even though the fulfilment has not yet come to pass, 'They'll be here all right, you needn't worry.' Cf. Note II.84, *Siang-siang pěrgi-lah dia ka-kěbun,* 'As soon as it's light, off they'll go . . .'

61 ta' sědar-sědar : duplication to cover variety, not any sign of consciousness at all. Cf. *běrgěrak-gěrak* in line 31 above.

62 'Tapi luka, patah, ta' ada : note the absence of a conjunction.

63 Děrebar ka-mana? : *ka-* is used because the idea of 'motion towards' is implicit in the situation. He has been taken *to* the place where he now is.

64 Baring dalam kěreta itu : *itu* refers to the whole phrase, not to the word *kěreta.*

65 Biar saya pěrgi tengok : in such sentences, with a 1st person actor, the *mě-* derivative is not used after *pěrgi*. The syntax is probably this: 'Allow that I go (and) allow that I see.' Cf. Note II.32.

68 Apa machan baba? : note, again, the impersonal form of the question.

> *baba:* a title used in addressing Chinese born in Malaya.

71 hĕndak balek : no *mĕ-*, because *balek* is a verb of movement.

79 tĕrbelok : note the *tĕr-*, for the involuntary turn which his car performed.

81 Mahu belok sĕlekoh / macham mana pula . . . : note, again, the absence of a subordinating conjunction. Sentence Pattern II.6.

> *mahu:* in this context (*i.e.* for mere futurity) *mahu* is bazaar Malay. Most Malays would use *hĕndak* here. See Note VII.5.
>
> *pula:* in surprised protest at the very thought of it.

83 tuan-tuan : more formal than *awak*. The word *tuan* (*lit.* 'master') is used as a 2nd person pronoun even among relatives when conversation is on a serious level, *e.g.* when people are talking together in a *surau*. It is the correct pronoun to use to a *haji* (*i.e.* a man or woman who has made the pilgrimage to Mecca), and to a man whose personal name is preceded by *Sayid* or a woman whose name is preceded by *Sharifah* or its abbreviation *'Pah* (*i.e.* a descendant of the Prophet's family). In a love-pantun (see VIII.84) it may refer either to the man or to the girl. It is the pronoun used by Malays to European men, by editors to readers, by radio-announcers to listeners.

89 Saya tĕngah bĕrdiri : more casual and leisurely than *Saya bĕrdiri*.

90 awak : an informal 2nd person pronoun used between equals. The sergeant knows Din. The 2nd person pronoun *ĕngkau*, on the other hand, always has a 'downward slope', from 'superior' to 'inferior'. For a non-Malay speaking to a Malay the best form of address is the name or the title of the listener.

91 biar di-tuliskan-nya : the impersonal construction is used because the important thing is that the writing should be done, not that the sergeant in particular should do it.

95 pĕngĕnalan : the affixes *pĕ-* . . . -*an* (sometimes *pĕr-* . . . -*an*) create nouns and adjectives: *kĕnal*, 'recognize'; *pĕngĕnalan*, 'recognition'. For the nasal infix *-ng-* and the dropping of the initial *k* compare the verbal form *kachau / mĕngachau* in Note III.90.

98 di-naikkan orang : *orang* is used here in the same way as 'they' is used in English, referring to nobody in particular. It is very common with the impersonal *di-* construction, *e.g. Baik simpan bĕsikal, kalau-kalau di-churi orang;* 'You had better put your bicycle away, in case it gets stolen' (*lit.* '. . . wondering-if there-should-be-stealing by-a-person'). Note that a noun, as well as the 3rd person pronoun *-nya*, may indicate the agent after a *di-* construction.

SCENE IV: TAKING STOCK

3. INI and ITU

    i. belonging to a noun-group:

        Susah | měreka hěndak rapat itu.
        It is difficult for them to get near.

5. NUMERAL COEFFICIENTS

    (e) *orang* for human beings:

        sa-orang sergeant, 'a sergeant'

6. PRONOUNS

    (a) Personal

        ii. *tuan* is used in a formal context:

            Siapa antara tuan-tuan di-sini yang nampak kěreta itu běrlanggar
                tadi?
            Which of you saw the collision?

        awak is used informally between equals:

            Tolong bagi nama děngan alamat awak.
            Please give your name and address.

        Note. In Sentence Pattern VIII.2 you will find *awak* as a
        1st person pronoun.

        iv. *-nya*

            c. as an object pronoun after *mě-*, and after compound
                prepositions:

                Apa yang mělanggar-nya?
                What was it that ran into it?
                Dia běrtanya kapada-nya. He asks her.
                Orang becha itu pun di-naikkan orang ka-dalam-nya.
                They lift the rickshaw man into it.

    (c) the relative *yang*

        iii. when *yang* draws attention to a particular action, by a par-
            ticular actor, the verb-word takes the prefix *mě-*:

            Apa yang mělanggar-nya? 'What was it that ran into it?'

10. AFFIXES

    (a) *běr-*

        ii. making an intransitive verb:

            Orang ramai běnar běrkěrumun.
            People were crowding round in great numbers.

(*b*) *mě-*

    i. as a verbal noun after a preposition:

        Dia běrlari balek dari měngaji Kor'an.
        She is running home after her Kor'an lesson.

    ii. as a finite verb after a 3rd person subject, closely linking action with actor:

        Apa yang mělanggar-nya? 'What was it that ran into it?'

(*c*) *pě- . . . -an* creating a noun or adjective:

    kěnal, 'recognize'; *pěngěnalan*, 'recognition'; *card pěngěnalan*, 'identity card'.

(*e*) *těr-*

    ii. for a sudden and unexpected happening:

        Orang becha itu těrchampak ka-dalam parit.
        The rickshaw cyclist was thrown into the ditch.
        Kěreta saya těrbelok ka-sini.
        My car swung round into this position.

(*f*) *di-*

    i. for a particular action with agent specified, either (as in the first example) as the predicate word, or (as in the second example) following the predicate word.

        Orang becha itu pun di-naikkan orang ka-dalam-nya.
        They lift the rickshaw man into it.
        Tolong bagi nama biar di-tuliskan-nya.
        Please give your name, so that he can write it down.
        (*lit.* Allow-that there-should-be-writing-down by-him.)

(*h*) *kě- . . . -an*, noun or adjective affixes

    i. creating an abstract noun:

        jahat, 'wicked'; *kějahatan*, 'wickedness'

    ii. creating an adjective (or noun) denoting possibility:

        Zaharah kělihatan běrlari-lari balek.
        Zaharah is to be seen racing home.

II. PUN

    ii. to draw attention to the subject of a main statement which follows a subordinate time-statement (usually written style):

        Sěrta sampai sahaja ia ka-rumah, Che' Mahmud pun běrtanya kapada-nya.
        The moment she reached the house, Che' Mahmud began to question her.

    iii. in written Malay, when a predicate word is fixed by *-lah*, a subject word which *precedes* it is lit by *pun*:

        Měreka pun sampai-lah, 'They arrived.'

12. JUGA

    ii. indicating mental reservation:

        Těrok juga, 'Rather serious.'

13. PULA

    i. for surprise or protest:

        Mahu belok sělekoh macham mana pula lari kuat?

        Would I be likely to be going fast when I was just taking a corner?

14. -LAH

    i. for emphasis

        b. in written Malay, by marking out a predicate word and so, as a rule, confirming an action which the reader has been led to expect:

            Měreka pun sampai-lah.

            They arrived.

            Sa-kětika itu sampai-lah sa-orang sergeant.

            A moment later, along came a police-sergeant.

            Sa-kějap lagi sampai-lah.

            It'll be here in a moment.

            Pada kětika itu tiba-lah kěreta sakit.

            At that moment the ambulance arrived.

            Kěna jadi saksi-kah?—Kalau pěrkara ini sampai ka-mahkamah, kěna-lah.

            Shall I have to be a witness?—If the case comes into court, yes, you will.

        c. by singling out one particular word:

            Kachau-lah saya.

            H'm. I shan't like that! (*lit.* Confused I (shall be).)

15. PREPOSITIONS

    (*c*) *ka-*

        i and ii. used whenever 'motion towards' is implied:

            Děrebar ka-mana? 'Where's the driver?'

16. CONJUNCTIONS

    i. omission of co-ordinating conjunction:

        Luka patah ta' ada.

        There's no wound, and there are no bones broken.

    ii. omission of subordinating conjunction: (See also No. 22.iii)

        Mahu belok sělekoh macham mana pula lari kuat?

        When I was just going to turn a corner, how should I be going fast?

18. BOLEH and BIAR

    (*b*) *biar*, in speech, for purpose:

        Tolong bagi alamat awak, biar di-tuliskan-nya.
        Give him your address, please, so that he can write it down.

22. THE NOUN-GROUP

    i. as a description, attached to another noun indicating place or time:

        Di-těmpat kěreta běrlanggar.
        At the spot where the collision took place.
        (*lit.* At the place of-a-car-colliding.)

    iii. declaring the attendant circumstances:

        Mahu belok sělekoh | macham mana pula lari kuat.
        When I was going to turn a corner, how should I be going fast?
        Dapat kita alas kěpala | sudah-lah.
        As long as we get something under his head, that's all that matters.

    iv. as subject of a sentence:

        Susah | měreka hěndak rapat itu.
        It is difficult for them to get near.
        (*lit.* That they-intending-near (is) difficult.)

23. SUDAH

    i. stressing completion:

        'Dah ada-kah orang pěrgi měmanggil kěreta sakit?
        Has somebody gone for the ambulance?

    ii. stressing the state that has come about:

        Pa' Abu sa-orang, saya 'dah tahu.
        Pa' Abu for one, that I already know.

25. IMPERSONAL EXPRESSIONS

    ii. an impersonal approach, to elicit a personal opinion:

        Apa macham, baba?
        How are you feeling, baba?

26. SAHAJA meaning 'only', 'just', 'merely', 'all . . .'

        Sěrta sampai sahaja ia . . .
        No sooner had she arrived than . . .
        Gopoh sahaja nampak-nya.
        You seem all flustered.

SCENE IV: SENTENCE PATTERNS

1. *kĕ-* . . . *-an*

a. **Zaharah kĕlihatan bĕrlari-lari balek.**
Zaharah is seen running home.

b. **Kalau chuacha baik, pulau itu kĕlihatan dari bukit ini.**
In fine weather the island can be seen from this hill.

c. **Dalam hutan ini tiada apa yang kĕdĕngaran kĕchuali bunyi riang-riang sahaja.**
Here in the jungle there is nothing to be heard except the noise of the cicadas.

d. **Ada orang 'nak mĕnumpang tidor, kata-nya dia kĕmalaman di-sini.**
There are some people asking if we can put them up. They say they will have to spend the night here.

e. **Pada tahun dahulu sawah kĕkĕringan, anak kampong ramai yang kĕkurangan padi.**
Last year the rice-fields suffered from drought, and many of the peasants were short of grain.

2. *hĕndak* for 'time to . . .', 'hope to . . .', etc.

a. **Rah ta' sĕmpat hĕndak pĕrgi mĕnengok.**
I didn't have time to go and see.

b. **Dia bĕrjanji 'nak datang ka-sini pukul sa-puloh.**
He promised to come at ten o'clock.

c. **Saya harap hĕndak mĕmasokkan anak pĕrĕmpuan ka-sĕkolah Kĕrajaan tahun dĕpan.**
I hope to get my daughter into the Government school next year.

d. **Saya chadang 'nak mĕngganti pokok gĕtah bila lapang sadikit.**
I am planning to replant my rubber when I can find the time.

e. **Ta' ada pĕluang hĕndak mĕngganti atap. Hari hujan sahaja.**
I never get a chance to repair the roof. It rains every single day.

3. *tĕr-*. i. accidental; ii. completion; iii. ability to complete

i. Accidental

a. **Orang itu tĕrchampak ka-dalam parit.**
The man was thrown into the ditch.

b. **Bola itu tĕrlambong ka-tĕngah-tĕngah orang ramai.**
The ball bounced right into the middle of the crowd.

c. **Manis bĕnar kopi ini. Tĕrbanyak sadikit gula-nya.**
The coffee is very sweet. I put more sugar in it than I meant to.

d. **Pada saya, biar tĕrbanyak, jangan tĕrkurang.**
As far as I'm concerned, I'd rather you put too much than too little.

e. **Mĕmbĕlah kĕlapa itu jaga-jaga sadikit, jangan tĕrkĕrat jari.**
Be careful splitting that coconut. Mind you don't cut your fingers.

ii. Completion

a. Di-atas meja itu banyak buku tĕrator.
There were many books set out on his table.

b. Kain basohan pagi tadi sĕmua tĕrsidai di-tĕngah panas.
All the clothes that had been washed in the morning were hung out in the sun.

c. Tĕrpĕranjat dia mĕnengok pĕti duit-nya tĕrbuka.
He was startled to see his cash-box wide open.

d. Gambar chalun itu tĕrpampang pada pĕlĕkat bĕsar.
Portraits of the candidates were displayed on large posters.

e. Banyak kĕreta tĕrhĕnti di-situ. Ada kayu tumbang mĕlintang jalan.
Many cars were held up at that point, because a tree had fallen across the road.

iii. Ability to complete

a. Pasokan pĕkan itu ta' tĕrlawan dek pasokan kampong.
The town team was too strong for the village team.

b. Bĕrapa hari baharu tĕrsudakhan dek awak kĕrja ini?
How many days will it take you to finish the job?

c. Kalau had $5 sa-bulan, tĕrbayar-lah dek saya.
If it's not more than $5 a month, I can pay it.

d. Saya ta' tĕrdaya lagi dĕngan budak 'ni.
I simply don't know what to do with this child!

e. Tĕrok sakit-nya itu, ta' tĕrubat agak-nya.
He is seriously ill. I doubt if he will recover.

4. *ramai* and *banyak*

a. **Orang ramai bĕnar bĕrkĕrumun.**
The people were crowding round in great numbers.

b. Ramai budak kĕluar ka-pĕkan hari ini, 'nak mĕnengok pĕraduan sĕnaman.
There are crowds of children going in to town to-day to see the drill competition.

c. Mari kita ikut jalan kiri ini. Malas saya 'nak lalu di-chĕlah-chĕlah orang ramai itu.
Let's go by this path on the left. I don't feel like threading my way through that crowd.

d. Ta' banyak orang datang mĕnengok wayang. Lĕbat sangat hujan pĕtang sa-malam.
Not many people came to the concert. It rained heavily yesterday afternoon.

e. Tĕmpat yang banyak udang galah ia-lah di-kuala sungai Linggi.
A place where lobsters abound is the mouth of the Linggi river.

5. A 'free' statement, for an English subordinate clause

a. **Dapat kita alas kĕpala-nya / sudah-lah.**
As long as we get something under his head that will do.

b. 'Nak jual kĕrbau ini / pulang modal / jadi-lah.
If I get my money back when I sell the buffalo, I'll be content.

c. Musim susah ini / lĕpas makan anak-bĕranak / chukup-lah.
  In these hard days, if you have enough to support your family that's all you can ask.

d. 'Dah buat kira-kira yang abah suroh tadi / 'dah-lah.
  If you have finished those sums that I set you, that's all you need do.

e. Dapat kita siapkan kĕrja ini sa-bĕlum hari minggu / sudah-lah.
  If we manage to get through this by Sunday, it will be all right.

f. **Mahu belok sĕlekoh / macham mana pula lari kuat?**
  When I was just going to take a corner, I wouldn't be likely to be going fast, would I?

g. Hĕndak mĕmbuat rumah / chari-lah tanah-nya dahulu.
  If you are going to build a house, get the land for it first of all.

h. Sampai sahaja saya ka-rumah / hari pun hujan.
  No sooner had I arrived at the house than it began to rain.

i. Kaki-nya sakit / 'nak main bola juga.
  Although he has hurt his foot he is going to play football, all the same.

j. Puas mĕnunggu-nya / ta' datang / saya balek sahaja-lah.
  When I had waited for him until I was tired (and he still didn't come), I just went off home.

SCENE V

DI-RUMAH ORANG KAHWIN

A MALAY WEDDING (PART I)

1 Pada hari ini Mr. Martin tĕlah di-bawa oleh Che' Mahmud dĕngan Che'
2 Normah pĕrgi ka-rumah orang kahwin kĕrana hĕndak mĕnunjokkan kapada-
3 nya sĕrba sadikit 'adat isti'adat majlis pĕrkahwinan Mĕlayu. Mĕreka tiba
4 pagi masa orang sĕdang bĕrsiap-siap. Biasa-nya orang tidak pĕrgi pagi ka-
5 rumah orang kahwin tĕtapi kĕrana hĕndak mĕnunjokkan kapada Mr. Martin
6 sĕmua pĕrkara bĕrkĕnaan dĕngan majlis itu maka mĕreka pun pĕrgi pagi.

*On this-day Mr. Martin has-been-brought by Che' Mahmud with Che' Normah
a-going to-the-house of person-marrying because wishing-to show to-him all-varieties a-little
customs (and) ceremonial of-an-assembly of-a-Malay-wedding. They arrive morning,
time (of) persons-in-the-middle-of-getting-ready. The usualness-of it, people not go
morning to-house of person marrying but because wishing-to show to Mr. Martin all
things connected with that-gathering (punctuation word), they go morning.*

To-day Che' Mahmud and Che' Normah have taken Mr. Martin to a house
where there is a wedding in progress, because they want to show him something of the customary ceremonial which is observed during the celebration
of a Malay wedding. They arrive in the morning, when everybody is busy
with preparations. It is not usual to pay a morning visit to the house where the
ceremonies are to be held, but they do so in this case because they want to
show Mr. Martin everything that is connected with the ceremony.

7 MAH. **Ini-lah rumah-nya.   Di-mana agak-nya tuan rumah,**
This (is) the house-in-question.   Where, the guess-of-it, people of-
This is the house.   I wonder where they are, so that we

8 **boleh kita bagi tahu kita 'dah sampai.**
the-house, able we give to-know we have arrived.
can tell them that we have arrived.

9 NOR. **Biar saya pĕrgi bagi tahu.   Pĕrgi-lah bawa Mr.**
Allow-that I go give-to-know.   Go, conduct Mr. Martin a-seeing-
I'll go and tell them.   You take Mr. Martin to have a look

10 **Martin mĕnengok-nengok.**
seeing.
round.

11 Che' Normah pĕrgi mĕnchari tuan rumah ka-bĕlakang.
Che' Normah goes a-seeking people of-the-house to-the-back.
Che' Normah goes round to the back to look for the host and hostess.

MAH. **Mari-lah.**

Come along.

Che' Mahmud měmbawa Mr. Martin masok ka-kawasan rumah itu. Kawasan rumah itu ada běrpagar děngan pokok bunga raya sa-kěliling-nya.

Mr. Martin měnunjok kapada bangsal yang ada těrdiri di-hadapan rumah itu.

Che' Mahmud conducts Mr. Martin entering into the enclosed-land of-the-house. The enclosed land, there-exists (this fact) (it is) be-fenced with plants of-the-common-flower all around it.

Mr. Martin points to shed which exists erected at-front of-the-house.

Che' Mahmud takes Mr. Martin into the compound of the house. It has a hibiscus hedge all round it.

Mr. Martin points to a booth which has been erected in front of the house.

MAR. **Ada dia buat rumah kěchil pula.**

It-is-that they make a-little-house in addition.

Oh, they've built another little house.

MAH. **O, itu balai nama-nya. Bangsal pun dia juga.**

O, that, 'pavilion' (is) the name of it. 'Booth' also it (is). The-

Oh, that's called a *balai*, or a *bangsal* if you like. The other

Yang satu lagi sa-bělah sana itu khemah. Dua-dua

(one)-which (is) one more, on-the-side yonder (is) a tent. All-two

one over there is a *khemah*. They are both of them places

itu těmpat orang makan.

those (are) places of-people-eating.

where you eat.

MAR. **Balai itu ada lantai, dalam khemah itu ada kěrusi**

The pavilion, there-is a-floor, in the-tent there-are chairs tables

There is a floor in the pavilion, but in the tent there are

meja sahaja. Siapa kěna pěrgi makan di-balai?

only. Who incurs going-eating in-pavilion? Who, further, incurs

only chairs and tables. Who has to eat in the pavilion

Siapa pula kěna pěrgi makan dalam khemah?

going-eating in tent?

and who in the tent?

MAH. **Itu ta' kira. Siapa-siapa suka sahaja. Orang suka**

That (is) not-calculation. Whosoever likes, simply. People

There's no rule about it. You just please yourself. If you

makan běrsila pěrgi makan ka-balai. Orang suka

wishing eat sitting-cross-legged, go eating into pavilion. Persons

prefer to eat sitting on the floor, then you go into the

26   **makan atas meja pĕrgi makan ka-dalam khemah.**
         wishing eat on table, go eating into tent.
         pavilion to eat.   If you prefer to eat from a table then you
         go into the tent.

27   Che' Normah datang balek mĕndapatkan Che' Mahmud dĕngan Mr.
28   Martin.
         Che' Normah comes-returning going-up-to Che' Mahmud and Mr. Martin.
         Che' Normah comes back to Che' Mahmud and Mr. Martin.

29 NOR.   **Suka bĕnar hati tuan rumah mĕndĕngar Mr. Martin**
         Happy, truly, the-heart of-master of-house hearing Mr. Martin wish
         Our host is delighted to hear that Mr. Martin wants to see
30   **mahu mĕnengok-nengok kĕnduri dia ini. 'Tapi**
         seeing-seeing this-feast of-him. But, says he, this-feast of-him
         everything that is going on.   But the feast that he is giving,
31   **kata dia kĕnduri dia ini kĕnduri kĕchil, jangan tidak.**
         (is) small-feast, let-it-not-be not.   The-making give-pleasure-to
         he says, is only a little one, just a token, to please the young
32   **Buat mĕnyukakan hati budak-budak.**
         the hearts of-the-young-people.
         people.

33 MAH.   **Hai! Tumbang lĕmbu sa-ekor, kĕchil juga kata**
         Hai! There falls an-ox one-tail-of, just-small says he?   Wishing
         Ha!   He kills an ox, and calls it 'just a little feast', does he?
34   **dia? 'Nak macham mana lagi?**
         how, still?
         What more could you want?

35 NOR.   **Ah, sĕngaja dia mĕnyĕbut-lah. Ta' kan dia 'nak**
         Ah, purposely he is-saying.   Not-likely he going-to say this-feast
         Oh, he's just saying that for the sake of saying it.   You
36   **mĕngatakan kĕnduri dia ini bĕsar. Siapa pula**
         of-his (is) big.   Who, I-ask-you, is-prepared himself enter basket,
         wouldn't expect him to say that he was giving a grand
37   **hĕndak, sĕndiri masok bakul sĕndiri angkat!**
         himself lift (it)!
         feast.   Who would undertake to get into the basket and
         carry it himself?

MAR. **Masok bakul . . . apa itu? . . . saya ta' faham.**
Enter basket . . . what, that? I not understand.
Get into the basket. . . . What was that? . . . I didn't
understand.

NOR. **Sĕndiri masok bakul sĕndiri angkat. Itu satu pĕpa-**
Oneself enter basket, oneself lift. That (is) a-saying. Meaning-
'To get into the basket and then lift it yourself' is a saying
tah. Ĕrti-nya mĕmuji diri sĕndiri atau pĕrbuatan
of-it, praising self of one-self or the-doings of oneself.
that we have. It means to praise yourself, or your own
sĕndiri.
performances.

MAR. **Orang ramai ini sĕmua mĕnolong buat kĕrja, ia?**
These people in-numbers all are-helping doing work, yes?
All these people here, they are all helping with the work,
I suppose?

MAH. **Ia. Sĕmua-nya boleh katakan sanak saudara atau**
Yes. All-of-them, able to-be said, kith-and-kin or friends of
Yes. Pretty well all of them, you can say, will be relatives
kawan-kawan tuan rumah ini. Bukan hari ini
master of-this-house. Not this-day only they come, working.
or friends of the host. It isn't only to-day that they have
sahaja dia datang bĕkĕrja. Ada sa-tĕngah-nya itu
There-exists (this fact), the half-of-them, it-has-become one week,
come. Some of them have been helping for as long as a
'dah sampai sa-minggu mĕnolong.
helping.
week.

NOR. **Mari kita tengok ka-bĕlakang sana pula.**
Come we look to-the-back, yonder, in addition.
Let's go and see what's happening at the back, now.

Di-sabĕlah bĕlakang rumah itu ada sa-buah lagi bangsal.
On the side of-the back of-the house there-is one-unit, still, shed.
Behind the house there is another booth.

MAR. **Ini satu lagi pula bangsal.**
This (is) one still, further, booth.
Here's another booth.

50 NOR. **Ia. Bangsal tĕmpat orang masak. Tengok-lah pĕr-**
Yes. Shed, the place of-people-cooking. See, the utensils in-the-
Yes. The shed where the cooking is done. Look, all the

51 **kakas-nya sĕmua bĕsar-bĕsar. Yang bulat itu**
case all rather big. That (one) which (is) round, cauldron the name
pans are larger than usual. That round one is called a *kawah*.

52 **kawah nama dia. Tĕmpat mĕnjĕrang-nya ini**
of-it. This place of-putting-it-over-the fire, (is) the trivet-of-stones.
This place that you put it on, to heat it, is the *tungku.*

53 **tungku.**

54 MAR. **Apa orang masak dalam kawah ini?**
What, people cook in this cauldron?
What do they cook in the *kawah?*

55 NOR. **Apa-apa pun boleh. Nasi boleh, gulai pun boleh.**
Anything-at-all can-be. Rice can be, curry can be. Provided-
Anything you like—rice, or curry if you like—so long as it

56 **Asalkan banyak boleh-lah. Kalau ta' bĕrapa ban-**
that much, can-be. If not many people, using-of frying-pan only.
is a large quantity. If you are cooking for a few people

57 **yak orang pakai kuali sahaja.**
you just use a *kuali.*

58 Ia mĕnunjok kapada kuali yang ada dĕkat di-situ.
She points to frying-pan which there-is near there.
She points to a *kuali,* near by.

59 **Ini dia kuali-nya. Kĕchil sadikit. Lagi pun dia ada**
This (is) it, the frying-pan under-discussion. Small a little.
Now here's a *kuali.* It's a bit smaller. And it has

60 **bĕrtĕlinga. Tengok-lah yang bĕkĕrja di-sini banyak**
Moreover it, there-is (this fact) (it is) be-eared. See, (those) who
handles. Notice that most of the people working here are

61 **orang pĕrĕmpuan.**
are-working here, most (are) persons female.
women.

62 MAH. **Jangan-lah ingat orang pĕrĕmpuan sahaja yang**
Don't think women only who work. People male have cut up ox.
Don't think that it is only women who are doing the work.

63 **bĕkĕrja. Orang laki-laki 'dah potong lĕmbu. Ten-**
See the meat in-heaps. Work of choosing husked-rice, rolling
The men have cut up the ox. Look at the piles of meat.

gok daging bĕrtimbun itu. Kĕrja mĕmileh bĕras,
spices, shredding coconuts, trimming vegetables able, in turn,
Picking over the rice, grinding the spices, shredding the
mĕnggiling rĕmpah, mĕngukor kĕlapa, mĕnyiang
women do.
coconuts, preparing the vegetables, the women in their
sayor itu boleh-lah pula orang pĕrĕmpuan buat.
turn can see to all that.

NOR. **Ta' ada apa lagi hĕndak tengok di-tanah ini. Mari**
There-is-not anything still wishing see on-the-ground this. Come
There's nothing else that we want to see down here. Let
kita naik ka-rumah pula.
we go up to-house next.
us go back up into the house.

Pada masa itu mĕreka bĕrdiri dĕkat dĕngan tangga dapor.
At that time they are-standing near with staircase of kitchen.
They are now standing near the kitchen staircase.

MAH. **Ini ada satu tangga, tĕtapi ta' elok kita naik ikut**
This (is the case), there-is a staircase, but not good we go-up
Here is a staircase, but it wouldn't be proper for us to go
tangga bĕlakang. Kita kĕna naik tangga dĕpan.
following staircase back. We have-to go-up staircase front.
up by a back staircase. We must use the front one.

Mĕreka kĕtiga pun naik ka-rumah sa-tĕlah mĕnanggalkan kasut di-tangga
hadapan. Mĕreka tĕrus ka-sĕrambi.
They all-three go up to-the-house, there-having-been make-to-drop-off shoes on steps
front. They straight to verandah-room.
The three of them go up into the house, after taking off their shoes on the
front staircase. They go straight on into the *sĕrambi*.

MAR. **Chantek tikar ini.**
Beautiful (are) these mats.
These are beautiful mats.

NOR. **Di-sĕrambi ini memang di-bĕntang tikar chantek-**
In the sĕrambi, this, naturally, there-is-a-spreading mats very
It is here in the *sĕrambi* of course that they put down their
chantek. Di-sini-lah tĕmpat pĕngantin laki-laki
pretty. Here (is) place of-bridegroom-sitting, time of-marriage
best mats. It is here that the bridegroom sits when the

77   **dudok masa akad nikah.**
     contract.
     marriage contract is made.

78   Měreka masok ka-těngah rumah. Che' Normah měnunjok kapada
79 pělamin.
     They enter to-mid-house. Che' Normah points to bridal dais.
     They go into the living room. Che' Normah points to the bridal dais.

80   **Těmpat dudok chantek běrbunga-bunga ini nama-**
     This place-of-sitting, beautiful, be-decked, name of it, bridal-
     This decorated dais is called the *pělamin*. It is here that
81   **nya pělamin. Di-sini-lah kita běri pěngantin dudok**
     couch. Here we give-to-sit (i.e. *seat*) *the bridal pair, time of the*
     the bridal couple are put to sit during the *bersanding*
82   **masa běrsanding.**
     'enthronement'.
     ceremony.

83   Che' Mahmud měnunjok kapada nasi běsar yang ada těrlětak děkat
84 pělamin itu.
     Che' Mahmud points to cooked-rice, large, which is-present, placed near dais.
     Che' Mahmud points to a large tray of rice, placed near the bridal dais.

85   MAH. **Di-děpan dia kita lětak nasi běsar ini.**
     In front of-it we place this large cooked-rice.
     In front of it we place this large tray of rice.
86   NOR. **Mari kita tinjau pula ka-dalam bilek pěngantin ini.**
     Come, we peep, further, into the room of the bridal couple.
     Let's have a look into the bridal chamber now.

87   Kětiga-tiga měreka pěrgi ka-pintu bilek pěngantin.
     All three they go to-door of room of bridal-couple.
     The three of them go to the door of the bridal chamber.

88   **Banyak běnda běrtěkat di-sini. Sěpěrai katil itu**
     Many (are) *the things embroidered here. The draping of-bed* (is)
     Most of the things here are embroidered. The draping
89   **běrtěkat, muka bantal itu běrtěkat, tikar sila itu**
     embroidered, the faces of pillows (are) *embroidered, the mat for-*
     round the bedstead is embroidered, and the pillow-ends,

běrtěkat.
sitting-on (is) embroidered.
and the mat on which the bridegroom sits.

MAR. **Chantek sunggoh, ia.**
Pretty truly, yes.
It's very pretty, isn't it?

MAH. **Orang sudah mula běrsiap hěndak běrkhatam nam-**
People have begun making-ready going-to complete studies, the look
They have begun to make ready for the completion-of-the-

pak-nya. Mari kita dudok ka-sěrambi.
of it. Come, we sit to-the verandah.
Kor'an ceremony, I see. Let us go and sit in the *sěrambi*.

Che' Mahmud běrjalan pěrgi ka-sěrambi. Che' Normah tidak běrgěrak
dari děkat pintu bilek pěngantin itu.
*Che' Mahmud walks going to the verandah. Che' Normah not stirs from near the
door of room of bridal couple.*
Che' Mahmud goes to the *sěrambi*. Che' Normah does not move from the
door of the bridal chamber.

MAR. **Che' Normah tidak-kah kěluar ka-sěrambi?**
Che' Normah not come out to verandah-room?
Isn't Che' Normah coming out on to the *sěrambi*?

NOR. **Tidak. Saya dudok di-těngah rumah ini sama**
No. I sit in-mid-house this, same with women other.
No. I shall stay here in the living-room, the same as the

děngan orang pěrěmpuan lain-lain.
other women do.

Mr. Martin pěrgi měngikut Che' Mahmud. Che' Normah tinggal di-
těngah rumah. Orang pěrěmpuan lain-lain masok ka-těngah rumah itu dari
dapor lalu dudok běrtimpoh di-atas tikar sama-sama děngan Che' Normah.
*Mr. Martin goes following Che' Mahmud. Che' Normah remains in mid-house.
Women, other, enter to mid-house from kitchen then sit with-feet-to-the-right on the mat
together with Che' Normah.*
Mr. Martin goes with Che' Mahmud. Che' Normah remains in the living-
room. The other women come into the living-room from the kitchen and sit
down, *běrtimpoh*, on the mat with Che' Normah.

E

SCENE V: NOTES

1 tělah di-bawa . . . pěrgi: *tělah* in the written language represents *sudah* (used as an auxiliary) in the spoken language.

　　bawa pěrgi: lit. 'conducts, going', *i.e.* 'takes (him) to'. See Note 13 below.

2 rumah orang kahwin: *lit.* 'house of person marrying'. The simple form of the word is used in the same unrelated way in the expression *kěrja kahwin*, covering all the preparations, the ceremonies, and the entertaining in connection with a wedding.

6 maka: a punctuation-word, used freely in literary Malay (less commonly in modern written Malay) to mark the beginning of a clause. In Malay script, which is an adaptation of Arabic script, punctuation marks are an innovation.

13 měmbawa dia masok: *lit.* 'conducts him, entering', *i.e.* 'takes him into'. This is the same construction as in line 1 above (*tělah di-bawa . . . pěrgi*). In both cases the participial verb of the Malay sentence (*i.e.* the second verb of motion) is best translated by a preposition in English. The idiom is illustrated in Sentence Pattern 1.iii. In the illustrations the participial word begins with *mě-*. In the present examples there is no *mě-* because *pěrgi* and *masok* belong to the group of verbs of movement which do not take that prefix. Cf. *Dia měmbawa kěluar*, 'He took it out.' *Dia mělompat turun*, 'He jumped down.' *Dia běrjalan naik*, 'He walks up.' *Susu gětah měleleh turun ka-dalam chawan*, 'The latex flows down into the cup.' *Anai-amai itu měmanjat naik sampai ka-bumbong itu;* 'The white ants climbed up right into the roof.' See Note II.22.

14 Kawasan rumah itu ada běrpagar: *běr-* may be taken here as a possessive, 'having a fence'.

　　ada: the word indicates the existent state of affairs, but its omission would make only a very slight difference in the meaning, 'It was a fenced garden', rather than 'The garden was fenced'. In Sentence Pattern VII.2.ii and iii you will find examples of both constructions, with 'possession' stressed in the first group and 'existence' stressed in the second. For your own use, *Meja ini běrlachi* and *Meja ini ada běrlachi* will do equally well as a translation of 'The table has a drawer', but *Meja ini ada lachi*, spoken without a pause (*i.e.* using *ada* to mean possess, with an inanimate subject), verges on bazaar Malay. If it is spoken with a pause in the middle the first two words become a statement of topic ('This table / there is a drawer') as in Note 21 below.

19 Yang satu lagi itu: 'the other one'. Note the idiom. Cf. *Ada dua ekor anjing, yang sa-ekor-nya běsar, yang sa-ekor lagi itu kěchil;* 'There were two dogs, one of them big, and the other small.'

21 Balai itu / ada lantai: this may be *translated* 'The pavilion has a floor', but the pause after *itu* indicates clearly that in the Malay sentence *balai itu* is a statement of topic, and that *lantai* is the subject of *ada*, not an object. See Note 14 above.

24 Orang suka makan běrsila: not *orang yang suka,* because the thought is not, 'those persons who like sitting cross-legged go and eat in the pavilion', but, 'A person liking to sit cross-legged, (*i.e.* If a person . . .) in that case, going-eating is to the pavilion'. Again the speaker's intonation makes the syntax clear. Listen for the pause after *běrsila.*

27 měndapatkan: Sentence Pattern VIII.2 illustrates the various uses of the word *dapat.*

29 měnděngar: the speaker omits the *d*, as is often done. Similarly, *b* after a nasal is sometimes dropped in speech, *e.g. sěmilan* for *sěmbilan*, 'nine'.

31 jangan tidak: a common colloquial use of the expression, implying that the performance in question is just a mere 'better than nothing' in token of something more elaborate, *e.g. Saya ini měmungut duit jamuan budak-budak. Běri sa-ringgit pun jadi-lah, jangan tidak;* 'I'm collecting for the children's party. A dollar will do, just to "show willing".' The phrase is also used as a direct double-negative imperative, *e.g. Jangan tidak balek lěkas,* 'Be sure to come back in good time.'

32 Buat měnyukakan hati: this is a colloquial use of *buat (lit.* 'the making of . . .', 'the providing of . . .' *e.g. Saya 'nak tanam sa-baris bunga di-sini buat tanda sěmpadan děngan kěbun awak;* 'I'm going to plant a row of flowers here, for a boundary mark between your garden and mine.' Cf. Note VIII.27. In bazaar Malay this use is extended, so that *buat* becomes an equivalent of the English word 'for', even in such phrases as 'for me'. Do not imitate this.

33 Tumbang lěmbu sa-ekor: *tumbang,* 'to fall', of things which fall over from their base, *e.g.* trees, masts, slaughtered cattle. Malay is rich in such specialized words. Other 'falling' words are *rěbah,* 'collapse', 'fold up' (of a person fainting), the heavier word *roboh,* 'collapse' (of a house), and the still heavier word *runtoh,* 'come tumbling down' (of a landslide, of the sky in a fable). There are many other such groups of words which need to be used with precision.

sa-ekor: lit. 'one tail of'. This is the numeral coefficient for *all* living creatures other than human beings.

When *sa-* + *coefficient* precedes a noun, it usually corresponds to English 'a', meaning 'a particular one' (*e.g.* I.29, *Nampak sa-buah kapal tĕrbang;* 'An aircraft is seen'). When *sa-* + *coefficient* follows its noun, it stresses the numeral value of *sa-*. In this example it is not one particular ox that is thought of, but the fact that a whole ox is provided for the feast. (The size of the beast that is killed—goat, ox or buffalo—is the measure of the scale of the festivities.)

35 sĕngaja dia mĕnyĕbut-lah: *-lah* for emphasis, stressing the content of the word: 'He's only *saying* that, he doesn't really mean it.'

37 sĕndiri angkat: 'himself lift it.' A pronoun object is not put in if it can be gathered from the context. (*Note.* It would probably be more accurate to say that in such sentences there is no object, that the statement is merely 'himself do the lifting'.)

43 boleh katakan: for the written form *boleh di-katakan, lit.* 'able, it-to-be-said', *i.e.* 'one might say'.

sanak saudara: the first word is Arabic, the second Sanskrit. Another such alliterative coupling (without conjunction) is *kaum kĕluarga,* also meaning 'kith and kin'. Arabic and Sanskrit supply the two main streams of foreign loan-words in Malay. The Sanskrit words came in during the pre-Islam period, when Hindu civilization was the dominant cultural influence in the Archipelago. The Arabic words are still coming in.

45 Ada sa-tĕngah-nya: 'some of them'; *sa-tĕngah* need not mean an accurate numerical half. *Sa-paroh* is used in the same way.

46 'dah sampai sa-minggu mĕnolong: note the idiomatic turn of the sentence. The real statement is *sudah.* Cf. *Dia itu sudah bĕrjam-jam mĕmbacha;* 'He has been reading for hours' (*lit.* 'Him, it has become hour after hour, he-reading').

50 tĕmpat orang masak: *lit.* 'place of people cooking'. When a root-word begins with *m* the prefix *mĕ-* is seldom used.

pĕrkakas sĕmua-nya bĕsar-bĕsar: duplication used to modify, not to emphasize. Cf. *Budak-budak dalam darjah ini pandai-pandai bĕlaka;* 'The children in this class are all of them pretty good.'

55 Apa-apa pun boleh: duplication to allow for all possible variety. For the *pun* see Note I.81.

56 Kalau ta' bĕrapa orang / pakai kuali sahaja: here *pakai* is itself the subject of the sentence. 'There is the practice of using.' The *kalau* might have been omitted, in which case the first phrase would be a 'free' noun-group (like *orang suka makan bĕrsila* in line 24 above), giving the circumstances, setting the scene as it were, for the statement which follows.

59 Kĕchil sadikit: 'a bit smaller'. Colloquial Malay usually allows comparison to be gleaned from the context. See Note VIII.90.

dia ada bĕrtĕlinga: see Note 14 above.

60 yang bĕkĕrja: the *r* of the prefix is omitted before *kĕrja* because of the *r* in the root.

banyak orang pĕrĕmpuan: short for *yang banyak-nya orang pĕrĕmpuan*, *i.e.* not 'there are many women' but 'most of them are women'.

63 'dah potong lĕmbu: *potong* here refers both to the killing and to the cutting up of the ox. Among themselves the Malays always use the correct word *sĕmbĕleh* for killing beasts for food in accordance with Islamic ordinance.

64 Kĕrja mĕmileh bĕras: *lit.* 'the work, picking over the rice', an example of the *mĕ-* derivative used as a verbal-noun.

pileh bĕras: the husked rice is spread on a *mĕngkuang* mat, and the odd grains of unhusked padi (*antah*) are picked out.

65 mĕngukor: this might be from *ukor*, 'measure', since roots which begin with vowels take the infix *-ng-*, but the context tells you to choose the other alternative, *kukor*, 'to rasp'.

mĕnyiang sayor: 'prepare the vegetables'. Like the English word 'prepare', the Malay word *siang* includes all the required processes, such as *kupas*, 'peel'; *chinchang*, 'chop', etc.

70 Ini ada satu tangga: the 'circumstantial' use of *ini*, usually to be translated as 'Here is . . .' Do not think of the sentence as meaning 'This is a staircase', using *ada* as a copula. That would be bazaar Malay. The *ini* is not the staircase itself, but the circumstance of there being a staircase there, *lit.* 'This (is) there-being-a-staircase.' Cf. Note II.10, *Ini Mr. Martin 'dah sampai.*

naik ikut tangga bĕlakang: 'go up *by* the back staircase', in written Malay *naik mĕngikut*. See Note 13 above.

72 Mĕreka kĕtiga: *tiga*, 'three'; *kĕtiga*, 'the three of them'. In line 87 below, the duplication further strengthens the 'group' idea, *kĕtiga-tiga mĕreka*, 'all three of them'. *Kĕtiga* also means 'thirdly', and *yang kĕtiga* means 'the third'.

sa-tĕlah mĕnanggalkan kasut: causative suffix *-kan*; *tanggal*, 'dropped off'; *tanggalkan*, 'make to drop off', *i.e.* 'remove'. In speech, *sudah buka kasut*.

75 Di-sĕrambi ini: the circumstantial *ini*, not 'on this verandah' but 'here, on the verandah'.

di-bĕntang tikar: the impersonal *di-* construction followed immediately by the object, with no agent necessarily mentioned because the idea is expressed quite generally. If the agent *were* mentioned it would have to come immediately after the verb, before the object, *di-bĕntang orang tikar, lit.* 'there-is-a-spreading by-people (of) mats' *i.e.* 'they spread mats'. See Notes II.36, and VIII.66.

81 kita běri pěngantin dudok: cf. Note II.75. *Ia měmběri dia pakai těrompah.*

83 nasi běsar: this will be *pulut* rice on a large tray which is placed on a stand. From it the bride and bridegroom will each in turn take a few grains to place in the mouth of the other partner as a symbolic act. The rice will be stuck round with some of the coloured eggs (on sticks) which have been prepared for distribution to the guests. See line 101 in Scene VI.

88 sěpěrai katil: usually 'bed-spread', but here used of the silken hangings sewn, temporarily, to the edge of the sheet (*kain chadar*).

    sěpěrai itu . . . muka bantal itu . . . tikar sila itu: the writer has used no *pun* here because he is giving a catalogue of things which would naturally occur together. If one is embroidered they will all be embroidered. Thus he is not seeking to re-focus the attention with each new thing that he mentions, as, *e.g.*, in line 55 above, *Nasi boleh, gulai pun boleh.* The level tone of the speaker in line 88 makes the difference quite clear. Cf. line 64 above, *měmileh běras, měnggiling rěmpah*, etc., a catalogue of naturally associated actions.

92 orang sudah mula: *orang* used in its 'general' sense, corresponding to English 'they'.

    běrsiap hěndak: 'getting ready *to* . . .' The inherent futurity in *běrsiap* requires *hěndak* before the following verb-word. Cf. Note IV.12 and Sentence Pattern IV.2.

SCENE V: TAKING STOCK

3. INI and ITU

    ii. *ini* indicating circumstance

        Ini | ada satu tangga, 'Here's a staircase.'

5. NUMERAL COEFFICIENTS

    (*f*) *ekor* for living creatures (non-human)

        Pada suatu masa ada sa-ekor lěmbu . . .

        ' Once there was an ox . . .'

        Tumbang lěmbu sa-ekor.

        An ox falls. (*i.e.* one whole ox is to be eaten at the feast.)

    Note: sa- + coefficient *before* the noun = 'a certain'

                sa- + coefficient *after* the noun = 'one'

6. PRONOUNS

(a) personal

iv. b. -nya used impersonally, meaning 'in question'

biasa-nya, 'as a rule'.
Ini-lah rumah-nya, 'This is the house'.
Pĕrkakas-nya sĕmua bĕsar-bĕsar.
The utensils used are all rather large.
Ini dia kuali-nya.
Now this (is what I mean by) a *kuali*.

(c) the relative pronoun *yang*

ii. equivalent to 'the one', 'the ones', 'those':

Yang satu lagi itu khemah.
The other one is a tent.

7. DUPLICATION

i. to show variety:

Apa-apa pun boleh, 'Anything at all (can be cooked in it).'

ii. to moderate:

Pĕrkakas-nya sĕmua bĕsar-bĕsar.
The utensils are all rather large.

iii. to emphasize:

Kĕtiga-tiga mĕreka pĕrgi ka-pintu.
All three of them go to the door.

10. AFFIXES

(a) bĕr-

i. possessive:

Kawasan rumah itu ada bĕrpagar.
The garden is fenced.
Kuali itu ada bĕrtĕlinga.
There are handles to the frying-pan.

ii. forming an intransitive verb:

Che' Normah tidak bĕrgĕrak dari dĕkat pintu.
Che' Normah does not move from the doorway.

(b) mĕ-

i. as a verbal noun:

d. in apposition to another noun—

Kĕrja mĕmileh bĕras.
The work (of) picking over the rice.

iii. participial:

> *a.* after a verb of movement, and corresponding to an English preposition—
>
> > *Mr. Martin pĕrgi mĕngikut Che' Mahmud.*
> > Mr. Martin goes with (*lit.* following) Che' Mahmud.
> > *Dia datang balek mĕndapatkan Che' Mahmud.*
> > She returns to (*lit.* coming up to) Che' Mahmud.

Reminder: 'coming and going' verbs do not take *mĕ-*:

> > *Dia bĕrjalan pĕrgi ka-sĕrambi.*
> > He walks into (*lit.* going into) the verandah.
> > *Che' Mahmud mĕmbawa dia masok ka-kawasan rumah.*
> > Che' Mahmud takes him into (*lit.* entering into) the front garden.

(*d*) *-kan*

i. causative:

> *tanggal,* 'dropped off'; *tanggalkan,* 'make to drop off', 'take off'

(*e*) *tĕr-*

i. completed state:

> . . . *nasi bĕsar yang ada tĕrlĕtak dĕkat pĕlamin itu.*
> . . . a large tray of rice, placed near the bridal dais.

(*f*) *di-*

ii. for action, with no specified agent:

> *Di-sĕrambi ini memang di-bĕntang tikar yang chantek-chantek.*
> Here in the *sĕrambi,* naturally, they put down their finest mats.
> (*or* . . . The finest mats are always laid in the *sĕrambi.*)

(*i*) *kĕ-*

i. used to create group-numbers:

> *mĕreka kĕtiga,* 'the three of them'

11. PUN

i. with *juga* to draw attention to a word which balances some previous word:

> *Bangsal pun dia juga,* 'It's called *bangsal,* too (as well as *balai*).'

13. PULA

ii. for recurrence, repetition:

> *Mari kita tengok ka-bĕlakang sana pula.*
> Let's go and see what's going on at the back, now.
> *Ini suatu lagi pula bangsal.*
> Here's another shed.

14. -LAH

  i. *c.* or emphasis, by singling out a word from others in the same
  category.

  > *Ah, sěngaja dia měnyěbut-lah.*
  > Oh, he's just *saying* that (he doesn't *mean* it).

15. PREPOSITIONS

  (c) ii. *ka-* for implied 'motion towards':

  > *Dia pěrgi měnchari tuan rumah ka-bělakang.*
  > She goes and looks for the host at the back of the house.
  > *Mari kita tengok ka-bělakang.*
  > Let's go and have a look at the back.
  > *Mari kita dudok ka-sěrambi.*
  > Let's go and sit on the verandah.

18. BOLEH and BIAR

  (a) *boleh* used colloquially for purpose:

  > *Di-mana agak-nya tuan rumah, boleh kita bagi tahu.*
  > I wonder where I shall find the host, so that we can let him know.

22. THE NOUN-GROUP

  i. as a description, attached to a noun of place or time:

  > *rumah orang kahwin*
  > a house where a wedding is going on
  > *těmpat orang makan*
  > the place where you eat
  > *bangsal těmpat orang masak*
  > the shed in which they do the cooking
  > *těmpat měnyěrang-nya*
  > the place on which you put it, to get hot
  > *těmpat pěngantin laki-laki dudok*
  > the place where the bridegroom sits
  > *těmpat pěngantin dudok masa 'akad nikah*
  > the place where the bridegroom sits at the time when the marriage-
  > contract is made
  > *Měreka tiba pagi masa orang běrsiap-siap.*
  > They arrive in the morning when the people are in the middle of
  > their preparations.

  ii. a noun declaring the topic:

  > *Balai itu | ada lantai.*
  > *lit.* The pavilion, there's a floor there.

  iii. a noun-group declaring the circumstances:

  > *Orang suka makan běrsila | pěrgi makan ka-balai.*
  > If you like sitting cross-legged to eat, you go to the pavilion to
  > have your meal.

v. an unprefixed 'verb' as the subject-noun (*pakai, pĕrgi*) :

Kalau ta' bĕrapa orang / pakai kuali sahaja.

If there aren't many people, a frying-pan is used.

Orang suka makan bĕrsila / pĕrgi makan ka-balai.

If you like sitting cross-legged to eat, you go to the pavilion to have your meal.

23. SUDAH

i. meaning 'has'. In written Malay *sudah* used thus as an auxiliary is replaced by *tĕlah:*

Ia tĕlah di-bawa pĕrgi ka-rumah orang kahwin.

He has been taken to a house where a wedding is going on.

24. ADA

This word denotes existence; it does not mean 'is', 'are', but 'there is', 'there are':

Dalam khemah itu ada kĕrusi meja sahaja.

In the tent there are only chairs and tables.

Kawasan rumah itu ada bĕrpagar.

The ground round the house is fenced in.

Dia mĕnunjok kapada bangsal yang ada tĕrdiri di-hadapan rumah itu.

He points to a shed, erected in front of the house.

Ada dia buat rumah kĕchil juga.

Oh, they've built a little house as well.

Balai itu, ada lantai.

When it's a *balai*, there is flooring.

Dia ada bĕrtĕlinga.

There are handles to it.

Nasi bĕsar yang ada tĕrlĕtak dĕkat pĕlamin itu.

A large tray of rice, placed there near the bridal couch.

(See also Sentence Patterns III.3.i and ii)

SCENE V: SENTENCE PATTERNS

1. *mĕ*: i. 'goes a-seeking'; ii. 'goes to seek' iii. 'takes a-crossing'

i. Verb of movement + *mĕ-*

a. **Che' Normah pĕrgi mĕnchari tuan rumah ka-bĕlakang.**

Che' Normah goes and looks for the host at the back of the house.

b. Che' Asmah itu datang mĕnĕngok anak-nya di-rumah sakit.

Che' Asmah came and visited her child at the hospital.

c. Hari itu abang saya datang mĕminjam duit sadikit.

That day my brother came and borrowed a small sum of money.

d. Gajah itu mĕngawaikan bĕlalai-nya mĕngambil pisang yang di-hulorkan budak itu.
The elephant curled its trunk and took the banana that the child was holding out to it.

e. Kĕreta api ini baharu masok mĕnyorok Bukit Bĕrapit.
The train has just entered the Bukit Bĕrapit tunnel (lit. entered tunnelling).

ii. Verb of movement + *hĕndak* + *mĕ-*

a. Dia pĕrgi ka-kĕdai 'nak mĕnchari tĕmbakau.
He went to the shop to get some tobacco.

b. Sa-malam dia datang 'nak bĕrjumpa saya, 'tapi saya ta' ada di-rumah.
He came to see me last night, but I wasn't in.

c. Adek saya datang hĕndak mĕminjam duit tiga ratus ringgit. Di-mana-lah saya 'nak charikan!
My young brother came along to borrow $300. Where was I to find $300 for him?

d. Lĕpas itu di-tinjau-nya 'nak mĕnengok apa yang kurang.
After that she took a look round to see what was wanted.

e. Di-panjat-nya tiang lampu itu nak mĕngambil layang-layang-nya yang tĕrsangkut di-situ.
He climbed up the lamp-post to get his kite which had caught in it.

iii. Verb of movement + verb of movement with *mĕ-* (= English preposition)

a. Dia mĕmbawa kĕreta mĕngikut jalan raya.
He drove the car along the main road.

b. Orang pĕrahu itu kĕrja-nya mĕmbawa orang mĕnyĕbĕrang sungai.
The boatman's job is to take people across the river.

c. Kapal kami kĕna ribut masa bĕlayar mĕnuju ka-Colombo.
Our boat ran into a storm as we were making for (or sailing towards) Colombo.

d. Gajah kalau di-bawa mĕrĕntas sawah banyak-lah padi yang rosak.
If you take an elephant across a rice-field a lot of the rice will be spoilt.

e. Kapal bĕsar ta' dapat bĕlayar mĕnĕrusi Sĕlat Tĕbĕrau.
Large ships cannot sail through the Johore Strait.

2. i. *bukan*; ii. *tidak*; iii. *bukan* or *tidak*; iv. *ta'*

i. *bukan*

a. **Bukan** (or Bukan-nya) **hari ini sahaja dia datang bĕkĕrja.**
It isn't only to-day that they have come to help.

b. Ahmad itu bukan orang-nya yang boleh di-suroh mĕmanjat. Badan-nya gĕmok.
Ahmad isn't the sort of person that you would tell to climb a tree. He's too stout.

c. Kĕnyang pun makan juga-lah sadikit. Awak bukan (or bukan-nya) datang hari-hari ka-sini.
Do have something to eat, even though you aren't hungry. It isn't every day that you come to see us.

d. Kata Che' Ali awak 'nak balek besok.—Bukan. Lusa.
Che' Ali says you're going home to-morrow.—No. It's the day after.

e. Osman-kah měnyanyi těngah malam tadi, těrjaga sěmua orang?—Bukan
Was it you who were singing last night, Osman, waking everybody up?—No, it wasn't me!

ii. *tidak*

a. Tidak di-běnarkan orang luar masok ka-kawasan askar itu.
Strangers are not allowed inside the military area.

b. Měmotong gětah pun tidak, běrtanam padi pun tidak. Apa-lah kěrja-nya dudok di-kampong?
He's not a rubber tapper, nor a padi planter. What does he do, then, living in a village?

c. Kalau tidak 'nak beli pun, ta' měngapa. Tengok sahaja-lah.
It's quite all right, even if you don't want to buy anything. Just have a look round.

d. 'Nak balek besok-kah?—Tidak. Lusa.
Is it to-morrow that you are going home?—No. The day after.

e. Osman měnyanyi-kah dalam wayang malam tadi?—Tidak.
Did you sing at the concert last night, Osman?—No, I didn't.

iii. *bukan* or *tidak*

a. Bukan-kah (*or* Tidak-kah) měmbuang duit sahaja měmběli baju nipis itu? Bukan-nya tahan.
Isn't it just a waste of money to buy that thin coat? It won't last any time.

b. Barang apa nasihat kita, bukan (*or* tidak) sahaja pada dia.
What ever advice you give him, he just flouts it.

c. Měngapa-lah susah-susah sangat měnchari surat khabar itu? Kalau hilang pun bukan (*or* tidak) měnjadi rugi.
Why are you going to so much trouble trying to find that newspaper? It isn't serious, even if it is lost.

d. Hěndak běli-kah ěnche'?—Tidak (*or* Bukan). 'Nak tengok-tengok.
Do you want to buy it?—No, thank you. I was just looking.

e. Měrchun běsar ini bukan (*or* tidak *or* ta') boleh di-běri budak-budak měmasang-nya.
You can't let children fire off big crackers like this.

iv. *ta'*

a. Ta' kan sudah kěrja kita malam ini. Banyak běnar yang ta' siap lagi.
We'll never get through all this to-night. There's a great deal that we haven't done yet.

b. Tidak-lah 'nak siap malam ini juga. 'Tapi ta' boleh lengah sangat.
No, we shan't get it done to-night. But we mustn't loiter over it, all the same.

c. Gugor sa-biji mumbang kělapa. Mujor ta' kěna kěpala budak itu.
A young coconut fell. It was lucky that it didn't drop on the child's head.

d. Di-pandang-nya kapal tĕrbang itu sampai ta' nampak.
He followed the plane with his eyes until it was out of sight.

e. Ta' (or Tidak) bĕrbaju tĕbal ta' tahan kĕluar rumah dalam musim sĕjok.
You won't be able to go out without an overcoat during the winter.

3. *tĕmpat* + noun-phrase for '(the place) where'

a. **Ini bangsal tĕmpat orang masak.**
This is the shed where they do the cooking.

b. Di-pasir itu-lah tĕmpat kami bĕrkelah.
That's the beach where we had our picnic.

c. Tolong tunjokkan tĕmpat kĕreta itu jatoh.
Show me the place where the car went over the edge.

d. Kalau nak mĕngganti ubat lampu ini, di-sini tĕmpat mĕmbuka-nya.
If you want to put a new battery in the torch, this is where you undo it.

e. Di-pĕkan itu-lah tĕmpat saya lahir.
That's where I was born.

DI-RUMAH ORANG KAHWIN LAGI

A MALAY WEDDING (PART II)

1 Che' Mahmud dĕngan Mr. Martin dudok di-sĕrambi bĕrsama-sama dĕngan
2 orang lain yang sudah ramai di-situ.

Che' Mahmud with Mr. Martin sit on-sĕrambi together with other people who have-become many there.

Che' Mahmud and Mr. Martin are sitting in the *sĕrambi* with the other guests, many of whom have already arrived.

3 MAR. **Kita orang laki-laki sahaja di-sini, ya? Orang**
We, people male only, here, yes? People female sit in-mid-house.
It is just we men who sit here, is it? The women sit in the
4 **pĕrĕmpuan dudok di-tĕngah rumah.**
inner room.

5 MAH. **Memang. Dalam majlis macham ini orang laki-laki**
Habitually. In assembly this-sort, men not mix with women.
Yes, that's always so. In a gathering of this sort the men
6 **tidak bĕrchampor dĕngan orang pĕrĕmpuan.**
don't mingle with the women.

7 MAR. **Orang sa-bĕlah sana lain sadikit pakaian di-kĕpala**
People side yonder, other a-little the-wear on-the-heads-of them?
Those people over there are wearing something different on
8 **dia?**
their heads?

9 MAH. **Orang itu sĕmua orang ahli agama. Sĕrban di-**
Those people, all, people specialists of-religion. Turban on-heads-
They are all of them men versed in religion. The turban
10 **kĕpala-nya itu pakaian orang sudah pĕrgi naik hajji**
of-them, the-wear of persons completed going upon pilgrimage to
that they wear is the headgear of a person who has made
11 **ka-Mĕkkah. 'Tapi orang yang bĕlum naik hajji pun**
Mecca. But, persons who not yet go on pilgrimage, there is, to a
the pilgrimage to Mecca. But there are some people who
12 **ada juga pakai sĕrban. Orang dudok dĕkat jĕndela**
certain extent, a-wearing of turban. The person sitting near the
wear it, even though they have not made the pilgrimage.

13   **itu bukan haji.**
window (is) a-non-haji.
That man sitting near the window there, he's not a *haji*.

14   Ada sa-orang datang mĕmbawa pĕrasap dari tĕngah rumah.
It is that one-person comes bringing an incense-burner from inner room.
Somebody comes out of the living-room, carrying an incense-burner.

15 MAR. **Ini apa pula di-bawa orang ini?**
This what, I wonder, there-is-a-bringing by-this-person?
What is this that this person is bringing in?

16 MAH. **Pĕrasap nama-nya. Di-dalam-nya ada bara api.**
Censer name-of-it. In it there-are embers of-fire. The-smoke of-
It's called a *pĕrasap*. There are live coals inside it. The

17   **Asap bara itu mĕnjadi wangi bau-nya sĕbab ada di-**
the-embers, becomes fragrant, the smell of it, because it-is-that there-
smoke from it is scented because they have sprinkled

18   **taborkan kĕmian. Kita pakai pĕrasap ini bila hĕn-**
is-a-scattering of-benzoin. We use this censer when there-is-going-
benzoin on it. The incense-burner is always used when some

19   **dak mĕmulakan satu-satu kĕrja agama macham ini.**
to begin one-or-another religious ceremony this-sort. A-little,
religious rite, such as this, is about to begin. Presently we

20   **Sadikit lagi kita dĕngar-lah pĕngantin pĕrĕmpuan**
still, we hear bride reading Kor'an.
shall hear the bride reading the Kor'an.

21   **mĕmbacha Kor'an.**

22 MAR. **Mana dia ta' kĕluar lagi?**
Where she, not come-out still?
Where is she, that she hasn't come out yet?

23 MAH. **Dia tidak kĕluar. Dia mĕmbacha di-tĕngah rumah**
She not come-out. She reads in-mid-house in gathering of women
She doesn't come out. She recites it in the living-room

24   **dalam kumpulan orang pĕrĕmpuan sahaja.**
only.
among the women only.

25   Pada kĕtika itu pĕngantin pĕrĕmpuan mulaï mĕmbacha Koran. Sakalian
26 yang hadzir pun mĕnyambut bachaan-nya itu apabila sampai ka-hujong
27 satu-satu surah. Sa-tĕlah habis bĕrkhatam itu mulaï pula majlis marhaban.

28 Pada masa sampai kapada těntang bachaan sěmua orang městi běrdiri, tuan
29 rumah kěluar ka-sěrambi měmbawa bunga rampai děngan ayer mawar.
30 Ayer mawar itu di-rěnjis-nya kapada baju tiap-tiap sa-orang yang ada dan
31 bunga rampai itu di-běri-nya sa-orang sa-bungkus.

*At moment that, bride begins reading Kor'an. All who are-present receive the
reading of-her whenever arrive to end of each-one section. When ended the-completing
of-study, begins, in turn, assembly of 'marhaban'. At time arriving to place-in-reading of
all-persons-must-stand, master of house comes out to verandah-room carrying mixed-flowers
with rose-water. The rose-water, there-is-a-sprinkling-by-him to coats of-each one-
person who is-present and the mixed flowers, there-is-a-presenting-by-him one-person one-
package.*

At that moment the bride begins to read the Kor'an. All those present take
up the reading at the end of each *surah*. When that is over, the *marhaban*
chanting begins. When they come to the point in the reading where everybody must stand, the host comes out into the *sěrambi* bringing scented petals
and leaves and rose-water. He sprinkles the rose-water on the clothes of every
guest, and gives each one a packet of *bunga rampai*.

32 MAH.   **Orang ini měmberi bunga rampai pula.**
      This-person is-giving flowers, various, next.
      He is giving out *bunga rampai* now.

33 MAR.   **Buat apa ini?**
      Doing what, this?
      What for?

34 MAH.   **Ta' ada apa-apa guna-nya. Buat wangi sahaja.**
      Not-is anything the-use-of-it. Make fragrant only. In-inside-of
      Not for anything in particular. Just for the sake of the
35   **Di-dalam-nya macham-macham jěnis bunga děngan**
      it all-sorts varieties of-flowers with leaves of-pandan, a species of
      perfume. Inside the packets there are various sorts of
36   **daun pandan, satu bangsa daun wangi.**
      leaf, scented.
      flowers, and scented *pandan* leaves.

37   Lěpas marhaban itu di-angkat orang teh děngan kueh-kueh kěring sěrta
38 sadikit kueh basah ia-itu wajek, dodel, agar-agar.

*After the-'marhaban' there-is-lifted up, by-people, tea, with dry-cakes together-with
small-quantity wet-sweets, that-is-to-say diamond-shaped sweetmeats, 'fudge', and sea-weed
jellies.*

After the *marhaban* chanting tea is brought in, with cakes and some sweetmeats—*wajek, dodol* and sea-weed jellies.

39 MAR.   **Běras-kah di-buat orang wajek ini?**
      Rice, there-is-a-making, by people, these 'wajek' sweetmeats?
      Are these *wajek* cakes made with rice?

-0 MAH. **Běras juga, tětapi bangsa mělěkit bila di-masak.**
Rice, granted, but a-sort being-sticky when there-is-cooking.
Yes, it's rice, but a particular kind that goes sticky when

-1 **Běras pulut nama-nya. Dodol ini pun běras pulut**
'Pulut' rice the name of it. This dodol, 'pulut' rice too,
it's cooked. It's called *pulut* rice. They make this *dodol*

-2 **juga di-buat orang. Tětapi běras itu di-tumbok**
there-is-a-making by people. But the rice is-pounded first be-
too from *pulut* rice. But the rice is first pounded into

-3 **dahulu měnjadi těpong. Lěpas minum ini kita**
coming flour. After this-drinking we return first. Evening pre-
flour. When we have finished eating these, we'll go home.

-4 **balek dahulu. Pětang 'karang datang sa-kali lagi.**
sently, come one-time more. Not the-trouble we come eat rice.
This afternoon we shall come again. There is no need for

-5 **Ta' payah kita datang makan nasi. Ta' ada apa**
Not there-is any thing intending see, time the-rice-eating.
us to come to the luncheon. There is nothing that we

-6 **běnda 'nak tengok masa makan nasi itu.**
want to see during the meal.

-7 Sa-tělah minum teh itu orang jěmputan sěmua balek dahulu.
Has-been that drinking of tea, invited people all go-back first.

-8 After the refreshments the guests all go home.

-9 Di-rumah Che' Mahmud Mr. Martin běrtanya kapada Zaharah. Zaharah
baharu balek sěkolah.
*At-house of Che' Mahmud, Mr. Martin asks to Zaharah. Zaharah newly returned
from school.*
At Che' Mahmud's house Mr. Martin questions Zaharah, who has just come
home from school.

-0 MAR. **Pagi tadi Zaharah sěkolah, ta' pěrgi ka-rumah orang**
Morning just-gone-by Zaharah at-school, not go-to-house of-
This morning you were at school. You didn't go to the

-1 **kahwin. Pětang ini pěrgi ta'?**
person-marrying. This afternoon, go, or not?
wedding. Will you be coming this afternoon?

-2 ZAH. **Ta' boleh juga, fasal Rah 'nak měngaji Kor'an.**
Not able, too, reason Rah about-to study Kor'an.
No, I can't come this afternoon, either, because I shall be
going to Kor'an school.

53   Che' Mahmud děngan Che' Normah dan Mr. Martin datang lagi pada
54 pukul lima pětang kěrana měnengok isti'adat běrsanding.   Pada masa měreka
55 sampai itu orang sudah ramai běrhimpun di-halaman kěrana měnanti pěn-
56 gantin laki-laki.

*Che' Mahmud with Che' Normah and Mr. Martin come more at strike 5 afternoon
because seeing ceremony sitting-in-state.   At the time of-them-arriving people have-become
many in-courtyard because-of awaiting bridegroom.*

Che' Mahmud and Che' Normah and Mr. Martin return at 5.0 p.m. in
order to see the *běrsanding* ceremony.   When they arrive there is already a
crowd gathered in the courtyard to await the bridegroom.

57 NOR.   **Biar saya těrus ka-rumah.   Tadi tuan rumah pěsan**
            Allow-that I straight to-house.   Earlier, people-of-house send
            I'll go straight in.   They sent me a message asking if I
58   **minta siapkan pěngantin pěrěmpuan.**
            message asking make-ready bride.
            would help to get the bride ready.

59 MAH.   **Kalau sudah ada kěrja měngapa ta' bagi tahu dari**
            If has-been there-is work, why not give-to-know from earlier, able
            If you had something to do, why didn't you say so before,
60   **tadi, boleh kita datang lěkas sadikit.   Ini bukan-kah**
            we come promptly a-little.   This, is-it-not, it-has-become almost-
            so that we could have come a little early.   You're cutting
61   **'dah suntok?**
            too-short time?
            it a bit fine now, aren't you?

62 NOR.   **Tidak.   Hěndak siapkan barang-barang ěmas-nya**
            Not.   Going-to make-ready things gold in-question only.   Hair,
            No.   I'm only going to see to the jewellery.   There are
63   **sahaja.   Rambut, bědak, kain baju sěmua 'dah ada**
            face-powder, clothes, all, has-been there-are other people making-
            other people seeing to the hair-dressing and the cosmetics
64   **orang lain měnyiapkan-nya.**
            ready-them.
            and the clothes.

65   Che' Normah pun naik ka-rumah.   Sa-jurus lěpas itu tiba-lah pěrarakan
66 pěngantin laki-laki.

*Che' Normah goes-up to-house.   One-moment past that, arrives procession of-bride-
groom.*

Che' Normah goes into the house.   A moment or two later the bridegroom's
procession arrives.

MAH. **Tengok-lah pĕngantin itu pakai tĕngkolok di-**
See, the-bridegroom, wears kerchief on-head-of-him.
Look. The bridegroom is wearing a kerchief head-dress.
kĕpala-nya.

MAR. **Macham gambar dalam stamp, ia?**
Sort picture in stamp, yes?
Like the picture on the stamps, isn't it?

MAH. **Ia. Dalam stamp itu gambar raja. Pĕngantin pun**
Yes. In the stamps, picture of raja. Bridegroom, people call ruler
Yes. On the stamps it is a likeness of the ruler. A bride-
orang panggil raja juga, raja sa-hari. Dia bĕr-
too, ruler of-one-day. That him-being-protected-by-umbrella too,
groom, too, is called a raja—a 'one-day raja'. He has an
payong itu pun macham raja juga. Dahulu bila
(is) like ruler. Before, when bridegroom has arrived near, like
umbrella held over him too, like a raja. In earlier times,
pĕngantin sudah sampai dĕkat macham ini dia tidak
this, he not more go on-foot. There-is person come a-carrying-
when the bridegroom was as close as this he would not
lagi bĕrjalan kaki. Ada orang datang mĕnandu-
him on shoulders.
walk any further. A man would come and carry him on
nya atas bahu.
his shoulders.

Apabila sampai ka-halaman pĕngantin itu di-dudokkan atas kĕrusi di-tĕpi
halaman itu. Gong sĕrta gĕndang pun di-palu orang kĕrana hĕndak bĕrsilat.
*When arrive to-courtyard, the bridegroom, there-is-a-seating on chair at-edge of-the-
courtyard. Gongs with drums, there-is-a-beating by-people because going-to-be perform-
dagger-dance.*
When they come into the courtyard they seat the bridegroom on a chair at
one side. Gongs and drums are beaten to announce the *silat* performance.

Pĕrmainan ini bĕrsilat nama-nya. Sudah ini ba-
This performance, dagger-dancing name-of it. Completed, this,
This performance is called *bĕrsilat*. It has to take place
haru-lah pĕngantin di-bawa naik bĕrsanding. Pada
newly bridegroom is-brought going-up sitting-ceremonially. At
before the bridegroom is conducted to the dais for the

80 **masa pĕngantin sampai ka-tangga 'karang boleh**
time bridegroom arrives to-stairs presently able see, there-is person-
bĕrsanding ceremony. When he reaches the steps you'll

81 **tengok ada orang mĕnabor bĕras, nama-nya bĕras**
scattering husked-rice, name of it rice washed. Use-of-it
see somebody scattering rice, it's called 'washed rice'. It

82 **basoh. Guna-nya jadi tanda sĕlamat datang.**
acts as sign safe come.
is a symbol of welcome.

83 Sa-tĕlah sĕlĕsai bĕrsilat itu pĕngantin pun di-bawa naik ka-rumah.
When brought-to-end the-dagger-dance, bridegroom, is brought mounting to-house.
When the *silat* performance is over, the bridegroom is brought up into the house.

84 MAR. **Tiga pasang orang bĕrsilat ini, ia?**
These pairs persons doing-dagger-dance, yes?
Three couples of fencers, is it?

85 MAH. **Ia. Tiga pasang. Konon-nya ta' boleh gĕnap.**
Yes. Three pairs. The-report-of-it, not can even-number. If
Yes, three couples. They say that it mustn't be an even

86 **Kalau tidak tiga pasang mĕsti lima pasang atau pun**
not three pairs must five pairs or-else seven.
number. If it isn't three pairs then it must be five, or

87 **tujoh.**
seven.

88 Pada masa pĕngantin sampai ka-tangga ada sa-orang pĕrĕmpuan tua
89 mĕnabor bĕras basoh. Apabila sampai ka-kĕpala tangga oleh pĕrĕmpuan itu
90 di-rĕnjis-nya sadikit ayer kapada kaki pĕngantin sa-bagai ganti mĕmbasoh
91 kaki-nya. Sa-tĕlah itu pĕngantin pun di-bawa ka-pĕlamin. Pĕngantin
92 pĕrĕmpuan sudah ada sĕdia di-dudokkan di-situ. Orang ramai pun bĕr-
93 dahulu-dahuluan naik ka-rumah kĕrana hĕndak mĕnengok bĕrsanding.

At time bridegroom arrives to-stairs, there-is one-person old-woman scattering washed-rice. When arrival to-head of-stairs, by-the-woman, there-is-a-sprinkling-by-her a-little water to feet of-bridegroom, as substitute of-washing feet-of-him. Has-been that, bride-groom, there-is-conducting to-bridal couch. Bride, it has-come-to-be, ready, seated there. People in-large-numbers pressing-one-in-front-of-the-other come-up to-house because-of going-to see-the-bridal-couple-seated-side-by-side.

As the bridegroom reaches the stairs, an old woman scatters 'washed rice'. When he reaches the top of the stairs she sprinkles a few drops of water on his feet as a token 'washing' of his feet. After that he is led to the bridal dais. The bride has already been seated on it. The guests crowd up the stairs pressing forward to get a good view of the seated couple.

4 MAH. **Mari kita pula naik.**
Come we, in turn, go-up.
Let us go up, too.

5
6 Mr. Martin pun naik ka-rumah měngikut Che' Mahmud. Děngan menin-
jau di-chělah orang ramai itu dapat-lah ia měnengok pěngantin běrsanding.
Mr. Martin goes-up to-house, following Che' Mahmud. With craning-to-see at-chinks of-people-in-numbers, successful, they-seeing bridal pair sitting together.
Mr. Martin goes up after Che' Mahmud. They peep through the spaces
between the people in the crowd and manage to see the bridal couple sitting
in state.

7 MAR. **Dudok macham itu sahaja-kah běrsanding ini?**
Sit like that, only, this-běrsanding?
Is that all that *běrsanding* is, just sitting like that?

8 MAH. **Dudok bagitu sahaja-lah. Ta' ada apa-apa lagi.**
Sit like-that only. Not is anything still.
Yes that's all. Just sitting like that. Nothing more.

9 Sa-tělah měnengok běrsanding itu měreka pun běrkira-lah hěndak balek.
0 Měreka běrdiri di-halaman měnanti Che' Normah. Datang sa-orang
1 měmběri bunga tělor.
Has-been seeing the sitting-together, they reckon going-to return. They stand in-court-yard waiting Che' Normah. There-comes a-person giving flowers of-egg.
Having seen the *běrsanding*, they decide to go home. They stand in the
courtyard and wait for Che' Normah. Somebody brings them coloured eggs.

2 MAR. **Apa pula ini?**
What, further, this?
What's this, now?

3 MAH. **Bunga tělor. Měnjadi tanda kita sudah ada datang**
Egg-decorations. Acting-as sign, we, has-been, there-is coming to
Decorated eggs. As a sign that we have been present at
4 **ka-majlis ini.**
this assembly.
this gathering.

5 Kěmudian nampak-lah Che' Normah datang dari bělakang.
Then is-seen Che' Normah coming from back.
Then they see Che' Normah coming from the back of the house.

6 MAR. **Itu dia Che' Normah.**
That (is) she, Che' Normah.
There's Che' Normah.

107 NOR. **Saya lengah sadikit.   Lama-kah mĕnanti?**
I delay a-little.   Long waiting?
I'm a bit late.   Have you been waiting long?

108 MAH. **Tidak.   Mari-lah kita balek.   Orang 'dah banyak**
Not.   Come, we return.   People, it-has-become many returning,
No.   Let's be getting home.   Many people have already

109 **balek nampak-nya.**
the appearance-of-it.
gone, I see.

110 Mĕreka pun balek.
They go home.

SCENE VI : NOTES

2 yang sudah ramai: note that *ramai* and *banyak*, although not
descriptive adjectives, are used with *sudah* to denote a state of
affairs which has newly come about.   Contrast Scene IV.39,
kĕrana orang ramai bĕnar bĕrkĕrumun, 'because the people are
crowding round in large numbers'.   In that sentence the writer
is concerned merely with the fact that that is the existing state of
affairs.   Whether it has only recently come about or not is
irrelevant.   But the point in the present example is that they are
not the first arrivals, there are already many people in the courtyard when they arrive.

7 Orang se-bĕlah sana / lain sadikit pakaian . . . : note the
difference in idiom.   Malay states first the main broad topic and
then comes down to the particular detail in question, *e.g.* 'The
water of that river is very muddy' becomes in Malay, *Sungai itu
kĕroh sangat ayer-nya, lit.* 'That river, very muddy is the water of it.'

di-kĕpala dia: *dia*, not *-nya*, for the genitive, to emphasize the fact
that *they* wear something different, but in the next line *kĕpala-nya*
because 'their' is now taken for granted, and the important word
is *sĕrban*.

11 orang yang bĕlum naik hajji pun / ada juga / pakai sĕrban:
be content to leave the syntax fluid, as suggested in the literal
translation, with *orang . . . pun* as an initial statement of topic:
'Even the people who haven't been to Mecca / there exists also /
turban-wearing.'

13 bukan haji: it is always *bukan* (not *tidak*) that is used when one
definite word is negatived, *e.g. pĕnuntut yang bukan Mĕlayu*, 'non-
Malay students'.

14 pěrasap: 'incense-burner' from *asap*, 'smoke'. If a temporary 'live' derivative were required (*e.g.* for 'smoke-bomb') the more usual formation with infix *-ng-* would probably be used, *bom pěngasap*.

18 Kita pakai pěrasap ini: *kita* used in its 'general' sense, meaning 'you', 'they', 'one'. Contrast line 20 below, where *kita* includes the listener and means 'we'.

19 měmulakan: *-kan* causative, 'make to begin', 'set in train'.

satu-satu: duplication for variety, 'any particular religious ceremony that you might mention'.

20 kita děngar-lah: *-lah* for confirmation. Che' Mahmud has already told him that there is going to be a Kor'an ceremony, 'You'll be hearing it, you'll find, in a minute or two.' Cf. Note IV.59: *Sa-kějap lagi sampai-lah;* 'It'll be along in a minute or two, you'll see.'

25 mulaï měmbacha: the verbal suffix *-i* is much less common than *-kan*. This root-word *mula*, 'beginning', always takes *-i* except when it is definitely causative, as in *měmulakan* in line 19 above.

But the *-i* suffix, which is probably related to the preposition *di-*, 'at', 'in', usually has a feeling of 'place' about it, *e.g.* *měnděkati*, 'drawing near *to* . . .' (contrast *di-děkatkan* in Note III.40, 'brings something near'); *měliputi*, 'flowing *over* . . .'; *mělempari*, 'throwing (something) *at* somebody' (contrast *mělemparkan*, 'to throw, or hurl, something').

26 apabila sampai: *apabila* is the written form for 'when', meaning 'on the occasion (*or* occasions) when'; in speech, as you have seen, it is always shortened to *bila*.

27 surah: a short section of the Kor'an comprising one topic only.

31 sa-orang sa-bungkus: note the word-order, ending with the word of quantity. English usually puts it the other way round, 'one package each'. So also, 'three apiece', *sa-orang tiga biji;* 'twice a week', *sa-minggu dua kali;* 'once a year', *sa-tahun sa-kali.*

36 daun pandan: the scented variety, not the sort that is used for mat-making. The scented petals and leaves would be wrapped in a piece of banana-leaf and 'pinned' together with a bit of palm-leaf vein (*lidi*).

37 kueh-kueh kěring: 'dry cakes', *i.e.* small cakes baked in moulds, such as *kueh bahulu*, 'sponge cakes'.

44 balek dahulu: for the *dahulu* (which it is difficult to show in translation) cf. Note II.45, *Dudok-dudok-lah dahulu.*

Pětang 'karang: 'this evening', *lit.* 'the evening, presently', the time mentioned being regarded as a continuation of the present time. Contrast *Pětang ini* in Note I.81, '*this* evening' (as distinct from to-morrow evening, or any other evening).

47 orang jěmputan: *lit.* 'invited people', *i.e.* the guests (also called *orang panggilan,* 'summoned people'). The suffix *-an* is used to create adjectives and nouns which sometimes have a passive meaning.

59 Kalau sudah ada kěrja: *i.e.* if that had become the existent state of affairs (which you already knew about). Cf. *Kalau sudah ta' ada duit, měngapa pěrgi juga?* 'If you had no money, then why did you go?'

60 Ini / bukan-kah 'dah suntok?: circumstantial *ini,* 'as things are'.

    bukan-kah: bukan with a question mark is not contradictory, it means 'Isn't it so? (you know it is)'. See Note I.11.

    suntok: usually implies that there is time enough left (to do something), but only just enough.

63 Rambut, bědak, kain baju sudah ada orang měnyiap-nya: note how Malay brings the topic words to the front of the sentence, whereas English tends to keep important words for an emphatic position at the end of a sentence. This is sometimes done in Malay too, but as a general rule you will be safe in bringing to the beginning of the sentence any word at all that you wish to emphasize.

    -nya could not be omitted here, because it picks up and gathers together the catalogue of nouns already mentioned. When it is omitted, the 'understood' object is fresh in the hearer's mind, *e.g. Ini salah. Bětulkan,* 'This is wrong. Correct it.'

    sudah ada: see Note 59 above, and Sentence Pattern III.3.i.

65 Sa-jurus lěpas itu, tiba-lah pěrarakan: *-lah* for confirmation of an impression already formed, 'along came the procession (as we had expected)'. The verb precedes its subject because it is the *arrival,* not the procession itself, that you are talking about.

70 Pěngantin pun / orang panggil raja juga: when the object is brought to the front of the sentence (because it is of primary importance) the verb will not take the *mě-* prefix even with a 3rd person subject, because the agent is of secondary importance. See also VIII.66 *ad. fin.*

71 Dia běrpayong itu pun / macham raja juga: *itu* belongs to the whole noun-group ('the fact of him having an umbrella held over him') which is the subject of the sentence. Cf. *Dia běrmain bola itu / 'nak měnchukupkan orang sahaja, bukan-nya pandai;* 'He only played in order to make up the team. He isn't really a footballer.'

78 Sudah ini baharu-lah pěngantin di-bawa naik: for *baharu-lah* meaning 'then and only then' see Sentence Pattern II.7.

81 měnabor: from *tabor.*

89 oleh pĕrĕmpuan itu di-rĕnjis-nya : this is a common variation of the usual pattern. Here the agent is mentioned first, and then picked up again by the usual 3rd person pronoun *-nya* after the *di-* verb.

90 sa-bagai ganti mĕmbasoh : *lit.* 'as a replacement of washing', a modern but well-established use of *sa-bagai*, 'like'.

92 orang ramai pun bĕrdahulu-huluan : *ramai* is here predicative and *bĕr-* verbal, 'the people are in numbers pressing forward'. Cf. Note IV.39.

    bĕrdahulu-huluan; bĕr + duplication + *an* combining to strengthen the idea of interconnection, 'each one striving to get in front of the next one'. The simple root *hulu* (*lit.* 'head', 'first part of') has been duplicated. Sometimes the compound root *dahulu* is duplicated.

96 dapat-lah ia mĕnengok : 'he does manage to see'. In such a sentence it is in the word *dapat* that the statement lies, as is shown by *-lah*. The rest of the sentence ('he-seeing') is the subject, the thing that ' succeeded'. Cf. *Sudah saya suroh* in Note I.64. For *dapat* see Sentence Pattern VIII.2.iii.

99 mĕreka pun bĕrkira-lah : the usual pattern for narrative style, when the reader's attention is already on the actors. Contrast line 100 below, *Datang sa-orang mĕmbĕri bunga tĕlor*, where the *arrival* of the person is the first that the reader knows about him; so also, *Nampak-lah Che' Normah* in line 105 below, and *tiba-lah pararakan* in line 65 above.

108 Orang 'dah banyak balek : *lit.* 'the people have become many, returning', *i.e. banyak* is predicative. Cf. Note 2 above.

SCENE VI: TAKING STOCK

3. INI and ITU

    i. *itu* with a noun-group:

        Dia bĕrpayong itu pun macham raja juga.

        And the fact that he has an umbrella held over him, that, too, makes him like a ruler.

    ii. *ini* (indicating the circumstances) as subject, with a noun-group as complement:

        Ini | bukan-kah 'dah suntok?

        As it is, haven't you left it rather late?

6. PRONOUNS

(a) iv. *-nya*

c. as object, after a *mĕ-* derivative:

> *Rambut, bĕdak, kain baju sudah ada orang mĕnyiapkan-nya.*
> Her hair, and the cosmetics, and her clothes, there are other people in charge of all those.
>
> *Ada orang datang mĕnandu-nya atas bahu.*
> A man would come and carry him on his shoulders.

8. TIDAK and BUKAN

(b) iii. *bukan* denying one word:

> *Orang dudok dĕkat jĕndela itu bukan haji.*
> That person sitting near the window is not a *haji*.

9. NO TENSE-FORMS

ii. time indicated by adverbial expressions:

> *Mĕreka datang lagi pada pukul lima pĕtang.*
> They will come again at five o'clock.
>
> *Mĕngapa ta' bagi tahu dari tadi?*
> Why didn't you mention it earlier?

10. AFFIXES

(a) *bĕr-*

iv. with duplication and *-an* to indicate interconnection:

> *Orang ramai pun bĕrdahulu-huluan.*
> The people crowded forward, pushing in front of each other.

(b) *mĕ-*

i. as verbal-noun

a. after a preposition:

> *kĕrana mĕnengok*, 'for seeing'
> *dĕngan mĕninjau*, 'by peeping'

c. after a transitive verb:

> *mulaï mĕmbacha*, 'begins the-reading-of'

iii. as participle:

a. after a verb of movement, for a simultaneous action:

> *Ada sa-orang datang mĕmbawa pĕrasap.*
> A man came in, bringing an incense-burner.
>
> *Ada orang datang mĕnandu-nya atas bahu.*
> A man would come and carry him on his shoulders.

(d) *-kan*

i. causative:

> *Tuan rumah minta tolong siapkan pĕngantin pĕrĕmpuan.*
> They have asked me to help make the bride ready.
>
> *Pĕngantin itu di-dudokkan atas kĕrusi.*
> They seat the bridegroom on a chair.

(f) di-

    i. for an action, with the agent specified:

        Bunga rampai itu di-běri-nya sa-orang sa-bungkus.

        He gives a package of the scented petals to each person.

        Ayer mawar itu di-rěnjis-nya kapada baju tiap-tiap sa-orang.

        He sprinkles the rose-water on the garments of all the guests.

        Oleh pěrěmpuan itu di-rěnjis-nya sadikit ayer kapada kaki pěngantin.

        The woman sprinkles a little water over the bridegroom's feet.

        Di-angkat orang teh.

        Tea is brought in.

        Běras-kah di-buat orang wajek ini?

        Is it from rice that they make this *wajek* sweetmeat?

        Gong sěrta gěndang pun di-palu orang.

        Gongs and drums are beaten.

    ii. with no agent mentioned:

        Pěngantin itu di-dudokkon atas kěrusi.

        They seat the bridegroom on a chair.

        Wangi bau-nya sěbab ada di-tabor kěmian.

        It is scented because they have sprinkled benzoin on it.

(g) -an

    i. creating a noun or adjective with passive meaning:

        orang jěmputan, 'invited people', *i.e.* guests.

    iii. creating a collective noun:

        kumpulan, 'a gathering'; *pakaian*, 'clothing'

(j) -i, a verbal suffix used with a limited number of roots:

    mulaï měmbacha, 'begins to read'

11. PUN

    i. with *juga* to draw attention to a word, or word-group, which balances some previous word:

        Pěngantin pun orang panggil raja juga.

        A bridegroom too (not only a ruler) is called *raja*.

        Dia běrpayong itu pun macham raja juga.

        And the fact that he has an umbrella (not only the name given to him), that, too, makes him like a ruler.

13. PULA

    i. surprise:

        Ini apa pula? 'What's this, I wonder?'

    ii. sequence:

        Sa-tělah habis běrkhatam itu mulaï pula majlis marhaban.

        When the Kor'an reading was over, the *marhaban* chanting began.

        Mari kita pula naik.

        Let us go up too.

14. -LAH

   i. for emphasis:

      a. by confirming an impression already suggested—

         Dudok bagitu sahaja-lah.
         Yes, just sitting like that.

      b. by marking the predicate-word and so, as a rule, confirming an expected action—

         Sa-běntar lagi kita děngar-lah pěngantin pěrěmpuan měmbacha Kor'an.
         In a minute or two we shall hear the bride reciting the Kor'an.
         Sa-jurus lěpas itu tiba-lah pěrarakan pěngantin laki-laki.
         A moment later, along came the bridegroom's procession.
         Děngan měninjau di-chělah orang dapat-lah ia měnengok pěngantin.
         By peering through the gaps in the crowd they did manage to get a glimpse of the bridegroom.

   ii. after an imperative:

      Tengok-lah pěngantin itu pakai těngkolok di-kěpala-nya.
      Look! The bridegroom is wearing a kerchief on his head.

15. PREPOSITIONS

   (c) i. *ka-*, for 'motion towards':

      Biar saya těrus ka-rumah.
      I'll go straight into the house.

17. 'WHEN'

   (c) as a subordinating conjunction, in writing, *apabila*:

      Apabila sampai ka-hujong satu-satu surah . . .
      When they came to the end of each section . . .

18. BOLEH and BIAR

   (a) *boleh* used colloquially for purpose:

      Měngapa ta' bagi tahu dari tadi, boleh kita datang lěkas sadikit.
      Why didn't you mention it sooner, so that we could have come a bit early? (*or* 'then we could have . . .')

19. BAHARU

   i. for 'not until', 'then and only then'

      Sudah ini baharu-lah pěngantin di-bawa naik běrsanding.
      This has to take place before the bridegroom is taken upstairs for the *běrsanding* ceremony.

22. THE NOUN-GROUP

i. as a description, after a place-word:

> . . . *kapada tĕntang bachaan sĕmua orang mĕsti bĕrdiri.*
> . . . to the point in the reading where everybody must stand up.

ii. a noun, with adjunct, declaring the topic:

> *Orang sa-bĕlah sana | lain sadikit pakaian-nya.*
> Those people over there, they're dressed rather differently.
> *Orang yang bĕlum naik haji pun | ada juga | pakai sĕrban.*
> But people who have not made the pilgrimage do sometimes wear the turban.
> *Dodol ini pun | bĕras pulut juga di-buat orang.*
> This *dodol* sweetmeat, they make this too with sticky rice.

iv. a noun-group as subject, and as complement:

> *Dia bĕrpayong itu pun | macham raja juga.*
> The fact that he has an umbrella held over him, that, too, is like a ruler.
> *Ini | bukan-kah | 'dah suntok?*
> As it is, isn't it rather late?
> (*lit.* This-state-of-affairs, (is) it not, having-become-late?)

v. an un-prefixed 'verb' as the subject-noun | (*pakai*):

> *Orang yang bĕlum naik haji pun | ada juga | pakai sĕrban.*
> But people who have not made the pilgrimage do sometimes wear the turban.
> (*lit.* In the case of people . . ., there exists also, wearing-the-turban.)

23. SUDAH

ii. for 'has become':

> . . . *bĕrsama-sama dĕngan orang lain yang sudah ramai di-situ.*
> . . . together with the many other people who were already there.
> *Pada masa mĕreka sampai itu, orang sudah ramai bĕrhimpun.*
> By the time they arrived quite a large number of people had collected.
> *Kalau sudah ada kĕrja mĕngapa ta' bagi tahu dari tadi?*
> If you had some work to do, why didn't you say so earlier?
> *Ini bukan-kah 'dah suntok?*
> Isn't it almost too late, now?
> *Orang 'dah banyak balek.*
> Many people have already gone home.

SCENE VI: SENTENCE PATTERNS

1. 'Who' and *yang*: i. with or without *yang*; ii. with *yang*;
iii. without *yang*

i. *yang* optional

a. **Sĕrban di-kĕpala-nya itu pakaian orang sudah pĕrgi naik hajji ka-Makkah** (or yang sudah).

The turban he is wearing is the dress of a pilgrim (or *of a person who*).

b. Di kampong itu ta' ada orang pandai bĕrsilat (or yang pandai).

In that village there is nobody skilled in the art of dagger-defence (or *who is skilled*).

c. Siapa lambat bĕrjalan boleh-lah pĕrgi dahulu (or yang lambat).

Anybody who is a slow walker can go on in advance (or *who walks slowly*).

d. Dalam pĕpĕreksaan elok jawab soalan sĕnang dahulu (or yang sĕnang).

In an examination it is best to answer easy questions first (or *the questions which are easy*).

e. Orang bĕrdiri di-hujong dalam gambar itu bukan ahli pasokan (or yang bĕrdiri).

The man standing at the end in the photograph is not a member of the team (or *who is standing*).

ii. *yang* essential, as a distinguishing pronoun

a. Orang yang bĕrjanggut panjang itu baharu pindah ka-kampong ini.

The man with the long beard has only just moved to this village.

b. Di-sini ada-kah orang yang pandai mĕngajar silat?

Is there anybody in the village who can teach the dagger-dance?

c. Tolong pileh buah langsat ini.   Mana yang busok buangkan.

Go through these langsats, will you, and throw away any that are going bad.

d. Kĕrtas soalan yang bĕrhantar pada hari Sĕlasa itu ada sampai.   Yang lain bĕlum.

The papers that were sent off on Tuesday have arrived, but the others haven't.

e. Rumah yang banyak rosak-nya itu mahal lagi laku-nya daripada rumah baharu.

That house that was in such bad repair was sold for more than a new house.

iii. *yang* not used to add a second statement

a. Sa-kali pĕrsĕtua ada-lah sa-orang tukang kayu dudok di-kampong anu.

Once upon a time, there was a carpenter who lived (i.e. and he lived) in such-and-such a town.

b. Ada sa-orang tua bĕrjanggut baharu pindah ka-kampong ini.

There is an old man with a beard who has recently come to live in this village.

c. Di-dalam kampong itu ada sa-orang tua kĕrja-nya mĕngajar silat.

In the village there was an old man who earned his living by teaching the dagger-dance.

d. Kĕrtas soalan itu sudah lama bĕrhantar, tĕtapi ta' tiba pada hari pĕpĕrek-saan itu.

The question papers, which had been sent off in good time, had not arrived on the day of the examination.

e. Rumah itu memang burok masa di-bĕli-nya dahulu. Masa ini langsong-lah hĕndak roboh.

The house, which was in bad repair when he bought it, is in a completely ruinous condition now.

2. *pula*: i. sequence; ii. surprise

i. Sequence

a. Lĕkas-lah sadikit mĕmbĕli sayor itu, kita 'nak ka-kĕdai ikan pula.

Don't spend too long getting the vegetables, we're going on to the fish shop afterwards.

b. 'Dah tammat sĕkolah itu, ka-mana pula dia 'nak bĕlajar?

Where is he going to continue his studies when he has finished at that school?

c. Admad 'dah 'nak sudah. Siapa pula 'nak bĕrgunting?

I've nearly finished Ahmad. Who else wants a haircut?

d. Biar saya pula mĕmbawa bakul.

Let me carry the basket for a bit, now.

e. Di-mana pula kita dapat bĕrjumpa lagi?

Where can we meet again?

ii. Surprise

a. Apa pula di-gadohkan hal duit. Bila-bila pun boleh bayar.

But why are you bothering so much about the money? You can pay whenever you like.

b. Ka-mana pula Hashim itu, bĕrgopoh-gopoh 'aja dalam hujan ini?

Wherever is Hashim off to, hurrying along in the rain like that?

c. Siapa pula mĕrosakkan radio ini? Pagi tadi elok lagi.

Now who has made this wireless go wrong, I wonder? It was all right this morning.

d. 'Dah bĕkĕrja sa-pagi-pagi tadi sampai sudah. Kĕrja apa pula lagi?

We spent tho whole morning on the job, and we finished it. What else can there possibly be to do?

e. Di-mana pula di-simpan-nya sapu tangan saya.

Now where on earth has she put my handkerchieves!

3. *juga*

a. Ta' hĕndak roti lain. Hĕndak roti tadi juga.—Jangan jahat!

I don't want any other bun. I wanted that one.—Don't be so naughty!

b. Siapa juga datang, jangan di-bĕri masok.

Whoever comes, you are not to let him in.

c. 'Dah pandai-kah bahasa Mĕlayu?—Ĕrti juga, 'tapi 'nak bĕrchakap bĕlum bĕrani lagi.

Are you getting on, in Malay?—I can understand it pretty well, but I haven't the courage to talk yet.

d. Kalau dia 'nak měngikut kita, boleh juga.   Apa salah-nya?
If he wants to come with us, he can.   That's quite all right.

e. Saya datang dahulu pun, naik kapal těrbang juga.
When I came last time I came by air, too.

4. -*nya*: i. as agent and as genitive;   ii. as object, after *mě-*

i. As agent and as genitive

a. **Bunga rampai itu di-běri-nya sa-orang sa-bungkus**
He gave each person a packet of flower petals.

b. Pokok bunga itu di-siram-nya tiap-tiap pagi.
She waters the flowers every morning.

c. Orang yang puteh janggut-nya itu sa-orang 'alim běsar.
The man with the white beard is a well-known religious scholar.

d. Surat khabar-nya bělum datang lagi, macham mana kita 'nak tahu siapa
měnang lawan bola 'tu?
The paper hasn't come yet.   How are we to know the result of the match?

e. Kata chěrita-nya dia dapat lotěri.   Bětul-kah?
There is a rumour that he has won a prize in a lottery.   Is it true?

ii. As object after *mě-*

a. **Ada orang datang měnandu-nya.**
A man would come and carry him on his shoulders.

b. Choba buka tin susu itu, 'tapi měmbuka-nya itu jaga jangan tumpah.
Open that tin of milk, will you.   But be careful not to spill it when you're opening it.

c. 'Dah běrběntang tikar ini.   Siapa agak-nya měmběntang-nya?
The mats have been put down.   I wonder who put them down?

d. Macham mana měmasak-nya, tělor pěnyu ini?
These turtle eggs, how do you cook them?

e. Měmbuka pěrkakas jam itu sěnang, 'nak měmasang-nya balek saya ta'
sanggup.
*It's easy enough to take a watch to pieces, but I wouldn't undertake to put it together
again.*

SCENE VII

DI-LOMBONG BIJEH

ON A TIN MINE

Hari ini Che' Mahmud pĕrgi mĕmbawa Mr. Martin mĕnengok lombong bijeh di-Sĕrĕndah kira-kira dua puloh batu dari Kuala Lumpur. Lombong itu di-punyaï oleh sa-orang China kĕnalan Che' Mahmud. Che' Mahmud mĕmbĕrhĕntikan kĕreta-nya di-hadapan sa-buah rumah dĕkat simpang jalan ka-lombong itu. Ia tiada mahu mĕmbawa kĕreta mĕngikut jalan lombong itu kĕrana jalan itu burok bĕnar, batu-nya bĕsar-bĕsar. Ia bĕrchakap kapada sa-orang budak yang ada di-halaman rumah itu.

This-day Che' Mahmud goes conducting Mr. Martin seeing mine of tin-ore at Sĕrĕndah, about two tens mile-stones from Kuala Lumpur. The-mine is owned by one-person Chinese, acquaintance of Che' Mahmud. Che' Mahmud makes-to-stop car-of-him at-front of-one-unit house near junction of-the-road to-mine. He not willing take car following the-road of-mine because that-road (is) in-bad-repair truly, stones-of it fairly-big. He speaks to one-person young-person who is-present in-courtyard of the house.

To-day Che' Mahmud is taking Mr. Martin to see a tin mine at Sĕrĕndah, about twenty miles from Kuala Lumpur. The mine is owned by a Chinese who is an acquaintance of Che' Mahmud. Che' Mahmud draws up in front of a house near the turning which leads to the mine. He does not want to take his car along the mine road because it has a very bad surface, made of quite big stones. He speaks to a boy who is in the compound of the house.

MAH. **Awak ta' ka-mana-mana pagi ini?**
You not to-anywhere this-morning?
You are not going anywhere particular, this morning?

BUD. **Ta' ka-mana-mana ĕnche'. Bĕkĕrja-kĕrja di-rumah**
Not to-anywhere, sir. Work-working at-house only.
No, ĕnche'. I am just doing odd jobs about the house.
sahaja.

MAH. **Boleh ta' tolong tengok-tengokkan kĕreta?**
Able, not, help, look-look-at car?
Could you keep an eye on my car?

BUD. **Boleh itu boleh-lah ĕnche'. 'Tapi tengok-tengokkan**
The-being-able, able, yes, sir. But look-look-at only?
Yes, I could. But . . . er . . . Just keep an eye on it?
sahaja-kah?

F   135

14 MAH. **Hai, ada-lah kira-kira-nya.   Jangan bimbang.**

Hi!   There-does-exist,   the   reckoning-in-the-case.   Don't (be)

Oh, I'll make it worth your while.   Don't worry about

anxious.

that.

15   Che' Mahmud děngan Mr. Martin běrjalan kaki ka-lombong itu.   Lom-
16 bong itu běrpagar děngan kawat běrduri.   Di-pintu pagar ada S.C. běrkawal.
17 S.C. itu sudah di-běri tahu oleh tuan-punya lombong itu měngatakan Che'
18 Mahmud hěndak datang.   Děngan sěbab itu těrus sahaja di-tunjokkan-nya
19 rumah kěpala lombong itu.   Kěpala itu sa-orang China yang měnjadi wakil
20 tuan-punya lombong itu.   Dia-lah yang měnjaga sakalian orang yang
21 běkěrja di-situ dan dia-lah juga yang měnyimpan bijeh yang di-dapati.

Che' Mahmud, with Mr. Martin, goes on-foot to-the-mine.   The mine (is) be-fenced
with wire be-thorned.   At-gate of-fence there-is S.C. keeping-watch.   The S.C., has-been
given-to-know by master-owning the mine, saying Che' Mahmud going-to come.   With
that-cause straight-away, merely, there-is-a-showing by-him the house of-the-overseer
of-the-mine.   The overseer (is) one person Chinese who acts-as representative of-owner of-
the-mine.   He (is the one) who supervises all persons who work there and he, precisely,
(is the one) who stores ore which is-got.

Che' Mahmud and Mr. Martin walk to the mine.   It is fenced round with
barbed wire.   At the gate of the fence a Special Constable is on sentry duty.
The owner of the mine has let him know that Che' Mahmud is coming, so he
at once points out the overseer's house.   The overseer is a Chinese, who acts
as agent for the owner of the mine.   It is he who superintends all the workers,
and it is he who is responsible for the tin-ore which is won.

22 MAH. **Tabek, kěpala.**

Greetings, overseer.

Good morning, overseer.

23 KĚP. **Tabek ěnche'.   Sudah tiba, ia?   Sa-malam taukeh**

Good day, ěnche'.   Have arrived, yes?   Yesterday taukeh speak

Good morning, ěnche'.   You've arrived!   The *taukeh* told

24 **chakap ěnche' mahu datang.**

ěnche' going-to come.

me yesterday that you were coming.

25 MAH. **Boleh kěnal kawan kita Mr. Martin.**

Able get-to-know friend of-me Mr. Martin.

Let me introduce my friend Mr. Martin.

26 KĚP. **Ha, tabek.**

Ha.   Greetings.

Good morning.

7 MAR. **Tabek.**
Greetings.
Good morning.

8 KĔP. **Boleh dudok.**
Can sit.
Take a seat.

9 MAR. **Tĕrima kaseh.**
Received favour.
Thank you.

0 KĔP. **Apa ĕnche' mahu tengok dahulu?**
What ĕnche' wants see first?
What do you want to see first?

1 MAH. **Apa-apa pun boleh.   Mr. Martin 'nak tengok sĕmua.**
Anything at all can-do.   Mr. Martin wanting see all.   He not-yet
Anything at all.   Mr. Martin wants to see everything.

2 **Dia bĕlum pĕrnah mĕnengok lombong bijeh.**
ever see mine of-tin.
He has never seen a tin mine before.

3 KĔP. **Saya boleh tunjok.   'Tapi ta' tahu chakap.   Chakap**
I can show.   But not know speech.   Speech of-people white, I
I can show him.   But I can't manage the talking.   I don't

4 **orang puteh saya ta' tahu.   Chakap Mĕlayu ta'**
not know.   Speech Malay, not how-much skilled.
speak English, and I am not very good at Malay.

5 **bĕrapa pandai.**

6 MAR. **Saya pun bukan pandai.**
I, too, not clever.
Neither am I.

7 Mĕreka bĕrjalan sampai ka-tĕmpat tinggi sadikit.   Dari situ boleh nampak
8 hampir-hampir sĕmua bahagian lombong itu.   Che' Mahmud mĕnunjok
9 kapada jĕntĕra pĕmanchut ayer.
They walk until to-place high a little.   From there able be-seen nearly all parts of-the-mine.   Che' Mahmud points to engine, pump (for) water.
They make their way to a spot that is higher than the rest of the mine. From there almost every part of the mine can be seen.   Che' Mahmud points to a monitor jet.

0 MAH. **Jĕntĕra di-bawah sana kĕrja-nya mĕmanchutkan**
Engine below there, work-of-it, pumping-out water very-strongly to-
That engine down there directs a jet of water, at great

41 **ayer kuat-kuat ka-tĕbing yang ada bĕrisi bijeh.**
bank which, it-is so, having-contents tin-ore. The-bank collapses.
pressure, against the bank that contains the tin ore. The

42 **Tĕbing itu runtoh. Tanah-nya bĕrchampor dĕngan**
Earth of-it mixed with water becomes mud, watery. In-it there-is
bank caves in, and the soil and the water together make a

43 **ayer mĕnjadi lumpor chayer. Di-dalam-nya ada**
ore. The-mud is sucked in by that large pipe, is pumped, mounting
watery mud in which is the ore. The mud is sucked in

44 **bijeh. Lumpor itu di-sĕdut dek pĕmuloh bĕsar itu,**
to top of that scaffolding.
by that large pipe and is pumped up on to that scaffolding.

45 **di-bomba naik ka-atas aram-aram itu.**

46 MAR. **Banyak bĕnar kayu-nya mĕmbuat aram-aram ini.**
Much, truly, the wood in-the-case, making this scaffolding.
It took an enormous amount of wood to construct that
scaffolding.

47 MAH. **Tĕntu-lah. Kata chĕrita-nya bĕsar bĕnar bĕlanja-**
Surely. Says the account of it, large truly expenditure in-the-case
It certainly did. They say it's a very expensive business

48 **nya mĕmbuat aram-aram ini. Lumpor chayer itu**
making this scaffolding. The watery-mud is-given to flow in
putting up the scaffolding. The thin mud is allowed to

49 **di-bagi mĕngalir dalam palong di-atas aram-aram**
trough on top of this scaffolding. Because there-is using that sluice,
flow along the sluice on top of the scaffolding. Because of

50 **ini. Sĕbab ada pakai palong itu lombong macham**
mine this-sort is-called by people sluice-mine.
the sluice this type of mine is called a sluice mine.

51 **ini di-panggil orang lombong palong.**

52 MAR. **Apa jadi dalam palong itu?**
What happens in the sluice?

53 MAH. **Pada masa lumpor chayer itu mĕngalir dalam**
At time the watery-mud flows in trough the-tin-ore which there-is
When the liquid mud flows along in the trough the ore

54 **palong bijeh yang ada di-dalam-nya turun ka-pĕrut**
in-it goes-down to-bed of-the-trough, gets-left there. The mud,
that it contains sinks to the bottom of the trough and there

palong itu tĕrtinggal di-situ. Lumpor itu habis-lah
the-last-degree-is-reached, it-floating into pool below there.   In the-
it remains.   All the mud floats off into the pool down below

hanyut ka-dalam kolam di-bawah sana. Pada pĕrut
bed of trough there-are partitions of-plank.   There the-ore sticks.
there.   There are wooden partitions along the trough,

palong itu ada sĕkat-sĕkat papan. Di-situ-lah bijeh
behind which the ore lodges.

itu mĕlĕkat.

MAR. **Rumah kĕchil di-atas aram-aram itu tĕmpat orang**
That-small-on-top-of-scaffolding house (is) place of person looking-
That little hut on top of the scaffolding is for the man who

mĕnjaga bijeh, bukan?
after ore, is-it-not-so?
takes charge of the tin, isn't it?

MAH. **Mĕnjaga bijeh pun ia juga, tĕtapi kĕrja orang yang**
Looking-after ore, yes, to-a-certain-extent, but work of-person who
Yes, he does take charge of the ore, but his real job when

dudok di-situ mĕmbuang batu. Dalam lumpor
sits there (is) throwing-out stones.   In the-watery-mud always
he sits up there is to throw the stones out.   Stones are

chayer itu sĕlalu ada batu. Tengok di-situ ada
there-are stones.   Look, there there-is heap of-stones.   Those-
always to be found in the liquid mud.   Look, over there,

timbun batu. Batu itu sĕmua di-buang dari rumah
stones, all, there-was-a-throwing from the-little house.
there's a heap of stones.   All of them have been thrown

kĕchil itu.
down from that hut.

Lĕpas itu mĕreka pĕrgi mĕnengok-nengok bĕrkĕliling lombong itu hingga
sampai ka-tĕmpat mĕnyimpan bijeh.
*That-having-been-let-go by, they go a-seeing around the-mine until arrive to-place
of-storing ore.*
After this they take a look round the mine, until they come to the place where
the tin-ore is stored.

KĔP. **Bijeh ini sa-pikul satu-satu guni.**
This ore, one-pikul, each-one sack.
Each bag holds a *pikul* of ore.

69 MAR. **Kĕchil sahaja guni ini.**
Small, merely, these sacks.
They are quite small, the bags.

70 KĔP. **Kĕchil. Bijeh bĕrat.**
Small.   Tin-ore (is) heavy.
Yes, they are small.   Tin ore is heavy stuff.

71 MAH. **Sĕkarang sĕmua orang kĕrja dudok dalam pagar, ia,**
Now, all work-people live within fence, yes, overseer?
Nowadays all the people who work on the mine live inside

72 **kĕpala?**
the fence don't they, overseer?

73 KĔP. **Bukan sĕmua ĕnche'.   Ada juga orang dudok dalam**
Not all, ĕnche'.   There-are, it must be said, people living in new-
Not all of them, ĕnche'.   There are some who live in the

74 **kampong baharu.**
village.
new village.

75 MAH. **Ada-kah lagi apa-apa boleh tengok, kĕpala?**
Is-there still something-or-other able see, overseer?
Is there anything else to see, overseer?

76 KĔP. **Ta' ada lagi.   Mari kita balek minum teh.   Kita**
There-is-not more-still.   Come we return, drink tea.   We have-
No, that's all.   Let's go back and have some tea.   We have

77 **sudah bĕrjalan lĕbeh satu jam.**
completed walking more (than) one hour.
been walking for over an hour.

78 MAH. **Boleh-kah Mr. Martin tengok-tengok sadikit rumah**
Able Mr. Martin see-see a-little house of-overseer?   He has seen
Could Mr. Martin see over your house, overseer?   He has seen

79 **kĕpala?   Dia sudah tengok rumah Mĕlayu.   Dia**
Malay-house.   He wishes see, further, house of-Chinese-person.
a Malay house.   Now he would like to see a Chinese house.

80 **'nak tengok pula rumah orang China.**

81 KĔP. **Boleh.   Apa salah?   'Tapi ini rumah orang bangsat.**
Can.   What (is) wrong (with that)?   But this (is) house of-poor
Yes, of course.   But this is a poor man's house.   If he goes

82 **Mr. Martin pĕrgi Kuala Lumpur boleh tengok**
person.   Mr. Martin go Kuala Lumpur, able see houses of-rich-
to Kuala Lumpur he'll be able to see the houses of the rich.

3 **rumah orang kaya.**
people.

4 MAR. **O. Saya pun bukan orang kaya.**
O. I, for-my-part, not rich-man.
Oh, I'm not a rich man myself.

5 MAH. **Lagi pun dia ta' mahu tengok rumah orang kaya.**
There-is-still (this), he not want see house of-rich-person. Houses
Moreover, he doesn't want to see a rich man's house. The

6 **Rumah orang kaya sĕmua sa-rupa ta' kira apa**
of-rich-people all one-appearance, not taking-into-account what (is
houses of wealthy people are all alike, whatever their

7 **bangsa.**
their) race.
nationality.

8 KĔP. **Itu bĕtul juga. Di-rumah orang kaya ta' ada lagi**
That (is) true, I-grant-you. At houses of-rich people not is still
That's quite true. In the houses of the rich they no longer

9 **pakai kĕrtas merah macham ini.**
a-using (of) red-paper, this-sort.
use red paper like this.

10 Sambil bĕrchakap itu ia mĕnunjok kapada kĕrtas merah tĕrgantong di-
11 muka pintu-nya. Kĕtiga-tiga mĕreka masok ka-dalam rumah. Mr. Martin
12 mĕnengok gambar bĕsar-bĕsar sĕrta tulisan China tĕrgantong pada dinding.
Together with that-talking, he points to red-paper hung at-front of his doorway. All three they enter into house. Mr. Martin looks-at pictures rather-large together-with Chinese-writing hung on wall.
As he speaks he points to some red paper hung over the doorway. The three of them go into the house. Mr. Martin looks at some large pictures, with Chinese characters, hanging on the wall.

3 MAR. **Chantek tulisan ini.**
Beautiful (is) this-writing.
Beautiful writing, isn't it?

4 MAH. **Chantek sunggoh. Orang China memang di-buat-**
Beautiful, truly. Chinese-people, as-a-habit, there-is-a-making-
Yes, very beautiful. The Chinese always use characters as

5 **nya pĕrhiasan.**
by-them (it) a-decoration.
decoration.

96   Kĕpala itu mĕnarek Mr. Martin ka-dĕkat topekong-nya.
The overseer draws Mr. Martin to-near his-altar-picture.
The overseer takes Mr. Martin towards the household shrine.

97   KĔP.   **Ini tĕmpat kita orang sĕmbahyang.**
          This (is) place of-us-praying.
          This is where we offer our prayers.

98   MAR.   **Api ini ta' pĕrnah padam-kah?**
          This-fire not ever goes-out?
          This fire never goes out?

99   KĔP.   **Ta' ada padam-padam.   Siang malam ada sahaja.**
          There-is-not any-going-out.   Daylight, dark, it-exists, simply.
          Never.   It burns day and night.

100   Che' Mahmud mĕmbuka sa-buah bakul, di-sabĕlah dalam-nya bĕrlapek
101 dĕngan tilam.   Bakul itu bĕrisi sa-buah tekoh teh.   Ia bĕrkata kapada Mr.
102 Martin.
     Che' Mahmud opens one-unit basket, on-the-part inside-of it, (it) has-as-a-protective-
layer a-pad.   The basket has-as-contents one-unit tea-pot.   He speaks to Mr. Martin.
     Che' Mahmud opens a basket, the inside of which is padded.   There is a
teapot in it.   He speaks to Mr. Martin.

103   MAH.   **Ini suatu barang ta' ada di-rumah Mĕlayu.**
          This (is) one-unit thing not-is in Malay house.
          This is something that you won't find in a Malay house.

104   MAR.   **Apa itu?**
          What (is) that?
          What is it?

105   MAH.   **Teh kosong.   Siapa-siapa pun masok ka-sini boleh**
          Empty-tea.   Anyone-whosoever-he-may-be entering to-here can drink.
          Plain tea.   Anybody who comes in can have a drink.

106   **minum.   Tĕmpat minum-nya ini dia, chawan kĕchil**
          Receptacles of-drinking it, these (are) they, these-small-cups.
          This is what you drink it from, these little cups.

107   **ini.**

108   MAR.   **Siapa-siapa pun boleh minum?**
          Anyone whatsoever can drink?
          Anybody at all can have a drink?

109   KĔP.   **Boleh.   Apa salah?   'Tapi ta' ada gula ta' ada susu.**
          Can.   What (is) wrong (with that)?   But not-is sugar, not is
          Yes, of course.   But there's no sugar in it, and no milk.

Teh kosong sahaja. Ta' usah minum ini. Kita
milk. Tea with-nothing-in-it, merely. No-need drink this. We
Just plain tea. Don't you drink this. We'll have our tea

minum sana.
drink there.
over there.

Měreka pun pěrgi minum teh di-meja makan.
They go drink tea at eating-table.
They go to have their tea at a dining table.

SCENE VII: NOTES

3 kěnalan: the suffix *-an* forms a noun or an adjective. Here the
derivative is a 'passive' noun, 'one who is known'. Cf. *orang
jěmputan* in Note VI.47, and *tulisan China* in line 92 below.
Sometimes the noun is active, *e.g. langganan*, 'one who subscribes'.
Sometimes it is an abstract noun, *harga langgagan*, 'the price of
subscribing' ('subscription', either abstract or concrete). Cf.
pěrhiasan in line 95 below.

4 měmběrhěntikan: causal suffix *-kan*, 'make to stop'. The base-
word is *hěnti*, but the *běr-* prefix has become so firmly attached
that *běrhěnti* is here treated as if it were itself the base. *Měrěntikan*
and *měmpěrhěntikan* are also in use. In the latter form the prefix
pěr- and the suffix *-kan* are both causal.

5 ia tiada mahu měmbawa kěreta: note this correct use of *mahu*,
'be willing'. For futurity, Malays use *hěndak, e.g.* (from a child)
Kalau ta' bagi duit aku 'nak lari; 'If you won't give me some money,
I'll run away.' In such a sentence *mahu* would be bazaar Malay.

8 Awak ta' ka-mana-mana pagi ini?: duplication indicating
vagueness. Cf. Note IV.24, '*Ada-kah siapa-siapa luka?* 'Is
anybody hurt?' and contrast line 105 below, *Siapa-siapa pun boleh
minum;* 'Anybody (whosoever he may be) can have a drink.'

9 Běkěrja-kěrja di-rumah sahaja: duplication for variety, 'doing
odd jobs' (such as fetching water, sweeping the drains, etc.).

11 Boleh ta' tengok-tengokkan kěreta?: duplication to tone down;
he would not be 'looking at' it the whole time. Cf. *Rumah saya
děkat sahaja. Tengok-tengok-lah saya bila lapang;* 'I live quite near.
Drop in to see me when you have time', and contrast with
Untong-lah ada Che' Dah tolong měnengokkan budak hari 'tu; 'It was
lucky that Che' Dah was kind enough to take charge of the
children that day.'

12 Boleh itu boleh-lah: a common colloquialism, 'Oh, yes, I can do it all right, but . . .?' Cf. *Kalau kita měmběli mesin měmbasoh kain, sěnang kěrja kita—Sěnang itu sěnang.* '*Tapi ingat-lah pula běrapa harga-nya.* 'If you buy a washing machine your work is much easier.—It is, no doubt. But just think what it costs.'

16 ada S.C. běrkawal: *S.C.* is usual in speech; in writing, *mata-mata khas,* 'special policeman', is used. For the verbal use of *běr-* see Sentence Pattern 2.i.

17 tuan-punya lombong: *tuan-punya* (written as one word in Malay script) is here a compound word. So also, *tuan-punya rumah* means definitely 'the owner of the house', whereas *tuan rumah* may refer to owner, tenant, host or hostess. The sentence 'Who owns that car?' may be translated *Siapa tuan-punya kěreta itu?* or *Kěreta itu kěreta siapa?* or *Kěreta itu siapa punya?* The sentence 'That car is mine' becomes *Kěreta itu kěreta saya* (*lit.* 'That car (is) my car') or *Kěreta itu saya punya* (*lit.* 'That car, I own it'). But *saya punya kěreta* (instead of *kěreta saya*) for 'my car' is, strictly speaking, bazaar Malay though it is freely used by Malays themselves.

　sudah di-běri tahu měngatakan: *lit.* 'information has been given, saying . . .', *i.e.* 'He has been informed that . . .' Malay has no colloquial word corresponding to the conjunction 'that'. In speech, no conjunction is required, *e.g. Kata dia dia 'nak balek;* 'He said (that) he was going home.' In writing, this participial form of *kata* ('say') is very common, as is also the expression *kata-nya.* There are others.

21 bijeh yang di-dapati: see Sentence Pattern VIII.2.1; *dapati* is used for 'get' when the 'getting' depends to a certain extent on chance. For 'get', see Sentence Pattern VIII.3.

22 Tabek kěpala: *Tabek* is the usual word of greeting between Malays and non-Malays (often followed by *Apa khabar?*). Its original meaning is 'pardon', *e.g.* in the colloquial phrase *Tabek-tabek chakap,* 'Forgive my saying so.'

23 taukeh chakap ěnche' mahu datang: *chakap,* for 'say', and *mahu,* for 'going to', are both bazaar Malay. The mine-overseer does not speak as good Malay as the driver in Scene IV, who, as we know from the title *baba* by which the sergeant addresses him, comes from a Chinese family which probably uses Malay as its home-language.

25 Boleh kěnal: *boleh* followed by a verb is commonly used in informal speech in place of an imperative. Cf. *Boleh dudok* in line 28 below, where a Malay, speaking more formally, would say *Dudok-lah* or, still more politely, *Dudok-lah dahulu.*

32 bělum pěrnah: used for a 'never' which is equivalent to 'not yet'. For an absolute 'never' use *ta' pĕrnah*, e.g. *Saya ta' pĕrnah minum arak;* 'I never take alcohol.'

33 saya boleh tunjok: a Malay might have said, '*Mĕnunjokkan itu, boleh-lah, 'tapi 'nak bĕrchĕritakan ta' tahu.*'

39 pĕmanchut ayer: 'a pump', from *panchut*, 'gush out'. The prefix *pĕ-* serves the same purpose as the suffixes *-er* and *-or* in the English words 'sweeper' and 'sailor', *i.e.* it indicates an instrument or an agent, *e.g. sapu*, 'sweep'; *pĕnyapu*, 'broom'; *nyanyi*, 'sing'; *pĕnyanyi*, 'singer'. The nasal infixes are, with some exceptions, the same as for the prefix *mĕ-*. Occasionally the prefix takes the form *pĕr-*, *e.g. pĕrasap*, 'incense-burner'.

40 mĕmanchutkan ayer: causative *-kan*, *lit.* 'make to gush out'.

43 ayer . . . chayer: the word *ayer* is pronounced in several different ways. In Kedah it is *ayak*, in Perak it is *ayor*. Here the speaker (from Pahang) says *ayi*, and considers that this pronunciation is so widely used that it may be counted 'standard'.

45 di-bomba naik ka-atas: 'is pumped up', *lit.* 'is pumped, rising'. See Note V.13 and Sentence Patterns V.1.iii.

51 lombong palong: 'sluice-mine'; a dredge-mine is *lombong kapal korek*, and a mining pool is *lombong tinggal*.

54 pĕrut palong: cf. *pĕrut sungai* for the bed of a river.

55 Lumpor itu habis-lah hanyut ka-dalam kolam: note this very common use of *habis*, often best rendered in English by 'all'. It is not the mud that is 'finished' but 'the-mud-floating-off-into-the-pool'. Cf. *Ayam itu habis-lah mati;* 'The chickens were all dead, every single one of them.' See Sentence Pattern 1.

57 ada sĕkat-sĕkat papan. Di-situ-lah . . . : note the difference in idiom. Malay makes two parallel statements, 'there are partitions. There the ore sticks.' English usually makes the second statement subordinate to the first, 'there are partitions, where the ore sticks'. When the English word 'where' means 'and there' it should not be translated by *di-mana* (which, except in newspaper Malay, is always interrogative), nor by *tĕmpat*, but by an adverb of place in a separate statement, *e.g.* 'He went to a large shop, where he bought ten yards of silk'; *Dia masok sa-buah kĕdai bĕsar, di-situ di-bĕli-nya sa-puloh ela kain sutĕra.*

63 ada timbun batu: short for *timbunan batu;* in writing it would probably be *batu bĕrtimbun*, 'stones, in a heap'.

68 satu-satu guni: duplication for variety, to cover 'each several sack'. The sack, in this case, is a narrow bag about 2 ft. long and 9 in. wide.

73 Ada juga orang dudok: *juga* in its limiting sense, 'there *are* some who . . .'

77 lĕbeh satu jam: for *lĕbeh daripada satu jam*, but in speech the preposition is seldom used, *e.g.* *'Dah lĕbeh pukul ĕmpat* or *'Dah pukul ĕmpat lĕbeh;* 'It's gone four o'clock.'

97 tĕmpat kita orang sĕmbahyang: a Malay would say *kami* instead of *kita* in this sentence, since the hearer is not included in the statement.

　　kita orang: all Malay pronouns can be used for one person or for more than one, but in speech there is a strong tendency to indicate the plural by adding either *orang* or *sĕmua.*

110 Teh kosong: *lit.* 'empty tea', *i.e.* with no milk or sugar.

SCENE VII: TAKING STOCK

8. TIDAK and BUKAN

　　(b) iii. *bukan* negatives one word:
　　　　Saya bukan orang kaya.
　　　　I am not a-rich-man.

10. AFFIXES

　　(a) bĕr-

　　　　i. indicating possession:
　　　　　　Lombong itu bĕrpagar dĕngan kawat bĕrduri.
　　　　　　The mine has a fence of barbed-wire.

　　　　ii. creating an intransitive verb:
　　　　　　Ada S.C. bĕrkawal.
　　　　　　There is a Special Constable on guard duty.

　　(b) mĕ-

　　　　iii. participial:
　　　　　　a. after a verb of movement, and corresponding to an English preposition—
　　　　　　　　Ia tiada mahu mĕmbawa kĕreta mĕngikut jalan lombong itu.
　　　　　　　　He did not wish to take his car along (*lit.* following) the road to the mine.

　　(c) pĕr- . . . -an, affixes which create a noun:
　　　　pĕrhiasan (from *hias*), 'decorations'

　　(d) -kan

　　　　ii. causative:
　　　　　　Jĕntĕra di-bawah sana kĕrja-nya mĕmanchutkan ayer.
　　　　　　That engine down there is used for pumping water.

　　(e) tĕr-

　　　　i. indicating completion:
　　　　　　Bijeh turun ka-pĕrut palong itu lalu tĕrtinggal di-situ.
　　　　　　The ore falls to the bottom of the trough and is left there.
　　　　　　Ia mĕnunjok kapada kĕrtas merah tĕrgantong di-muka pintu itu.
　　　　　　He points to the red paper hung over his doorway.

(g) -an

    i. creating nouns with a passive sense:

        kěnalan, 'an acquaintance; *tulisan*, 'writing'; *bahagian*, 'division'

(k) *pě-*

    A prefix which creates nouns denoting instrument or agent:

        panchut, 'gush', 'pour forth'; *pěmanchut ayer*, 'a thing which pours forth water', *i.e.* a pump.

12. JUGA

    ii. for reservation:

        Měnjaga bijeh pun ia juga.
        Yes, he does look after the ore, but . . .
        Ada juga orang dudok dalam kampong baharu.
        There are *some* who live in the new village.

13. PULA

    ii. sequence:

        Dia hěndak tengok pula rumah China.
        He wants to see a Chinese house next.

14. -LAH

    i. c. for emphasis, by singling out one word from others of the same category:

        Dia-lah yang měnjaga orang běkěrja.
        It is he who looks after the workpeople.

15. PREPOSITIONS

    (c) i. ka- for 'motion towards':

        Awak ta' ka-mana-mana pagi ini?
        You're not going anywhere in particular this morning?

22. THE NOUN-GROUP

    i. as a descriptive phrase dependent on a noun of place or time:

        . . . *hingga sampai ka-těmpat měnyimpan bijeh.*
        . . . until they came to the place where the ore is stored.
        Rumah kěchil itu těmpat orang měnjaga bijeh.
        That little hut is where the man in charge of the ore stays.
        Ini těmpat kita orang sěmbahyang.
        This is where we pray.

    [*Note.* In sentences such as those given above there is inherent an idea of purpose, 'a place in which to store the ore'. When the phrase 'in which' (or 'by which', 'with whom', etc.) in an English sentence serves not to indicate the purpose but to add further information, the Malay idiom makes a separate sentence of the second statement, *e.g.*:

There are wooden partitions along the trough, behind which the ore lodges.

Pada pĕrut itu ada sĕkat-sĕkat papan.   Di-situ-lah bijeh itu mĕlĕkat.

Che' Mahmud opens a basket, the inside of which is padded.

Che' Mahmud mĕmbuka sa-buah bakul, di-sabĕlah dalam-nya bĕrlapek dĕngan tilam.]

iii. declaring the circumstances attending the main statement:

Dia pĕrgi ka-Kuala Lumpur / boleh tengok rumah orang kaya.

If he goes to Kuala Lumpur, he will be able to see the houses of the rich.

26. SAHAJA

Kĕchil sahaja guni ini.

These bags are quite small.

Ta' ada padam-padam,   Siang malam ada sahaja.

It never goes out, day and night it is always there.

27. HABIS, belonging to a whole noun-phrase:

Lumpor itu habis-lah hanyut ka-dalam kolam.

The mud floats off, every scrap of it, into the pool.

SCENE VII: SENTENCE PATTERNS

1. *Habis* with a verbal word or phrase

a. **Lumpor itu habis-lah hanyut ka-dalam kolam.**
   The mud all floats off into the pool.
b. Habis bĕrsĕlekeh kain tutup meja ini, kĕna gĕtah manggis.
   This tablecloth is all covered with mangosteen stains.
c. Habis tumpah dawat itu di-singgong dek budak itu.
   The boy knocked his elbow against it and the ink was spilt, every drop of it.
d. Habis tĕrchĕngang orang mĕnengok orang main ular itu, mĕmbiarkan tangan-nya di-pagut ular.
   The audience were dumbfounded to see the snake-charmer allowing the snake to bite his hand.
e. Buku 'nak bawa ka-Tanah Mĕlayu elok di-sapu ubat dahulu.   Kalau tidak, habis di-makan gĕgat.
   You had better varnish any books that you are taking to Malaya, otherwise they will be riddled with silver-fish.

2. *bĕr-*: i. verbal; ii. possessive; iii. *ada bĕr-*; iv. miscellaneous
i. Verbal

a. **Di-pintu pagar ada S.C. bĕrkawal.**
   At the gate there is a Special Constable on sentry duty.
b. Di-lorong itu ada orang mabok bĕrgadoh.
   There are some drunken people quarrelling in the street.

c. Masa saya kěchil-kěchil dahulu, ada orang běrkědai goreng pisang di-simpang itu.
When I was a child there was a shop that used to sell banana fritters at that corner.

d. Di-těpi sawah itu ada kěrbau běrlaga.
At the edge of the rice-field there were two buffaloes fighting.

e. Di-padang itu ada budak-budak běrmain layang-layang.
On the playing field there were some children flying kites.

ii. Possessive or descriptive

a. **Lonbong itu běrpagar děngan kawat běrduri.**
The mine was fenced with barbed-wire (or *had a barbed-wire fence*).

b. Pokok-pokok di-něgěri panas běrdaun sa-panjang masa, pokok-pokok di-něgěri sějok ta' běrdaun dalam musim sějok.
The trees in hot countries keep their leaves all the year round, trees in cold countries have no leaves on them during the winter.

c. Jalan itu běrlampu letrek.
The road is lit by electricity (or *has electric lamps*).

d. Meja běrlachi itu elok daripada meja ta' běrlachi.
A table with drawers is better than a table without drawers.

e. Lampu pichit ini běrubat tiga.
This torch has three batteries in it.

iii. *ada + běr-*

a. Kata awak sěkolah itu ada běrpadang bola. Ta' ada saya nampak.—Ada. Jauh ka-bělakang.
You said the school had a football field, but it hasn't, I see.—Yes, it has. It's away at the back.

b. Pokok dalam gambar ini ada běrdaun. Bukan-kah awak tangkap dalam musim sějok?
The trees in this photograph have leaves on them. But you took it in winter, didn't you?

c. Jauh dari pěkan běsar jalan ini, 'tapi ada běrlampu.
This road is a long way out of town, but it's got street-lamps.

d. Meja ini ada běrlachi. Meja itu ada ta'?—Ta' ada.
This table has a drawer. Has that one?—No, it hasn't.

e. Lampu pichit ini ada běrubat, ta' mahu měnyala. Těrbakar agak-nya mentol-nya.
This torch won't work. It's got a battery, all right. I expect the bulb has gone.

iv. Miscellaneous

a. Dalam bilek itu ada lampu těrpasang.
The lights were on in the room.

b. Dalam bilek itu lampu těrpasang sampai siang.
The lights are left on in the room all night.

c. Dalam bilek-nya lampu běrpasang sampai siang.
Somebody had the lights on in the room all night long.

d. Pada pukul lima pětang lampu di-jalan itu di-pasang orang.
  The lamps in that road are put on at 5 p.m.
e. Anak saya (ada) těrjumpa duit di-těngah jalan.
  My son found some money in the road.

3. *pun*:   i. to re-focus attention;   ii. after a subordinate clause

i. To re-focus attention

a. **Saya pun bukan orang kaya.**
  I'm not a rich man myself.
b. Dalam majlis ini orang laki-laki pun ada, orang pěrěmpuan pun ada.
  In this assembly both men and women are present.
c. Buat bagini pun boleh, buat bagitu pun boleh.
  You can do it this way or that way.
d. 'Nak pěrgi ka-situ naik kěreta api pun boleh, naik motor-car pun boleh.
  You can go there by train or by car.
e. 'Nak pěrgi ka-situ ta' boleh-kah naik motor-car?—Boleh.   Naik kěreta api pun boleh juga.
  Can you go there by car?—Yes, but you can get there by train too.
f. Sělalu hujan susah, jarang sangat hujan pun susah.
  It's bad when it rains too much, but also when it rains too little.
g. Awak 'nak pěrgi saya pun 'nak pěrgi.
  If you go, I'm going.
h. Awak 'nak pěrgi, saya pun 'nak pěrgi juga.
  If you go, I'll go too.
i. Dalam kampong ini pěnghulu pun dia, kathi pun dia.
  In this village he is both pěnghulu and kathi.
j. Pěrgi běrjumpa dia sa-orang sudah-lah, kathi pun dia, pěnghulu pun dia juga.
  We shan't need to see anybody except him.   He's the kathi, and he's the pěnghulu too.

ii. After a main subject, preceded by a subordinate clause of time.

a. Lěpas di-bacha-nya surat itu, dia pun měnangis.
  When she had read the letter, she wept.
b. Sudah měngumpulkan sampah sarap itu, dia pun měmbakar.
  When he had gathered the rubbish together, he burned it.
c. Bila sampai ka-atas pěntas itu, dia pun měmandang kapada orang ramai.
  When he had gone up on to the platform, he surveyed the crowd.
d. Bila habis sumbu-nya těrbakar, měrchun itu pun mělětup.
  When the fuse was burnt through, the cracker went off.
e. Bila di-kěrat-nya sahaja pita itu, kapal itu pun mělunchor ka-laut.
  The moment she had cut the ribbon, the ship slid into the sea.

DI-TĔMPAT HIBORAN

AT THE AMUSEMENT PARK

1   Pada malam Minggu Che' Mahmud dĕngan Che' Normah pĕrgi mĕnjĕmput
2 Mr. Martin ka-hotel-nya kĕrana hĕndak mĕmbawa-nya pĕrgi mĕnengok-
3 nengok tĕmasha malam dalam pĕkan.

On eve of-Sunday Che' Mahmud with Che' Normah goes inviting Mr. Martin to-his-
hotel because going-to conduct-him going seeing shows of-the-evening in the-town.

On Saturday night Che' Mahmud and Che' Normah go to call for Mr.
Martin at his hotel, in order to take him to see the evening shows in the town.

4 MAR.   **Ka-mana kita malam ini?**
      Whither we this-night?
      Where are we going to-night?

5 NOR.   **Mula-mula kita pĕrgi ka-pasar Minggu, lĕpas itu**
      At-the-beginning we go to-Sunday-market, after that we go-in
      First of all we are going to the weekly market, and after

6   **kita masok mĕnengok Lucky World Park.**
      seeing Lucky World Park.
      that we'll go inside and see the Lucky World Park.

7 MAH.   **Elok kita bĕrjalan kaki sahaja. Bukan jauh pasar**
      Good we travel on-foot merely. Not far, the Sunday market.
      It will be better just to walk there. It's no distance to the

8   **Minggu itu. Dari situ kita mĕmotong kampong**
      From there, we cut-through land-round-houses, a few, merely, have
      weekly market, and from there we only have to take a short

9   **sadikit sahaja sudah sampai ka-Lucky World**
      arrived to Lucky World Park.
      cut through a few gardens and we shall be at the Lucky

10   **Park.**
      World Park.

11   Kĕtiga-tiga-nya pun bĕrjalan mĕnuju pasar Minggu.
    All-three-of-them walk making-towards Sunday market.
    The three of them walk in the direction of the weekly market.

12 MAR. **Ramai orang di-pasar Minggu ini, ia?**
In-large-numbers, the people at the Sunday market, yes?
My word, the market's crowded, isn't it?

13 NOR. **Ramai.   Dalam Kuala Lumpur di-sini sahaja orang**
In-large-numbers.   In Kuala Lumpur, here only, people able manage
Yes it is.   This is the only place in Kuala Lumpur where

14 **boleh dapat měmbĕli barang-barang buatan Mĕlayu.**
the-buying various-things (of) Malay-workmanship.
you can buy things that are made by Malays.

15   Che' Mahmud mĕnunjok kapada orang bĕrjual sateh.
Che' Mahmud points to person (who) sells sateh.
Che' Mahmud points to a *sateh*-seller.

16 MAH. **Tengok orang itu bĕrjual sateh.**
See, that-person sells sateh.
Look.   That man is selling *sateh*.

17 MAR. **Apa sateh itu?**
What (is) that-sateh?
What is *sateh*?

18 MAH. **Satu macham makanan.   Daging bĕrpotong nipis-**
One-unit kind of-food.   Meat cut-in-slices, very thin, pierced-
It's a way of preparing meat, by cutting it into thin pieces,

19 **nipis, bĕrchuchok dĕngan lidi.   'Ndak makan-nya di-**
through with palm-leaf-veins.   Intending eat it, there-is-roasting.
and skewering it on palm-leaf veins.   When you are going

20 **bakar.   Tengok-lah orang itu dudok makan dĕkat**
See, that man sits-eating, near the-place of-roasting, precisely.
to eat it you roast it.   Look.   That man is eating it, just

21 **tĕmpat mĕmbakar itu juga.**
near the fire there.

22 NOR. **Sudah mĕnengok-nengok 'karang boleh kita choba**
Completed seeing-seeing presently, able we try it.
When we've had a look round, we'll try it.

23 **makan.**

24   Mr. Martin mĕnunjok kapada tudong saji tĕrgantong di-dalam sa-buah
25 kĕdai.
   Mr. Martin points to some dish-covers hanging in a shop.

MAR. **Apa běnda bulat běsar ini? Macham topi.**
What things, round, large, these? Like hats.
What are these big round things? They are like hats.

NOR. **Tudong saji, buat tutup makanan.**
Covers of-served-food, making covering of-food.
Dish-covers, for covering food.

Měreka běrjalan sampai ka-těmpat orang běrjual buah-buahan.
They walk until to-place of-people selling fruit-of-all-sorts.
They go on till they come to the fruit-sellers' stalls.

MAH. **Buah-buahan kita tengok dalam dusun hari itu**
Fruits-of various sorts we see in orchard that-day, all, it-is-that
All the fruits that we saw in the orchard are on sale here.
sěmua ada orang jual di-sini.
people sell here.

Mr. Martin těrbau buah durian.
Mr. Martin finds-himself-smelling durian-fruit.
Mr. Martin gets a whiff of *durian*.

MAR. **Bau ini saya tahu. Těntu bau durian.**
This-smell I know. Certainly, smell of 'durian'.
I know this smell. It's *durian*, right enough.

Che' Normah měnunjok ka-hujong pasar.
Che' Normah points to-end of-market.
Che' Normah points to the further end of the market.

NOR. **Di-sabělah sana itu těmpat orang jual sayor pula.**
On-the-side over-there, place of-people-sell-vegetables, in-their-turn.
Over there are the vegetable stalls.

Lěpas itu měreka měmatah balek ka-pangkal pasar itu lalu běrhěnti di-
sabuah kědai kopi, kěrana hěndak minum sěrta makan sateh.
*After that they break-off, returning to-beginning of the-market, then stop at one-unit
coffee shop, because going-to drink together with eat 'sateh'.*
After that they turn round and come back to the beginning of the market,
and then stop at a coffee stall for a drink and some *sateh*.

MAH. **Lěpas makan ini boleh-lah kita těrus pěrgi ka-**
After this-meal able we straightway go to Lucky World Park.
When we have finished, we'll go straight to Lucky World

38   **Lucky World Park. Kalau lambat 'karang ta'**
If late presently not-in-time seeing opera.
Park.   If we are late we shan't be in time to see the Malay

39   **sĕmpat mĕnengok bangsawan.**
opera.

40 MAR.   **Pukul bĕrapa bangsawan itu mula?**
Strike how-many the-opera begins?
At what time does the opera start?

41 MAH.   **Pukul sĕmbilan.**
Strike nine.
Nine o'clock.

42 NOR.   **Apa-lah 'nak di-gadohkan sangat. Hari baharu**
What (is this?) going-to-be a-fussing overmuch.   The day newly
What are you worrying about?   It's only just eight o'clock.

43   **pukul 'lapan.**
strike eight.

44 MAH.   **Bĕtul-lah baharu pukul lapan tĕtapi ta' kan-lah**
True, newly strike eight, but not likely-to-be intending straight enter
I know it's only just eight o'clock, but we shan't want to

45   **hĕndak tĕrus masok panggong bangsawan sahaja.**
hall of-opera only.   Intending also see 'joget' before.
go straight in to the opera only.   We shall want to see the

46   **Hĕndak juga-lah mĕnengok joget dahulu.**
Malay dancing first.

47   Sa-tĕlah sudah minum mĕreka pun pĕrgi ka-Lucky World Park dĕngan
48 mĕngikut jalan mĕmintas dalam Kampong Baharu.   Apabila sudah masok
49 ka-dalam park itu Che' Mahmud tĕragak-agak ka-mana hĕndak pĕrgi.
    When completed drinking, they go to Lucky World Park with following path cutting-
through in Kampong Baharu.   When have entered into the-park Che' Mahmud finds-
himself-guessing whither going-to go.
    When they have finished their coffee, they go to the Lucky World Park by
a path that takes a short cut through Kampong Baharu.   When they get inside
the park Che' Mahmud hesitates, wondering which way to go.

50 NOR.   **Elok kita masok ka-kanan dahulu, mĕnengok joget**
Good we go-in to-right first, seeing modern Malay-dancing.   After
We had better go to the right first of all and see the *joget*

51   **modern.   Lĕpas itu baharu pĕrgi tengok joget bĕtul.**
that newly go see genuine-Malay-dancing.
modern.   Then, after that we can go and see the real Malay
dancing.

2 Měreka pun pěrgi hampir ka-pěntas joget modern. Di-atas pěntas itu
3 orang sědang měnari běrpasang-pasang.
They go near to-stage of modern 'joget'. On the-stage people (are) in-the-middle-of dancing being-in-pairs.
They go up to the stage of the modern-style *joget*. On the stage people are dancing, in couples.

4 MAH. **Ini tari Mělayu tětapi bukan macham dahulu lagi.**
This (is) Malay dancing but not like before still. Name of-it even
This is Malay dancing, but not as it used to be. Even its

5 **Nama dia pun sudah běrubah měnjadi joget modern.**
has become changed, becoming 'joget modern'.
name has changed into *joget modern*.

6 MAR. **Lagu-nya macham lagu barat.**
Tune-of it (is) like tune of-west.
The tune is like a western tune isn't it?

7 NOR. **Itu-lah sěbab di-namakan joget modern. Di-sabělah**
That (is) reason there-is-a-naming 'joget modern'. At the side-of
That's why it is called *joget modern*. Over there at the back

8 **bělakang sana ada joget chara lama. Mari kita**
the-back yonder there-is Malay-dancing old-style. Come we go see.
there is old style dancing. Let's go and see.

9 **pěrgi tengok.**

10 Měreka pun pěrgi měnuju těmpat joget (atau ronggeng) chara lama itu.
11 Sa-bělum sampai ka-situ měreka lalu děkat panggong wayang China.
They go making-towards place of 'joget' (or 'ronggeng') old style. Not-yet arrive to-there, they go-by near theatre of Chinese-performance.
They go towards the old-style dancing. Before they get there they pass by a Chinese theatre.

12 MAR. **Wayang ini sudah mula main.**
This-performance has begun play.
This show has begun.

13 NOR. **Wayang ini wayang China. Chěrita dia panjang.**
This-theatre (is) Chinese-theatre. Story-of-it (is) long. That
This is the Chinese theatre. The plays are very long. That

14 **Itu sěbab dia mula dahulu sadikit daripada wayang**
(is) the reason it begins before, a little, than Malay-theatre.
is why it starts a bit earlier than the Malay theatre.

15 **Mělayu.**

66   Di-atas pĕntas joget itu di-dapati mĕreka orang mĕnari.
On the 'joget'-stage there-is-a-discovering by-them people-dancing.
On the *joget* stage they find people dancing.

67 MAH. **Ini dia joget chara lama bĕtul. Tengok pĕrkakas**
This (is) it, 'joget' style old truly. See, instruments of-music in-
This is dancing of the real old style.   Look at the instru-

68   **bunyi-bunyian-nya. Bĕsi bulat yang di-pukul orang**
the-case. That iron, round, which, there-is-a-striking by-person
ments of the orchestra.   That round metal gong with a

69   **tĕntang bonjol-nya itu tĕtawak. Kuat bunyi-nya**
on the-boss-of-it (is) a-gong. Strong the sound-of-it if there-is-
boss, that he is striking, is called *tĕtawak*.   When it is

70   **kalau di-pukul bĕtul-bĕtul. Orang bĕrdua itu pula**
striking truly. Those persons being-two, in-their-turn, are beating-
struck with full force it has a very loud note.   And these

71   **mĕnĕpok gĕndang. Biola pun ada juga. Choba**
with-the-hand drums. Violin, you see, is present too. Try hear,
two people are drumming.   There's a violin too.   Listen

72   **dĕngar lagu-nya lagu Mĕlayu bĕtul.**
the tune-in-the-case (is) a Malay tune truly.
to the tune; it is a genuine Malay tune.

73 MAR. **Lĕmbut bĕnar lagu ini.**
Soft, truly, this-tune.
It's a very quiet tune.

74 MAH. **Lagu ini memang lĕmbut. Nama-nya *Lagu Ma'***
This-tune by-its-nature (is) soft. Name-of-it 'The Duenna's
Yes, this *is* a quiet tune.   It's called *Ma' Inang*.   If we

75   ***Inang*. Kalau kita nanti sa-kĕjap dapat kita dĕngar**
Tune'. If we wait one-wink able we hear true Malay dance-tune.
wait a bit we shall be able to hear a real *ronggeng* tune.

76   **lagu ronggeng bĕtul. Lagu ronggeng bĕtul itu tidak**
The tune of genuine 'ronggeng' (is) not soft.
The real *ronggeng* tune is not a quiet tune.

77   **lĕmbut.**

78   Tiada lama lĕpas itu habis-lah lagu *Ma' Inang* dan mulaï pula lagu ronggeng
79 bĕtul.
There-is-not length-of-time after that, ended (is) tune 'Ma' Inang' and begins in-its-turn tune of true Malay dance.
Not long afterwards the tune *Ma' Inang* comes to an end, and the real *ronggeng* tune begins.

NOR. **Aa. Ini dia lagu ronggeng bĕtul. Tidak lĕmbut lagi.**
Ah. This (is) it, tune of true Malay dancing. Not soft still.
Ah. This is the real *ronggeng* tune. It isn't quiet now.
Tari-nya pantas. Tidak lĕmah lĕmbut macham
Dancing in-the-case lively. Not weak, soft, sort just-now.
And the dancing is lively, not languorous as it was before.
tadi.

MAR. **Orang itu mĕnyanyi pula masa mĕnari?**
These people sing, strange-to-say, time of-dancing?
They are singing as they dance?

MAH. **Nyanyi itu kita namakan pantun. Dia bĕrpantun**
That singing we name 'pantun'. This them-singing (is) answer-
We call the songs *pantun*. When they sing *pantuns* the man
itu bĕrjawab-jawab antara laki-laki dĕngan pĕrĕm-
ing-turn between man with woman.
and the woman answer each other in turn.
puan.

MAR. **Apa kata dia itu? Saya ta' ĕrti sadikit pun.**
What the-saying of-them. I not understand a-little even.
What are they saying? I can't understand a word of it.

MAH. **Orang pĕrĕmpuan itu kata:**
The woman says:

> **'Dari mana hĕndak ka-mana?**
> *'From where intending to-where?*
> 'Coming whence and going whither?
> **Tinggi rumput dari padi.**
> *High (is the) grass than growing-rice.*
> Higher the grass than the grain.
> **Tahun mana bulan yang mana**
> *Year which, month the-which*
> What the month and what the year
> **Boleh kita bĕrjumpa lagi?'**
> *Able we meet more?'*
> When we two meet again?'

Orang laki-laki itu mĕnjawab:
The man answers;

94 **'Kalau ada kĕpok di-ladang**
' If there-is a-rice-bin in-the-rice-field,
' If there's a rice-bin in your field,

95 **Boleh saya mĕnumpang padi.**
Able I leave-with-you rice
With you I'll store my grain.

96 **Kalau ada 'umor panjang**
If there-is long-age
If length of years the Fates but yield,

97 **Dapat kita bĕrjumpa lagi.'**
Manage we meet more.'
We two shall meet again.'

98 Mĕreka tĕrlalai mĕnengok ronggeng hingga sudah dĕkat pukul sĕmbilan.
They linger-without-realizing, watching dancing, up-to-the-point-that it-has-become near strike nine.
They linger watching the dancing until they suddenly realize that it is nearly nine o'clock.

99 MAH. **Hari 'dah dĕkat pukul sĕmbilan. Mari kita ka-**
Day has-become near strike nine. Come we to-theatre of perform-
It's nearly nine o'clock. Let's go to the opera now.

100 **panggong wayang bangsawan pula.**
ance of Malay-opera, in-its-turn.

101 Mĕreka pĕrgi ka-panggong bangsawan lalu masok.
They go to-theatre of Malay opera then go-in.
They go to the hall where the performance is given, and go inside.

102 NOR. **Wayang bangsawan ini lĕbeh kurang macham opera**
This performance of-opera more less like opera in Europe but not
This *bangsawan* performance is something like opera in

103 **di-Eropah 'tapi tidak sĕmua mĕnyanyi.**
all singing.
Europe but it is not all singing.

104 Mĕreka pun dudok.
They sit down.

SCENE VIII: NOTES

1 Pada malam Minggu: 'On *Saturday* night'. For the names of
the days of the week see page 172. In that list *Hari Ahad* is given
for 'Sunday' (*ahad = Ar.* 'one'), but *hari Minggu* is frequently
used for 'Sunday' by Malays who would always use the Arabic
terms for the other days of the week.

malam Minggu: the word *hari* is used to cover the whole period
of twenty-four hours (beginning with sunset), not merely for the
daylight hours. Since the 'day' (*hari*) begins with sunset, the 'darkness' (*malam*) comes before the 'daylight' (*siang*), and thus the
period which we call 'Saturday evening' becomes 'the dark part
of *Sunday*'; so, *malam Khamis* is 'Wednesday evening', *malam
Juma'at* is 'Thursday evening', and *malam Sabtu* is 'Friday
evening'.

12 Ramai orang di-pasar Minggu ini ia?: *ramai* is predicative, as
in IV.39 and VI.92 (*i.e.* it is the thing which is *said* about the
subject). *lit.* 'the people (are) in-crowds'. Remember that
there is no *ada* in such a sentence; the 'are' of the English sentence
is a copula, not a verb of existence, as it is in 'There are two men
outside', *Ada dua orang di-luar.* The statement made in the text
is not that 'many people are there' but that 'the people there
(are) many'. Notice how both speakers emphasize the word by
putting the stress on the final syllable.

17 Apa sateh itu?: *itu* is used here in a general sense, not that
particular *sateh* that they were looking at, but, 'What *is* this thing
called *sateh*?' Cf. *Gajah itu běrtělinga běsar;* 'The elephant (not
any particular one) has large ears.' *Susu itu puteh;* 'Milk (not
any particular jugful) is white.'

18 Daging běrpotong . . . běrchuchok: *běr-* with a passive
significance. It is the action that is of interest here, with the actor
in the background: the meat has been sliced and skewered (by
somebody or other). Contrast *tudong saji těrgantong* in line 24
below, where it is the completed state, not the action which
brought it about, that is of interest.

19 'Ndak makan-nya / di-bakar: note, once again, how impersonal is the tone of the Malay sentence, merely the two ideas
set down side by side, with no mention of agent for either action,
lit. 'there being intention of eating it, roasting is carried
out'.

20 děkat těmpat měmbakar itu juga: *juga* used with its limiting
sense, 'quite near the brazier, just there, and nowhere else'.
See Note II.60 and Sentence Patterns VI.3.

26 Macham topi: the speaker's rising intonation shows that the two words are a new statement.

27 buat tutup makanan: *lit.* 'the making of food-covers', *i.e.* 'for food-covers'. See Note V.32. The speaker says *mangkanan;* cf. *mangkin* as a variant form of *makin.*

29 Buah-buahan itu sĕmua / ada orang jual di-sini: see Sentence Pattern 1. In this construction the verb will always be in the simple root form (*i.e.* unprefixed). *Lit.* 'All those fruits / there exists (this fact) / people sell (them) here'. See Note VI.70.

38 Kalau lambat 'karang ta' sĕmpat mĕnengok bangsawan: 'If we are late, there won't be time to see the opera.' Here the English sentence indicates future time in the main clause ('will not'), the Malay sentence in the subordinate clause, by the adverb *'karang,* 'presently'.

ta' sĕmpat mĕnengok: note that there is no *hĕndak* here, because there is no intention involved. It is merely a statement that 'there is no time for seeing'. Contrast this with *Rah ta' sĕmpat 'nak mĕnengok* in Scene IV.12. 'I didn't have time to go and look (as I should have liked to do,)' *i.e.* 'there was no time for me-wanting-to-see'. Contrast the two following sentences: *Lapar bĕnar ini. Pagi tadi ta' sĕmpat 'nak makan;* 'I'm terribly hungry. I didn't have time to eat my breakfast this morning'; and *Mari kita minum kopi. Pagi tadi ta' sĕmpat makan di-hotel,* 'Let's go and have some coffee. There wasn't time for any breakfast at the hotel this morning.'

49 tĕragak-agak: *lit.* 'finds himself guess-guessing'. The duplication gives a feeling of uncertainty, the *tĕr-* shows that the uncertainty has just 'come upon him'.

ka-mana hĕndak pĕrgi: 'uncertain where to go'. Since, in this sentence, the 'going' is necessarily future to the 'uncertainty', *hĕndak* must be used. See Note IV.12.

53 sĕdang mĕnari: the *mĕ-* derivative is always used after *tĕngah* and *sĕdang* meaning 'in the middle of doing'.

54 macham dahulu lagi: *i.e.* when it was 'still' those early days. Cf. Note IV.54, *Tadi lagi Pa' Abu pĕrgi ka-balai.*

66 di-dapati mĕreka orang mĕnari: *lit.* 'there-is-a-discovering-by-them people-dancing'. Remember that when two nouns (or noun-phrases) follow the *di-* construction, the *first* of them is the doer of the action expressed by the *di-* verb (*i.e.* the logical, though not the grammatical 'subject') and the second of them 'receives' the action (*i.e.* it is the logical 'object'). This fits in with the rule of syntax that the subject of a Malay verb may not be separated from that verb (except by a time-adverb such as *lagi*, 'still'; *bĕlum*, 'not yet'). Thus if two nouns (or pronouns) *precede* the verb it is the *second* of them (*i.e.* the one next to the verb) that is the actor. This order of words will occur when the writer or speaker wishes to stress the object by bringing it into the emphatic position at the head of the sentence, *e.g. Dia saya panggil;* 'I was calling *him* (not you)'. *Saya dia panggil;* 'It was *me* that she called (not you).' *Saya awak ta' bagi duit;* 'You didn't give *me* any money.' *Awak saya ta' bagi duit;* 'I'm not going to give *you* any money. *Note:* When the object is brought to the front of the sentence the verb will always be in its simple unprefixed form, because the agent is of secondary importance (see VI.70 and Note 29 above). But when the object is picked up again by *-nya* after the verb, the *mě-* form is used because the first word is merely a 'statement of topic' and the real object is *-nya*, *e.g. Surat itu dia měmbuka-nya,* 'He opened the letter'.

68 Běsi bulat yang di-pukul orang těntang bonjol-nya itu: the *itu*, clipping the phrase together, shows that the whole of it from *yang* to *-nya* is a description of *běsi bulat, lit.* 'the round metal thing which, there is a striking by a person on the boss of it'.

bonjol-nya: the relative pronoun *yang* is never preceded by a preposition, nor can it act as a genitive. In sentences such as this it is used as a nominative to which the required description may be attached, and the genitive is supplied by the pronoun *-nya, e.g. Orang yang kita běrjumpa anak-nya hari itu taukeh lombong;* 'The person *whose* son we met the other day is the mine-owner.' *lit.* 'The person *who,* we met the son *of him* . . .' *Rumah yang kita nampak měnara-nya itu masjid;* 'The building *of which* you can see the spire is the mosque.' *lit.* 'The building *which,* you can see the spire *of it* . . .' The Malay sentences sound less stilted than the corresponding English sentences.

78 habis-lah lagu Ma' Inang: *habis* is itself the statement here, 'the tune is over, finished'. Contrast line VII.55. *habis hanyut,* where *hanyut* is the statement and *habis* amplifies it, 'floats off, completely', as in Sentence Pattern VII.1.

84 Dia běrpantun itu / běrjawab-jawab: *itu* shows that *dia-běrpantun* is a noun-unit, the subject about which the statement (*běrjawab-jawab*) is made.

pantun: a four-lined verse consisting of two couplets, with end-rhymes (or assonances) *a, b, a, b.* The writer conveys his message in the second couplet only. The first couplet prepares the ear for the second couplet, by inner as well as by final assonances, but it usually has no connection with its meaning. Frequently, as in this instance, it is a flash-picture of some familiar scene. Cf. Sentence Pattern 2.iv.*e.*

90 tinggi rumput dari padi: 'the grass is higher than the grain'.

The full formula of comparison would be *lĕbeh tinggi daripada*, 'more high than', but comparison and equality are usually indicated in speech by the fewest words possible, *e.g.* 'The flag-staff was as tall as a coconut palm'; *Tiang bĕndera itu sa-tinggi pokok nyior.* 'The tree was taller than the house'; *Pokok itu tinggi daripada rumah.* Similarly, for the superlative degree the full form *yang tinggi sa-kali* is usually cut short in speech, *e.g. Lima hĕlai kain ini, yang murah itu, yang mahal ini;* 'Of these five sarongs that one is the cheapest and this one is the dearest.'

98 tĕrlalai: the prefix suggests that the time has slipped by without their realizing it.

99 Hari sudah dĕkat pukul sĕmbilan: for *hari*, see Note 1 above, and compare such expressions as: *Hari 'dah malam;* 'It is dark' *Hari 'dah hujan;* 'It has begun to rain.' *Ayam bĕrkokok tanda hari 'nak siang;* 'The cocks crowed, heralding the dawn.'

SCENE VIII: TAKING STOCK

3. INI and ITU

  i. *itu* used as a general, not a particular, demonstrative:
> *Apa sateh itu?*
> What is *sateh*?

6. PRONOUNS

  (*a*) Personal:

  iv. *c.* -*nya* as object after a *mĕ*- derivative:
> *Dia mĕmbawa-nya pĕrgi tengok tĕmasha.*
> He takes him to see the shows.
> *Hĕndak makan-nya di-bakar.*
> When you are going to eat it, you roast it.
> (Reminder: verbs beginning with *m* seldom show *mĕ*-.)

9. NO TENSE-FORM

  ii. time indicated by an adverbial word or phrase:
> *Kalau lambat 'karang ta' sĕmpat mĕnengok bangsawan.*
> If we are late, there will not be time to see the Malay opera.

10. AFFIXES

  (*a*) *bĕr*-

  i. verbal use:
> *Mĕreka bĕrjalan sampai ka-tĕmpat orang bĕrjual buah-buahan.*
> They walk to the place where people are selling fruit.

  iii. as a passive participle:
> *Daging bĕrpotong nipis-nipis, bĕrchuchok dĕngan lidi.*
> Meat, cut into thin pieces, and skewered with coconut-leaf veins.

(b) *mě-*

    i. as verbal noun:

        Di-atas pěntas itu orang sědang měnari běrpasang-pasang.
        On the stage, couples are (in the middle of) dancing.

    iii. participial

        a. after a verb of movement, and corresponding to an
           English preposition:

             Kětiga-tiga-nya pun běrjalan měnuju pasar Minggu.
             The three of them walk towards the Sunday market.
             Měreka pun pěrgi měnuju těmpat ronggeng chara lama.
             They go towards the place where the old-style
             dancing is going on.

(e) *těr-*

    ii. for sudden and involuntary realization:

        Dia těrbau buah durian.
        He gets a whiff of durian.
        Dia těragak-agak ka-mana hěndak pěrgi.
        He hesitates, wondering where to go.
        Měreka těrlalai měnengok ronggeng.
        They find they have stayed longer than they meant to,
        watching the dancing.

(f) *di-*

    i. with agent specified:

        Di-dapati měreka orang měnari.
        They find people dancing.

(g) *-an*

    ii. creating an abstract (or concrete) noun:
        buatan Mělayu, Malay workmanship.

    iii. creating a collective noun:
        bunyi-bunyian, music (*lit.* a variety of sounds).

12. JUGA

    iii. with a limiting function:
        . . . *děkat těmpat měmbakar itu juga.*
        . . . just next to the brazier there.

13. PULA

    i. surprise:
        Orang itu měnyanyi pula masa měnari.
        They are singing as they dance!

    ii. sequence:
        Habis-lah lagu Ma'Inang mulaï pula lagu ronggeng.
        When the tune *Ma'Inang* comes to an end, the *ronggeng* tune begins.

15. PREPOSITIONS

(c) ka-

i. for 'motion towards':

Ka-mana kita malam ini?

Where are we going this evening?

ii. for implied 'motion towards':

Měreka pěrgi měnjěmput dia ka-hotel-nya.

They go and call for him at his hotel.

19. BAHARU meaning 'newly':

i. for 'not until', 'then and only then'

Lěpas itu baharu pěrgi tengok joget bětul.

And then, when we've seen that, we'll go and see the genuine Malay dancing.

ii. for recently, 'only just'

Hari baharu pukul 'lapan.

It's only just eight o'clock.

22. THE NOUN-GROUP

ii. a noun, with adjunct, declaring the topic:

Buah-buahan itu sěmua | ada orang jual di-sini.

All those fruits, there are people selling them here.

iii. a noun-group declaring the circumstances attending the main statement:

Kita měmotong kampong sadikit sahaja | sudah sampai.

If we just cut through between a few of the houses, we're there.

Hěndak makan-nya | di-bakar.

When you are going to eat it, you roast it.

iv. a noun-group as subject, and as object:

Dia běrpantun itu | běrjawab-jawab.

Their singing, it alternates (first the man, then the woman).

Di-dapati měreka | orang měnari.

They find people dancing.

[*Note.* The position of *sudah* in several sentences which have received comment is an indication that the following subject and verb make a noun-group which is itself the subject of *sudah*, e.g.:

Sudah | saya hantar ka-hotel.

. . bila sudah | kita kupas.

. . sudah | kami kěluarkan.

Compare also:

boleh | kita pěrgi

Ta' dapat | kita měngambil-nya.

'Dah ada-kah | orang pěrgi měnanggil kěreta sakit?

Puas | měnunggu-nya.]

28. COMPARISON

usually inferred rather than expressed. (See Note VIII. 90):

Tinggi rumput dari padi.
The weeds are taller than the rice.

SCENE VIII: SENTENCE PATTERNS

1. *ada* followed by subject + simple verb

a. **Buah-buahan kita tengok hari itu sěmua ada orang jual di-sini.**
   Those fruits that we saw the other day, they are all of them on sale here.

b. Gula 'dah ada Ma' Minah běli sa-malam. Ta' payah běli lagi (*or* awak
   měmběli lagi).
   Ma' Minah bought some sugar yesterday. There's no need to get any more.

c. Kira-kira ini ada Che' Gu těrangkan sa-malam. Měngapa ta' faham juga
   lagi?
   I explained this sum to you yesterday. How is it that you still don't understand it?

d. Běrok ada orang ajar měmanjat kělapa, kěra ta' ada.
   You can teach the coconut monkey to climb a palm-tree, but you can't teach the long-tailed monkey.

e. Chěrita itu sudah ada orang masokkan dalam surat khabar.
   That story has already been published in the newspaper.

2. *dapat*: i. *di-dapati*; ii. *měndapatkan*; iii. *dapat*; iv. *měndapat*

i. *di-dapati*

a. **Di-dapati měreka orang měnari.**
   They found people dancing.

b. Di-sini jarang di-dapati orang yang pandai měmbuat kěris.
   You seldom come across a kris smith here.

c. Di-dalam sungai ini boleh di-dapati bijeh timah.
   Tin ore is to be found in this river.

d. Apabila sampai ka-pondok itu, di-dapati-nya sudah kosong.
   When they reached the hut they discovered that it was empty.

e. Pada masa hěndak balek, di-dapati-nya minyak kěreta-nya sudah habis.
   When he was about to go home, he discovered that he had no petrol left.

ii. *měndapatkan*

a. **Che' Normah balek měndapatkan Che' Mahmud.**
   Che' Normah returns to Che' Mahmud.

b. Dia pěrgi měndapatkan guru běsar, hěndak mintakan anak-nya chuti dua
   hari.
   He went to see the headmaster to ask for two days leave of absence for his son.

c. Běsikal-nya hilang, dia pun pěrgi měndapatkan mata-mata di-simpang itu.
   When his bicycle disappeared he went and reported it to the policeman at the crossroads.

d. Gĕtah sudah-lah murah, hujan pula hari-hari. Kĕna mĕndapatkan chĕti, nampak-nya.

Rubber was low enough already, and now it rains every day! It strikes me that I shall have to be paying a visit to the money-lender.

e. Che' Rashid yang mĕnjaga duit masjid. Biar saya suroh dia mĕndapatkan ĕnche'.

It's Che' Rashid who looks after the mosque funds. I'll ask him to call and see you.

iii. *dapat*

a. **Dĕngan mĕninjau di-chĕlah-chĕlah orang ramai itu dapat-lah ia mĕnengok.**

By peeping between the people in the crowd, they managed to see.

b. Sa-lama dudok di-sini dapat-lah mĕnyimpan duit sadikit.

Since I've been living here I've managed to save a bit of money.

c. Panas-panas bagini kalau dapat ayer batu, bagus-lah.

Seeing that it's so hot, it would be a good idea if we could get hold of some ice.

d. Kalau Kĕrajaan 'nak bĕli tanah itu, kita ta' dapat 'nak mĕmbuat apa-apa.

If Government wants to buy the land, we can't do anything about it.

e. Sudah kita bĕlah batang rumbia itu, dapat-lah mĕngambil sagu-nya.

When you split the trunk of the rumbia palm, then you can get at the sago.

iv. *mĕndapat*

a. Saya pĕrgi juga mĕnchari ikan hari itu, 'tapi ta' mĕndapat.

Yes, I did go fishing, but I didn't have much success.

b. Pĕrgi mĕngaji sama-sama dĕngan orang, orang mĕndapat, awak tidak.

I went to school with the rest of them. They got on, I didn't.

c. Bĕlajar bahasa China itu susah. 'Tapi kalau di-usahakan sunggoh-sunggoh, ta' banyak sadikit mĕndapat juga.

It isn't easy to learn Chinese. But if you persevere with it you will, at any rate, make some progress.

d. Suka bĕnar hati Che' Dolah. Dia banyak mĕndapat padi tahun ini.

Che' Dolah is feeling very pleased. He has had a good padi harvest this year.

e. Tinggi-tinggi si-matahari,
   Anak kĕrbau mati tĕrtambat.
Sudah lama saya mĕnchari,
   Ini-lah baharu saya mĕndapat.

*High above the sun in heaven,
   Lifeless lies the tethered foal.
Through the years in vain I've striven,
   Now, at last, I reach my goal.*

3. 'Get'

a. Pĕrgi ambil pĕnyapu ka-dapor.

Go and get the broom from the kitchen.

b. Dudok-lah sa-kĕjap, saya 'nak pĕrgi mĕmbĕli ikan ka-kĕdai.

Sit down for a bit. I'm going to the shop to get some fish.

c. Mat ta' ada di-rumah.   Dia pĕrgi mĕnchari kayu api ka-bĕlakang.
   Mat isn't in.   He's gone out behind the house to get firewood.

d. Bĕrapa dia dapat upah mĕmbuat sa-hĕlai kain songkit?
   How much does she get for making a gold-threaded sarong?

e. Ta' usah bĕrbual di-tĕmpat gĕlap itu, kĕna gigit nyamok 'karang.
   Don't stay there gossiping in the dark.   You'll get bitten by mosquitoes.

4. 'See, look'

a. **Kalau lambat 'karang ta' sĕmpat mĕnengok bangsawan.**
   If we are late we shan't be in time to see the opera.

b. Rugi-lah saya ta' mĕnengok rumah yang awak tunjokkan itu.   Awak
   panggil tadi saya ta' mĕmandang.
   *A pity I didn't see that house that you pointed out.   When you drew my attention I
   wasn't looking that way.*

c. Choba pĕrhatikan dalam kamus itu, ada-kah pĕrkataan yang kita bichar-
   akan tadi.
   *Have a look in that dictionary, will you.   See if that word we were discussing just
   now is in it.*

d. Nampak-kah kapal terbang lalu tadi?—Ta' nampak.   Mĕmĕrhatikan
   ayam bĕrlaga.   Rugi-lah.—Ta' mĕmandang macham mana 'nak
   nampak.
   *Did you see that plane go by?—No.   I was watching those cocks fighting.   What a
   shame!—If you don't look, how do you expect to see?*

e. Mĕngapa itu?—Mĕnengok-nengok buku ini.   'Tapi ta' bĕrchĕrmin mata
   ta' nampak tĕntang yang halus-nya.
   *What are you doing?—Having a look at this book, but I haven't got my glasses on, so
   I can't see the parts that are in small print.*

5. The verbal prefixes

a. **Di-sĕrambi ini di-bĕntangkan tikar yang elok.**
   Here on the verandah we put down our best mats.

b. Di-sĕrambi itu tĕrbĕntang (*or* di-bĕntang) tikar yang elok.
   On the verandah there were spread some fine mats.

c. Orang pĕrĕmpuan itu mĕmbĕntang tikar di-sĕrambi.
   The woman was spreading the mats on the verandah.

d. Sudah mĕnyapu sĕrambi itu, di-bĕntang-nya tikar.
   When she had swept the verandah she put down the mats.

e. Pada masa saya sampai tikar sĕmua sudah bĕrbĕntang.
   By the time I arrived all the mats had been put down.

G

INDEX TO STOCK AND PATTERNS

E

ĕngkau (See Note IV. 90)
ĕntah Patt. III. 4
-ever (See Note I. 81)

G

Generic Stock 21
Genitive Stock 4 and 6 (*a*) iv
'get' Patt. VIII. 3

H

habis Stock 27; Patt. VII. 1. (See also Note VII. 55)
hari (See Note VIII. 99)
hĕndak Stock 10 (*b*) i. *b*; Patts. I. 4, IV. 2, V. 1. ii. (See also Notes IV. 12
   and 39, V. 92 and VIII. 38 and 49)

I

-i Stock 10 (*j*). (See also Note VI. 25)
ia Stock 6 (*a*) iii. (For *ia-lah* see Note III. 34)
Impersonal expressions Stock 25
ini and *itu* Stock 3; Patts. I. 7, II. 2

J

jadi (See Note III. 4)
jangan Stock 8 (*c*); Patt. II. 3. (See also Notes I. 44, V. 32)
juga Stock 12; Patts. VI. 3

K

ka- Stock 15 (*c*)
-kah Patt. I. 3
kami Stock 6 (*a*) i
-kan Stock 10 (*d*)
kapada Stock 15 (*d*)
'*karang* (See Notes II. 59, VI. 44, VIII. 38)
kĕ- Stock 10 (*i*). (See also Note V. 72)
kĕ- . . . -an Stock 10 (*h*); Patt. IV. 1
kita Stock 6(*a*) i

L

-lah Stock 14
lalu (See Notes II. 22, III. 40)

M

maka (See Note V. 6)
malam (See Note VIII. 1)
mana Stock 6 (*b*) ii
masa Stock 17 (*b*); Patt. I. 2

mĕ- Stock 10 (*b*); Patts. V. 1, VIII. 5.   (See also Note II. 22)
  mĕ- + *m* before *b* and (*p*)
  mĕ- + *n* before *d* and (*t*); *j* and *ch*
  mĕ- + *ng* before *g* and (*k*); *h* and vowels
  mĕ- + *ny* before (*s*)
  mĕ- alone before all other initial consonants
memang (See Note III. 9)
mĕreka Stock 6 (*a*) iii

N

nampak (See Note I. 29)
Negatives Stock 8; Patts. II. 3, V. 2
Noun-groups Stock 22. i. as description, ii. as declaration of topic, iii. as
  declaration of attendant circumstances, iv. as subject, object, or complement, v. verb-noun as subject
-nya Stock 6 (*a*) iv; Patts. I 8, VI. 4

O

Object preceding the verb.   (See Note VIII. 66)

P

pada Stock 15 (*b*)
pĕ- Stock 10 (*k*)
pĕr- . . . *-an* Stock 10 (*c*)
'please' Patts. II. 1
Possession Stock 4
Prefixes Stock 10; Patt. VIII. 5
Prepositions Stock 15 (*a*) *di-*, (*b*) *pada*, (*c*) *ka-*, (*d*) *kapada*
Pronouns Stock 3. ii (demonstrative); Stock 6 (*a*) personal, (*b*) interrogative,
  (*c*) relative
pula Stock 13; Patt. VI. 2
pun Stock 11; Patt. VII. 3
punya (See Note VII. 17)
Purpose (colloquially) Stock 18

R

ramai Patt. IV. 4

S

sahaja Stock 26; Patt. III. 2
sahaya or *saya* Stock 6 (*a*)
sambil (See Note II. 49)
'see, look' Patt. VIII. 4
sĕrta (See Note II. 22)
sila Patt. II. 1
sudah Stock 23; Patt. III. 3.   (See also Notes I. 40, III. 10 and 27, VI. 2
  and 59)

T

těmpat Stock 22. i; Patts. II. 4, V. 3

Tense-forms, absence of Stock 9

těr- Stock 10 (*e*); Patts. IV. 3, VII. 2 vi, VIII. 5

'that' (*conjunction*) (See Note VII. 17)

tidak Stock 8; Patt. V. 2

tolong Patt. II. 1

tuan Stock 6 (*a*) ii. (See also Note IV. 83)

W

'what a . . .' Patt. I. 8

'when' Stock 17 and 22. i; Patt. I. 2. (See also Note II. 38)

'where' Stock 22. i; Patt. V. 3. (See also Note VII. 57)

'who', 'which' Stock 6 (*c*), 22 i; Patt. II. 4. (See also Note VIII 68)

Y

yang Patt. VI. 1. (See also Note VIII. 68)

FOR QUICK REFERENCE

THE NUMERALS

Cardinal	Ordinal
1. sa-, satu, suatu	1st. yang pĕrtama
2. dua	2nd. yang kĕdua
3. tiga	3rd. yang kĕtiga
4. ĕmpat	
5. lima	13th. yang kĕtiga-bĕlas
6. ĕnam	14th. yang kĕĕmpat-bĕlas
7. tujoh	
8. (dĕ)lapan	
9. sĕmbilan	30th. yang kĕtiga puloh
10. sa-puloh	31st. yang kĕtiga puloh satu
11. sa-bĕlas	100th. yang kĕsa-ratus
12. dua-bĕlas	101st. yang kĕsa-ratus satu

	Serial
20. dua puloh	
30. tiga puloh	*firstly:* pĕrtama
41. ĕmpat puloh satu	*secondly:* kĕdua
	thirdly: kĕtiga
100. sa-ratus	
200. dua ratus	Distributive
301. tiga ratus satu	*three apiece:* sa-orang tiga biji
	twice a week: sa-minggu duakali
1000. sa-ribu	
2000. dua ribu	
3452. tiga ribu ĕmpat ratus lima puloh dua	

1,000,000. satu juta *or* satu milion

THE DAYS OF THE WEEK

Monday: Hari Ithnain *or* Isnain *or* Sĕnin
Tuesday: Hari Thalatha *or* Sĕlasa
Wednesday: Hari Arb'a *or* Hari Rabu
Thursday: Hari Khamis *or* Kamis
Friday: Hari Juma'at
Saturday: Hari Sabtu
Sunday: Hari Ahad

Note. These Arabic names are in common use, except in the sea-ports, where they are often replaced by *Hari* followed by a Malay numeral beginning with *Hari Satu* for Monday. Sunday is *Hari Minggu.*

THE MONTHS OF THE YEAR

The Arabic names of the months of the lunar year are as follows:

1. Muharram—30 *days*
2. Safar—29 *days*
3. Rabi'il-Awwal—30 *days*
4. Rabi'il-Akhir—29 *days*
5. Jamadi'l-awwal—30 *days*
6. Jamadi'l-akhir—29 *days*
7. Rajab—30 *days*
8. Sha'ban—29 *days*
9. Ramadzan—30 *days*
10. Shawal—29 *days*
11. Dzi'l-ka'dah—30 *days*
12. Dzi'l-hijjah—29 *days*

(For business purposes the western calendar is in common use, *e.g.* '25th April 1954', *dua puloh lima hari bulan April tahun sa-ribu sĕmbilan ratus lima puloh ĕmpat.*)

THE COMPASS POINTS

North: Utara
South: Sĕlatan
East: Timor
West: Barat

NUMERAL COEFFICIENTS

(*a*) *sa-buah* kapal tĕrbang
(*b*) *sa-batang* pokok kĕlapa
(*c*) *sa-biji* buah pinang
(*d*) *dua bilah* kĕris
(*e*) *sa-ekor* lĕmbu
    lĕmbu *sa-ekor*
(*f*) *lima hĕlai* kain sarong

COLOURS

puteh : *white*
hitam : *black*
merah : *red*
merah muda : *pink*

biru : *blue*
biru tua : *dark blue*
hijau : *green*
kĕlabu : *grey*

VOCABULARY

Abbreviations used: *Ar.*—Arabic, *Ch.*—Chinese, *Dut.*—Dutch, *Eng.*—English, *Hind.*—Hindustani, *Jav.*—Javanese, *Pers.*—Persian, *Port.*—Portuguese, *Skr.*—Sanskrit, *Tam.*—Tamil.

abah father, daddy (used by children)

abang elder brother; also used by wife to husband, girl to lover

abu ashes

ada there exists, there is present; *běrada* have possessions, (in newspaper Malay) be present

'adat[1] *Ar.* traditional custom

adek younger brother or sister; also used by husband to wife, lover to girl

adu, měngadukan cause to compete; *pěraduan* competition

agak guess; *agak-nya* probably, I should think; *těragak-agak* hesitantly

agama, ugama *Skr.* religion

agar-agar seaweed, jelly

ahli *Ar.* expert in . . ., member of . . .

'aja[2] = *sahaja*

ajak, měngajak invite to do something

ajar, měngajar teach; *bělajar* learn

'akad *Ar.* marriage contract

akan about to, to; *ta' kan* not likely to

aku (*familiar*) I, me

'alamat *Ar.* sign, address

alas, měngalas put something under or behind something else, as foundation, or protection, or lining

'alim learned in religious matters

alir, měngalir flow

almari *Port.* cupboard

ambil, měngambil fetch, take, get (something which you know to be there)

anai-anai termites, white ants

anak child, the young of creatures; *běranak* bear a child, have a child, be born; *anak běranak* parents and children together; *pěranakan* born in Malaya, having one or both parents non-Malay

angin wind, air

angkat, měngangkat lift, raise, pick up and bring in (food, tea, etc.)

anjong room over porch in Malay house

ansor, angsor, běrangsor gradually

antah odd rice-grains left unhusked after padi has been pounded

antara *Skr.* between

anu such-and-such, what d'you call it; *si-anu* so-and-so

apa? what? *běrapa?* how many? how much? (*bě*)*běrapa* some, a certain number; *ta' běrapa* not very (*colloquial*); *měngapa?* why? *ta' měngapa* it doesn't matter; *apa-apa* anything at all; *siapa?* who?; *siapa-siapa* anybody at all

apabila (*written*) when, on the occasion(s) when

api fire, flame

---

[1] This reversed comma in front of an initial *a* is a sign that in the *Jawi* (i.e. Malayo-Arabic) script the word does not begin with the letter *alif*, as do most of the words under *a*, but with a letter called *'ain* which is pronounced something like the *aa* in a sheep's 'baa'.

[2] An initial apostrophe shows that the word has been abbreviated.

174

apit, mĕngapit squeeze between two surfaces; *bĕrapit* hemmed in

ara fig

arah direction, in the direction of

arak, bĕrarak I. go in procession; *pĕrarakan* procession. II. *Ar.* rice spirit, toddy, alcohol

aram-aram scaffolding

arang charcoal

asal *Ar.* source, origin; *bĕrasal* originating (from . . .); *asalkan* provided that

asap smoke; *pĕrasap* incense-burner

asing separate, apart; (*modern*) foreign

askar, ashkar *Ar.* soldiers, troops

atap palm-thatch, roof

atas top; *di-atas* on, (of Malay house) in

atau *Skr.* or, or else

atok grandmother

ator, mĕngator arrange; *atoran* arrangement; *tĕrator* arranged

awai, mĕngawaikan reach out for anything with a curving movement, as with arm, foot, or elephant's trunk (whereas *chapai* is to reach for something with a direct movement)

awak body; person; you; I

awal *Ar.* beginning

ayah (*polite*) father

ayam chicken

ayer water; liquid; juice; *ayer batu* ice

baba title for Chinese (and sometimes people of other races) born in Malaya

bacha, mĕmbacha recite, read; *bachaan* reading; *pĕmbacha* reader

badan *Ar.* body (as opposed to spirit, soul); physical build

bagai *Tam.* sort, kind; *bĕrbagai-bagai* of various sorts; *sa-bagai* like, as if, (*modern*) in the capacity of; *bagaimana?* how? *bagini* in this way, *bagitu* in that way

bagi I. for. II. (*colloquial*) give, allow to, cause to

bagini, bagitu v. *bagai*

bagus fine, very good

bahagi divide; *bahagian* division

baharu new, newly; *baharu tiga hari* only three days ago; *baharu-baharu ini* quite recently

bahasa *Skr.* language; courtesy

bahu shoulder

baik good, well

baju loose short coat of silk or cotton; *baju panas* overcoat; *bĕrbaju* wearing a coat

bakar, mĕmbakar burn, roast, toast; *tĕrbakar* afire, burnt

bakul basket

balai audience hall; temporary roofed platform-room with open balustrated sides, pavilion; police-station

balek reverse side, at the back of; return, go home

bandar *Pers.* port, town

bangkit rise, stand up

bangku *Port.* bench

bangsa *Skr.* race, sort, kind

bangsal shed, booth

bangsat poor, humble, destitute; vagrant

bangsawan *Skr.* high-born; *wayang bangsawan* Malay theatrical performance

bantal cushion, pillow

banyak many, much; *tĕrbanyak* too many, too much, more than one intended

bapa, bapak father

barang any, any . . . so ever; about, more or less; something, things, goods, luggage; *barangkali* perhaps

barat west

baring lying down

baris row, line; *bĕrbaris* in rows

basah wet

basoh, mĕmbasoh wash

batang stem; numeral coefficient for trees, etc.

batil *Tam.* metal bowl

batu rock, stone, mile-stone, mile

bau smell; *těrbau* catch a whiff of

bawa, měmbawa bring, convey

bawah the lower side of, below

bayar, měmbayar pay; *těrbayar* able to be paid

bechak *Ch.* rickshaw; *bechak roda tiga* tricycle with car for passenger

bědak face-powder, cosmetic rice-powder

běkal provisions (for picnic, journey)

běkas I. trace, mark, former, 'ex-'. II. receptacle

bělah, měmbělah split lengthwise, cut open; *sa-bělah* half, on the side of, one of a pair (*e.g.* hands, feet); *sa-bělah sana* over there

bělaka every one of them; completely

bělakang back, rear

bělalai trunk (of elephant)

bělanja expense, outlay

-bělas -teen; *sa-bělas* eleven

běli, měmběli buy

belok change direction, to right or left; *těrbelok* swung round out of its course

bělum not yet; *sa-bělum (conjunction)* before

běnang thread

běnar true, correct; *běnarkan* make correct, give permission for

běnda *Skr.* thing, article; affair

běntang, měmběntang spread out, unroll; *běrběntang, těrběntang* spread out, unrolled

běntar moment; *sa-běntar lagi* in a moment, a moment later

běrani brave, bold

běrapa? běběrapa v. *apa*

běras husked rice

běrat heavy

běrdiri v. *diri*

běri, měmběri give

běrok the coconut-monkey

běrseh clean

běsar large; *běsarkan* make large

běsi iron

běsikal *Eng.* bicycle

besok v. *esok*

bětis calf, leg

bětul correct, straight, upright; *bětulkan* make straight; *běrbětulan* coinciding

biar, měmbiarkan allow, suffer, let be

biasa *Skr.* usual, accustomed; *biasanya* as a rule

bichara *Skr.* discussion, court-case

bijeh tin ore

biji seed; numeral coefficient for small round things, *e.g.* eggs

bila 1. when?; 2. in speech, short for *apabila* on the occasion when; *bila-bila* whenever

bilah lath, strip; numeral coefficient for knives, daggers, etc.

bilek room

bimbang anxious

bin *Ar.* son of

binti *Ar.* daughter of

biola *Port.* violin

bising noise; noisy

bola *Port.* ball

boleh can, able

bomba *Port.* pump

bonjol swollen; swelling, bump, boss

buah fruit; numeral coefficient for largish things, *e.g.* houses, cars; *buah-buahan* fruit of various kinds

bual bubble up; *běrbual-bual* chatter, gossip; *pěrbualan* conversation

buang, měmbuang throw, throw away

buat, měmbuat do, make; *buatan* manufacture, workmanship; *pěrbuatan* performance, act, deed

budak young person, child

buka, měmbuka open, unfasten, (of clothes) take off; *těrbuka, běrbuka* open, opened

bukan no, not (correcting an erroneous impression); *bukan-kah?* is it not so? *bukan-bukan* empty, foolish, imaginary

bukit hill

buku I. *Eng.* book. II. node, knot, knuckle

bulan moon, month

bulat round

bumbong roof-ridge, roof

bunga flower; *bĕrbunga* flowered, decorated

bungkus package, bundle

bunyi sound; *mĕmbunyikan* make to sound, pronounce; *bunyi-bunyian* music

burok shabby, in disrepair; ugly

busok going rotten (of fruit)

chachar small-pox; vaccination; *bĕrchachar* vaccinated

chadang, mĕnchadangkan plan, scheme, make arrangements for

chadar *Hind.* kain *chadar* a sheet

chakap, bĕrchakap undertake to do; speak; *pĕrchakapan* style of speech

chalun candidate (for election, etc.)

champak throw, throw away; *tĕrchampak* hurled, thrown

champor mix, mingle, mixed; *bĕrchampor-champor* all mixed up

chantek pretty, beautiful

chara *Skr.* style, fashion

chari, mĕnchari seek, look for

chat paint; *sapu chat* to paint

chawan *Ch.* teacup

chayer watery, weak (of tea)

che' = ĕnche'

chĕkah, mĕnchĕkah split open by pressure

chĕlah chink, fissure

chĕlup, mĕnchĕlup immerse; dye

chĕngang, tĕrchĕngang amazed, open-mouthed, astonished

chĕpat quick; quickly

chĕrita *Skr.* tale, account; *chĕritakan* to relate; *bĕrchĕrita* to tell a story

chĕrmat careful, neat

chĕrmin mirror; *bĕrchĕrmin mata* wearing spectacles

cheti, chĕti *Malayalam.* chetty, money-lender

chili chillies

China Chinese

chinchang, mĕnchinchang cut into very small pieces

chita *Skr.* feeling, feelings

chium, mĕnchium sniff, smell; kiss

choba try; (*colloquial*) please (in a request)

chorong funnel, chimney

chuacha *Skr.* clear, bright, brightness (of weather)

chuchi, mĕnchuchi clean, cleanse

chuchock, mĕnchuchok pierce, prick; *bĕrchuchok* strung, skewered

chuchu grandchild

chukup enough

churi, mĕnchuri steal

chuti *Hind.* leave of absence

daerah *Ar.* district

daging flesh, meat

'dah = *sudah*

dahshat *Ar.* terrible, horrifying

dahulu before, formerly; ahead; *bĕrdahulu-huluan* pressing forward, each one trying to get in front of the next one

dalam inside, in

dan and

dapat get, manage to; *pĕndapatan* information gained, 'findings'; for *mĕndapat, mĕndapatkan, di-dapati* v. Sentence Patterns VIII.2

dapor cooking stove; kitchen

dari from, out of

daripada than; (made) out of

datang come

dato', datok grandfather, grandmother; elder, non-royal chief

daun leaf; *bĕrdaun* having leaves

dawat *Ar.* ink

daya stratagem, way; *ta' tĕrdaya lagi* at the end of one's resources

dek (*colloquial*) by; through the agency of

dĕkat near; nearly; *mĕndĕkati* to draw near to; *dĕkatkan, mĕndĕkatkan* to bring (something) near

dĕlapan, 'lapan eight

dĕngan with, in company with, by means of

dĕngar, mendĕngar hear, listen to

dĕpan = *hadapan*

dĕrebar *Eng.* driver

di- 1. *prep.* (before place-words) at, in, on; 2. *verbal prefix* (before simple verbs), v. Stock 10 (*f*)

dia he, she, it, they, him, her, them

diam be silent, remain quiet; live, dwell; *bĕrdiam diri* to remain quiet, do nothing

dinding screen, partition, wall

diri I. self. II. erect; *bĕrdiri* be standing; *tĕrdiri* erected

dodol a sweetmeat of toffee-like appearance, made of *pulut* rice, coconut-milk and sugar

dua two; *dua-dua* both together; *saya bĕrdua dĕngan* . . . the two of us; *kĕdua* 1. the two; 2. secondly; *yang kĕdua* the second

dudok sit; dwell; *dudokkan* to seat

duit *Dut.* small cash, cent

duri thorn; *bĕrduri* having thorns

durian fruit with a thorny skin

dusun fruit plantation; orchard

ejek, mĕngejek tease, mock

ekor tail; numeral coefficient for living creatures other than human beings

ela *Eng.* yard (of cloth)

elok fine; suitable, just right

ĕmak, mak mother

ĕmas, mas gold

ĕmbun dew, mist

ĕmpat four; *bĕrĕmpat* four together, being four

ĕnam six

ĕnche', che' polite form of address to any Malay, man or woman, who has no distinctive title

ĕngkau, (shortened to **'kau** in the south, and to **hang** in the north) you (familiar, or to one inferior to the speaker either in age or rank)

ĕntah a word indicating uncertainty. Cf. the literary interrogative suffix -*tah*.

ĕrti meaning; *mĕngĕrti* understand

esok, besok to-morrow

faham *Ar.* (usually pronounced *paham*) understand

fasal *Ar.* (usually pronounced *pasal*) section, topic; concerning; (*colloquial*) reason, cause

gadoh, bĕrgadoh fuss, take trouble over; quarrel noisily

gajah elephant

galah pole

gali, mĕnggali dig; *pĕnggali* a spade

gambar picture, representation

gambir gambier

ganas fierce, man-eating (of animals); *pĕngganas* terrorist

ganti, mĕngganti substitute

gantong hang, hang up, defer; *bĕrgantong, tĕrgantong* hung up, hanging

garis, garisan line, scratch

gĕgat silver-fish, moth

gĕlap dark

gĕmok fat, obese

gĕnap even (of numbers), complete, full (of a period of time)

gĕndang drum

gĕrak, bĕrgĕrak move, stir

gĕtah sap, latex; rubber

gigi tooth

gigit, mĕnggigit to bite

giling, mĕnggiling to roll, grind (spices)

gonchang, měnggonchang to shake (*e.g.* a bottle)

gong gong

gopoh, běrgopoh-gopoh in a hurry

goreng fry (with very little fat)

gu' = *guru*

gugor drop, fall (of fruit falling one at a time, whereas *luroh* is used when large quantities fall)

gula sugar; *gula-gula* sweets

gulai curry

guna *Skr.* advantage, use; *měnggunakan* make use of; *běrguna* useful

guni *Hind.* sack

gunting scissors; *měnggunting* cut with scissors; *běrgunting rambut* have one's hair cut

habis ended, finished, none left; utterly, completely

had *Ar.* limit; up to

hadap, hadapan (in speech **děpan**) front

hadzir *Ar.* be present

hairan *Ar.* surprised, astonished

haji *Ar.* one who has made the pilgrimage to Mecca

hajji *Ar.* the pilgrimage to Mecca

hal *Ar.* circumstances, particulars

halaman, 'laman open space round a Malay house

halus fine, delicate

hampir near, nearly; go near

hantar, měnghantar send, escort; *běrhantar* sent, dispatched

hanya except for, only

hanyut drift, float

harap hope

harga *Skr.* price

hari day, 24 hours; *hari-hari* every day

hati liver, heart; *pěrhatikan, měměrhatikan* take note of

hělai, 'lai numeral coefficient for paper, hair, grass, leaves, garments

hěmpas dash down, or against something; *těrhěmpas* dashed against

hěndak (usually shortened to **'nak** in speech) about to, intend to, wish to

hěnti, běrhěnti stop, halt; *těrhenti* stopped, halted; *měmpěrhěntikan, měmběrhěntikan* bring to a stop

hias, měnghiasi decorate; *pěrhiasan* decorations

hidang serve food; *těrhidang* served, (of food), (*modern*) presented (of entertainment)

hidong nose

hijau green

hilang be lost, disappear

himpit, těrhimpit squeezed between two surfaces

himpun, běrhimpun come together, collect together

hingga until, up to, up to the point that

hitam black, dark in colour

hitong enumerate, count

hujan rain

hujong end, part furthest away

hulor, hulorkan, měnghulorkan stretch out, hold out (something to somebody)

hutan jungle, forest

ia (*written*) I. he, she, it; *ia-itu* it, that is to say, namely, *i.e.*; *ia-lah* (usually gathering together, and restating, a lengthy subject) it. II. = *ya* yes

ibu mother; *ibu bapa* parents; *ibu rumah* main building of a Malay house

ikan fish

ikat, měngikat tie, fasten

ikut, měngikut follow

inang (*literary*) nurse, duenna

ingat bear in mind, remember

Inggěris English

ini this, these

isi contents, flesh (of fruit), inhabitants (of country); *běrisi* having content, containing

istěri *Skr.* wife (more formal than *bini*)

isti'adat *Ar.* customary ceremonial

itu that, those, the

jadi come into being, be born, happen, be; *měnjadi* be abundant, be heavy (of crops)

jaga *Skr.* be awake; *měnjaga(kan)* awaken; *těrjaga* wakened

jahat wicked, (of children) naughty; *kějahatan* wickedness

jahit, měnjahit sew

jalan path, road; *běrjalan* travel, move about; *běrjalan (kaki)* walk; *běrjalan-jalan* stroll about

jam *Pers.* clock, watch; hour; *běrjam-jam* for hours on end

jamu, měnjamu entertain; *jamuan* party

jangan do not; lest

janggut beard; *běrjanggut* bearded

janji, běrjanji agree, promise (to do)

jarang at wide intervals in space or time; seldom

jari finger, toe

jatoh fall; *těrjatoh* fallen by chance

jauh distant; *běrjauhan* far apart one from the other

jawab, měnjawab *Ar.* answer; *běrjawab-jawab* answering each other in turn

jěmput, měnjěmput invite to accompany, invite to attend; *orang jěmputan* guests

jěndela *Port.* window (originally of glass windows only, now frequently interchangeable with *tingkap*)

jěngok, měnjěngok peep at (from behind something)

jěnis *Ar.* sort, kind

jěntěra *Skr.* wheel; machine

jěrang, měnjěrang put over fire to heat

joget Malay dancing

jolok, měnjolok knock down (fruit, etc. with a pole)

jual, měnjual sell; *běrjual* be a seller of . . .; be on sale

juga all the same, nevertheless; fairly, to a certain degree; also, too

jumpa, běrjumpa meet, come across; *těrjumpa* come across unexpectedly

jurus, sa-jurus a moment

ka- to, towards

kachang bean

kachau, měngachau stir, stir up, refuse

kadzi, kathi, *Ar.* Muslim registrar and judge, authority on matters of birth, death, marriage, divorce

-kah interrogative

kahwin marry, marriage; *pěrkahwinan* marriage

kail, měngail fish with rod and line; *orang pěngail* fisherman, *pěrahu pěngail* fishing-boat

kain cloth; sarong; *kain baju* clothes

kaji, měngaji learn to recite the Kor'an; study; attend school

kakak elder sister

kaki leg, foot

kalam *Ar.* pen

kalau if; *kalau-kalau* if by chance, in case

kali time, occasion; *sa-kali* once, at the same time; most of all

kami we (excluding the listener)

kampong homestead; ground (planted with mixed trees) round a house; village

kamus *Ar.* dictionary

kanan on the right

kapada v. *pada*

kapal *Tam.* ship

kapor lime, chalk

karang, měngarang compose, put together

'karang = *sěkarang* (sign of futurity)

kaseh affection, love; *těrima kaseh* thank you

kasut shoes

kata, mĕngatakan say; *pĕrkataan* word

katil *Tam.* bedstead

kaum *Ar.* family

kawah cauldron

kawal, bĕrkawal keep watch, be on guard

kawan friend; herd; (*as a pronoun*) I; you; *bĕrkawan dĕngan* be friendly with

kawasan enclosed land round a building

kawat wire

kaya rich, wealthy

kayu wood

kĕbun plantation, garden

kĕchil small

kĕchuali not counting, excepting

kĕdai *Tam.* shop; *bĕrkĕdai* keep a shop

kĕjap flick of an eye; *sa-kĕjap* a moment

kĕjut, tĕrkĕjut startled

kĕlabu grey

kelah, bĕrkelah go on a picnic

kĕlak (*written*) an adverb indicating future time

kĕlapa coconut

kĕledek sweet potato

kĕliling around, encircling; *sa-kĕliling* all round; *bĕrkĕliling* around; (*modern*) circling round (of an air-craft)

kĕluarga *Skr.* kinsfolk

kĕmas, bĕrkĕmas tidy, neat

kĕmian, kĕmĕnyan benzoin, a fragrant resin

kĕmudian then, afterwards

kĕna come up against, incur; make contact, be right; *bĕrkĕnaan dĕngan* in connection with

kĕnal, mĕngĕnal recognize, be acquainted with; *bĕrkĕnal-kĕnalan* knowing each other; *kĕnalan* an acquaintance

kĕnduri *Pers.* feast, party

kĕnyang satisfied (with food), having eaten enough

kĕpala *Skr.* head; overseer

kĕpok rice-bin

kĕpong, mĕngĕpong surround (with something); *bĕrkepong, tĕrkĕpong* enclosed

kĕra the long-tailed monkey

Kĕrajaan v. *raja*

kĕrana, karna *Skr.* because, because of

kĕrat, mĕngĕrat cut (across a short axis), sever; *tĕrkĕrat* severed

kĕrbau buffalo; *anak k.* buffalo calf

kĕreta *Port.* carriage, car; *kĕreta api* train

kĕring dry; *kĕkĕringan* drought, suffer from drought

kĕring dry; *kĕkĕringan* drought

kĕris kris, creese, Malay dagger

kĕrja *Skr.* work; preparations in connection with a feast; *bĕkĕrja* to work

kĕroh muddy, turbid

kĕrtas *Ar.* paper

kĕrumun, bĕrkĕrumun crowd together

kĕrusi *Ar.* chair

kĕtika *Skr.* moment, time, season

kĕtua elder, minor headman

khabar *Ar.* news; *surat khabar* newspaper

khatam *Ar.* end; ended (of studying the Kor'an); *bĕrkhatam* bring to an end (by the ceremony which marks the completion of Kor'an study)

khemah *Ar.* tent

kichap soya-bean sauce

kipas fan, propeller

kira calculation; *bĕrkira* calculate, think; *kira-kira* approximately, (to a child) sums

kiri on the left

kisar revolve, change direction; *kisaran* a mill

kita we (including the listener); you (meaning 'one', 'anybody')

kokok, běrkokok crow (of cocks)

kolam *Tam.* pool

konon it is said

kopak open (of fruit); *těrkopak* opened

kopi coffee

kosong empty

kotor dirty

koyak torn

kuah sauce, liquid in which something has been cooked

kuala mouth of stream

kuali iron frying-pan

kuat *Skr.* strong

kueh cake, sweetmeat

kukor, měngukor rasp

kulit skin, rind, leather

kumpul, běrkumpul assemble, come together; *měngumpulkan* gather together (people, things); *kumpulan, pěrkumpulan* a gathering

kunchi *Hind.* lock; *běrkunchi* having a lock, locked; *kunchi mangga* padlock

kuning yellow

kupas, měngupas peel, skin; *běrkupas* peeled

kurang less; *kěkurangan* scarcity, suffering from scarcity; *těrkurang* less than one intended

lachi *Dut.* drawer; *běrlachi* having a drawer

lada pepper

ladang dry clearing for rice; estate (*e.g.* rubber)

laga, běrlaga crash together (of animals fighting), collide (of cars)

lagi still, more; *sa-lagi* as long as; *lagi pun* moreover

lagu tune

-lah suffix-particle attached to the key word of a sentence

lahir, dzahir *Ar.* clear, apparent; be born

lain other, different; *běrlain-lain* of many different sorts; *běrlainan* differing (one from another)

laki husband; *laki-laki* male

laku conduct, behaviour; *lakukan* to behave

lalai, těrlalai dawdling, inattentive

lalu pass by; *těrlalu* exceedingly; *sělalu* 'always'; *ta' lalu* unable to (*colloquial*)

lama long (of time); *sa-lama* as long as

lambai, mělambai to wave

lambat slow, late

lambong, mělambong surge up, bounce; *těrlambong* soaring up and away

lampu *Port.* lamp; *běrlampu* having lamps, lighted by lamps; *lampu pichit* electric torch

langgan, běrlanggan subscribe (money); *langganan* subscription

langgar, běrlanggar collide with; *mělanggar* run into

langsat a small fruit with thin yellowish rind

langsong forthwith, completely

lantai floor

lapang empty, unencumbered, free

lapar hungry

lapek pad, mat, any protective layer

lapis fold, layer; *běrlapis* in folds, in layers

lari run away; *běrlari* run; *běrlari-lari* racing along

lateh practised, trained; *latehan* practice, training

lauk meat, fish, eggs, etc., cooked to eat with rice

laut sea

lawan, běrlawan rival, compete with; *ta' těrlawan* unrivalled, not able to be defeated

layang-layang kite

layar a sail; *bělayar* to sail, travel by ship

lěbat heavy, luxuriant, dense

lěbeh more (than)

legar, běrlegar circle round, revolve

lĕkas immediate; immediately; early (*e.g.* for an appointment)

lĕkat, mĕlĕkat adhere, stick

lĕkit, mĕlĕkit become sticky

leleh, mĕleleh trickle

lĕmah weak; *lĕmah lĕmbut* gentle (of character)

lĕmbu ox, bull, cow

lĕmbut soft, tender (of meat)

lempar throw, hurl; *mĕlempari* throw at; *mĕlemparkan* pelt with

lengah dawdle, linger

lĕpas free, loose, unattached; *lĕpaskan* to set free; *lĕpas itu* after that, then

lesen *Eng.* licence

lĕtak, mĕlĕtakkan put down, place; *tĕrlĕtak* placed

letrek *Eng.* electric

lĕtup, mĕlĕtup explode

lidi vein of palm-leaf

lihat, mĕlihat see; *kĕlihatan* to be seen, visible

lima five

lintang, mĕlintang lie athwart, move across

liput, mĕliputi flow over, inundate

lombong a mine

lompat, mĕlompat jump up and down, jump

lorong lane, path, street

luar the outside of anything; *kaluar* (go) outside; *di-luar* (be) outside; *kĕluar* to go out; *kĕluarkan* to take out

luka wound, sore

lukis, mĕlukis draw, paint; *pĕlukis* artist

lumpor mud

lunchor, mĕlunchor slip down

lusa the day after to-morrow

mabok drunk, intoxicated

macham *Tam.* kind, sort; (*sa-*) *macham* like, resembling

mahal expensive, dear

mahkamah *Ar.* court of justice

mahkota, makota *Skr.* crown; *kĕmahkotaan* coronation (*modern*)

mahu wish, be willing; (as an auxiliary indicating future time) will (*bazaar*)

main, bĕrmain play; *pĕrmainan* game, toy; *main-main* make a pretence

majallah *Ar.* magazine, journal

majlis *Ar.* assembly, meeting

maju successful; make progress

mak = *ĕmak*

maka a punctuation word used in written Malay

makalah *Ar.* article (in newspaper or magazine)

makan eat, chew (betel-nut); food, sustenance; *makanan* food

makin . . . makin, sa-makin the more . . . the more

Makkah Mecca

maktab *Ar.* school, college

malam darkness, night; the dark period of the twenty-four-hour cycle, which begins at 6 p.m.; hence often 'the eve of . . .'; *samalam* last night; *kĕmalaman* overtaken by darkness

malas lazy; *malas 'nak . . .* reluctant to, not feeling inclined to

malu shy, ashamed

mana? which? (*di*)*mana?* where? (*ka-*)*mana?* whither? (*macham*) *mana?* how? *mana-mana* any

mangga *Skr.* mango

manggis mangosteen

manis sweet; affable (of disposition)

marhaban *Ar.* a certain point in the ceremonial reading of the Life of the Prophet when the audience stands up and sings certain hymns

mari here! (*colloquial*) come here; *mari kita. . .* let us . . .

mas = *ĕmas*

masa *Skr.* time, period

masak ripe, cooked; cook; *měmasak* cook

maseh still, up to the present time, up to the time in question

masing, masing-masing separately, severally; each

masjid, mčsjid *Ar.* mosque

masok enter; *masokkan, měmasokkan* put (something) in

mata eye; *mata-mata* policeman

matahari sun

matchis *Eng.* matches

mati dead; stopped (of engines, etc.)

mawar *Ar.* rose

meja *Port.* table

mělainkan but (implying 'on the contrary'); except

mělati *Skr.* jasmin

Mělayu Malay (*adj.*)

memang by its very nature, invariably, habitually

měnang win, succeed

měnara *Ar.* minaret, spire

měngantok be sleepy

měngapa v. *apa*

měngkuang the screw-pine, a plant used in the weaving of mats and baskets

měntah uncooked; unripe

mentol *Eng.* electric bulb, gas mantle

merah red

měrchun cracker, fireworks

měreka, měreka itu (*written*) persons; they

měshuarat *Ar.* counsel; council

mesin *Eng.* machine

městi *Jav.* must (*colloquial*)

minggu *Port.* week; *hari Minggu* Sunday

minta, pinta ask for; *mintakan* ask for (something) for (somebody); *pěrmintaan* request

minum to drink

minyak oil, grease; *minyak kěreta* petrol

modal *Tam.* capital

muda young; unripe; pale (of colour)

mujor luck; lucky, fortunate

muka face, front of

mula *Skr.* beginning; *mulaï, měmulakan* begin; *mula-mula* first of all; *sa-mula* over again from the beginning

mumbang unripe coconut

murah cheap

musim *Ar.* season, monsoon

nadi *Skr.* pulse

nafas *Ar.* breath

nah (*colloquial*) here you are! take it!

naik go up

nakal naughty

'nak = *hěndak*

nama *Skr.* name; *namakan* give a name to; *běrnama* named

nampak be visible; see

nanti, měnanti wait; *nantikan* await

nasi cooked rice

nasihat *Ar.* advice

něgěri *Skr.* country, state, settlement

nganga, měnganga gape, be wide open

nikah *Ar.* marry

nipis thin (of materials, slices, etc.)

nombor *Eng.* number

-nya of him, of her, of it, of them; after *di-* + *verb*, by him, etc.; after *mě-* derivative (and compound prepositions), him, her, it

nyala, měnyala blaze, give off light

nyamok mosquito

nyanyi, měnyanyi sing; *pěnyanyi* singer

nyata *Skr.* clear, obvious

oleh by (somebody), because of (something)

orang person, people; numeral co-efficient for human beings

otak brains

pa' = *bapak*

pada at (before other than place words), on, according to; *kapada* to (a person), on (a certain date); *daripada* than; made of (some material)

padam go out, be extinguished (of fire, light)

padang level open space, playing-field, plain; *bĕrpadang* having a playing-field

padi rice (in the husk)

pagar fence; *bĕrpagar* fenced

pagi morning

pagut bite (of a snake); peck (of a bird)

pakai, mĕmakai use; wear; *bĕrpakai* dress (oneself); used, worn; *pakaian* clothing

paling, bĕrpaling turn the head sideways, look round; *palingkan* turn (something) sideways

palong trough, sluice-box

palu, mĕmalu beat (with a stick)

pampang, tĕrpampang full in sight, spread out before one

panas heat (of sun); hot

panchut gush out; *mĕmanchutkan* make to gush out; *pĕmanchut* a pump

pandai clever, skilled, knowing how to . . .

pandan screw-pine

pandang, mĕmandang turn one's eyes towards, look at; *tĕrpandang* find oneself looking at

panggil, mĕmanggil call, summon, invite

panggong stage; theatre

pangkal first part (of road, limb, etc.)

pangsa section (of fruit)

panjang long; *panjangkan* lengthen

panjat, mĕmanjat climb (tree, pole, etc.)

pantas quick, nimble

pantun a four-lined verse (v. Note VIII. 84); *bĕrpantun* to make up, and sing or recite such verses

parang a wood-knife

parit ditch

paroh, sa-paroh a half

pasang, mĕmasang I. fix, put in working order, start going, switch on; *bĕrpasang, tĕrpasang* switched on, lighted (of lamps). II. *sa-pasang* a pair. III. *pasang* rising (of tide)

pasar *Pers.* market, bazaar

pasir sand

pasokan troop, company, team

pasu vase, pot

patah broken, snapped off; *mĕmatakhan* to snap, break off (something); *pĕpatah* a proverbial saying; *sa-patah kata* a (preliminary) word or two

patut becoming, fitting, proper

payah difficult; *ta' payah* don't (polite)

payong umbrella, parasol; *bĕrpayong* having an umbrella, sheltered by an umbrella

pĕchah broken, shattered

pĕdas hot (of pepper, chillies)

pĕkan shopping-centre, village, town

pĕlamin bridal bed

pĕlekat cotton cloth

pĕluang clear space; chance, opportunity

pĕmuloh pipe made from stems of bamboo (*buloh*)

pendek short

pĕngantin bride or bridegroom

pĕnghulu headman

pengsan in a faint, unconscious

pĕning giddy, dizzy

pĕnoh full; *pĕnoh dĕngan* full of . . .

pĕntas sleeping platform; platform

pĕnyu green turtle

pĕrahu boat

perak silver

Pĕranchis French

pĕrang war; *pĕpĕrangan* warfare

pĕranjat, tĕpĕranjat startled

pĕreksa, mĕmĕreksa *Skr.* examine, look into; *pĕpĕreksaan* examination

pĕrĕmpuan feminine; woman

pĕrgi go

pĕrkakas tools, utensils, equipment

pĕrkara *Skr.* affair, thing

pĕrlahan slowly

pĕrnah? ever? *ta pĕrnah* never; *bĕlum pĕrnah* not (ever) yet

pĕrsĕtua *Skr.* once upon a time

pĕrut stomach, womb; bed (of stream)

pĕsaka, pusaka *Skr.* heirloom

pĕsan give an order, message, request

pĕtang afternoon, evening

pĕti *Tam.* box

pichit, mĕmichit press between finger and thumb, pinch

pihak, pehak side, team

pikul, mĕmikul carry over shoulder (*e.g.* sack); *sa-pikul* = 100 *kati* (1 *kati* = 1⅓ lb.)

pileh, mĕmileh choose

pinang betel-nut, areca-nut

pindah, bĕrpindah move, change position

pinggan plate

pinggang waist

pinjam borrow

pintas, mĕmintas cut through, take a short cut

pintu door, gate

piring saucer

pisang banana

pita *Port.* ribbon, tape

pokok tree, plant; origin (of); capital sum

pondok hut

potong, mĕmotong cut, cut off; kill an animal for meat (*colloquial*); perform a surgical operation; *bĕrpotong* cut up, sliced

puas satisfied; *puas saya mĕnchari* I've looked for it in every possible place

puchat pale

puji, mĕmuji to praise

pukul, mĕmukul strike, beat

pula, pulak (particle expressing sequence, and sometimes surprise) in its turn; if you please! (not always to be translated)

pulang return to starting-place

pulasan small fruit with a rough skin

pulau island

puloh group of ten

pulut a type of rice which goes sticky when cooked

pun a particle which draws attention to the preceding word or phrase (usually not to be translated)

pungut, mĕmungut collect, gather, pick up

punya, mĕmpunyaï possess

pusing, bĕrpusing rotate

puteh white

putus severed (of a rope); broken off (of speech); concluded, settled; *mĕmutuskan* to settle, to break off (of negotiation); *kĕputusan* decision

raja *Skr.* ruler, prince; *Kĕrajaan* Government

rajin diligent

ramai in large numbers (of people)

rambut hair

rambutan fruit with a hairy skin

rampai mixed, of various sorts

rapat close up to, close together

rasa, mĕrasa taste, perceive, feel; *bĕrasa* taste, taste of; *pĕrasaan* feeling, opinion; *ta' pĕrasan* not conscious of, not realizing

ratus group of a hundred

raya great, main; *bunga raya* hibiscus

rĕbah collapse (through weakness), fall down

rĕban chicken coop

rĕmpah spices; ingredients (for a recipe)

rĕndah low

rengkas abbreviated; *rengkasan* summary, notes

rĕnjis, mĕrĕnjiskan to sprinkle

rĕntas, mĕrĕntas to cut a narrow path through

riang-riang cicada

ribu group of a thousand; *bĕribu-ribu* in thousands

ribut a storm

ringgit dollar (= 2*s*. 4*d*.)

roboh collapse with a crash or a roar (*e.g.* house, or landslide)

roda *Port.* wheel

rokok cigarette

ronggeng Malay dancing

rosak injured, spoilt, out of order

roti *Hind.* bread

ruang hollow space (*e.g.* between pillars), the 'walls' of fruit sections

rugi *Skr.* financial loss; (*colloquial*) a pity that . . . !

rumah building, structure, house

rumbia sago palm

rumput grass; *bĕrumput* covered with grass

runding, bĕrunding discuss, consider (a plan)

runtoh fall heavily, collapse, come crashing down

rupa *Skr.* appearance; *sa-rupa* alike; *rupa-nya* apparently

sa- one, a. *Sa-* is always attached to the word, usually quantitative, which follows it: *sa-ekor kuching* a (certain) cat; *sa-panjang jalan* all along the road; *sa-panjang ini* as long as this. N.B. The forms *satu* and *suatu* are not attached because they already consist of *sa-* + coefficient (*watu*, Javanese form of the Malay word *batu*).

sabar *Ar.* patient

sadikit a little

safrah, saprah a long narrow cloth laid along the floor for a Malay meal

sagu sago-pith

sahaja only, merely; (*colloquial*) nothing but, quite

saji, tĕrsaji *Skr.* served (of food)

sakalian all together

sakat, mĕnyakat annoy, tease

sakit sick, ill; *sakit hati* annoyed, resentful

saksi *Skr.* witness

salah error, wrong, wrong-doing; *apa salah?* why not?

salin, mĕnyalin change (clothes, etc.); translate; copy down

sama *Skr.* same, alike; *bĕrsama dĕngan* together with

sambal side-dishes for curry (usually referring to uncooked green-stuff)

sambil at the same time

sambut, mĕnyambut receive, greet

sampah rubbish

sampai arrive; up to, until; *mĕnyampaikan* cause to arrive, deliver

sana there, over there

sanak *Ar.* relatives; *sanak saudara* kith and kin

sanding, bĕrsanding sit ceremonially side by side (of bride and bridegroom)

sangat very, exceedingly, excessively, too

sanggup undertake to do

sangka *Skr.* think, be under the impression that . . . (often mistakenly)

sangkut, bĕrsangkut stick, be attached to, catch into; *tersangkut* stuck, caught

sapĕrti, sĕpĕrti like, as, as if

sapu, mĕnyapu wipe, wipe away, dust; apply (*e.g.* face-powder); *bĕrsapu chat* painted; *pĕnyapu* broom; *sapu tangan* handkerchief

sarap dust

sarkis *Eng.* circus

sateh, sate, satai *Tam.* kabobs

satu v. *sa-*

saudara *Skr.* brother, sister, relative

sawah irrigated rice-fields (in the south; in the north, *běndang*)

saya, sahaya *Skr.* I (*lit.* slave); *saya sěmua* we (all)

sayor vegetables

sěbab *Ar.* cause; because

sěběrang, sa-běrang the other side (of river or street); *měnyěběrang* to go across; *sěběrang-měnyěběrang* on both banks

sěbut, měnyěbut mention, pronounce

sědang medium; in the middle of

sědap good to taste; comfortable; pleasant

sědar conscious of . . .

sědut, měnyědut draw in, suck up, sniff up

sědia *Skr.* ready; *sědiakan* make ready (something); *běrsědia* make oneself ready

sehat, sihat *Ar.* health

sějok cold, cool

sěkarang now, presently

sěkat, měnyěkat hinder, obstruct; *sěkat-sěkat* a series of partitions

sěkolah *Port.* school; *běrsěkolah* attend school

sělalu v. *lalu*

sělamat *Ar.* safety

Selan Ceylon

sělasa, thalatha *Ar.* Tuesday

sělat strait, straits

sělekeh, běrsělekeh smeared, stained in patches

sělekoh twisting; bend, corner (of road)

sělendang woman's shoulder scarf, head scarf

sělěsai settled, brought to a conclusion

sělimut rug, blanket; *sělimutkan*, *měnyělimutkan* to wrap something round something else

sělit, těrsělit wedged into a small space, stuck into a crevice

sěmat, sěmatkan pin together (*e.g.* papers)

sěmata-mata, sa-mata-mata *Skr.* utterly, completely

sěmbahyang prayer (*sembah* offer homage, *yang* divinity)

sěmběleh slaughter beasts for food by cutting the throat, as prescribed by Muslim law

sěmbilan nine

sěmentara *Skr.* while, in the meanwhile

sěmpadan boundary

sěmpat just enough time (to do something)

sěmua *Skr.* all

sěnak sharp sudden pains; a sudden sharp blow in chest or abdomen

sěnam, běrsěnam stretch oneself; *sěnaman* drill, physical exercises

sěnang easy, comfortable; having spare time

sěndiri self

sěndok spoon; *měnyěndok* to ladle out

sěngaja purposely

sěnyum, těrsěnyum smile

sepah, běrsepah strewn about untidily

sěpěrai bedspread

sěrah, měnyěrah hand over; *běrsěrah* give oneself up

sěrambi roofed verandah-room in a Malay house

sěrba *Skr.* all; *sěrba sadikit* a certain amount, to a certain extent

sěrban *Pers.* turban worn by a Haji

sěronok enjoyable

sěrta *Skr.* along with, together with

sěsat astray, having lost one's way

sětering *Eng.* steering-wheel

sewa, měnyewa hire, rent

sharikat *Ar.* association, corporation, firm

siang I. daylight; *siang-siang* early in the morning. II. *siang, měnyiang* to trim and prepare for cooking (meat, fish, vegetables)

siap ready; *siapkan*, *měnyiapkan* make ready (something); *běrsiap* make preparations, make oneself ready

siapa v. *apa*

sibok busy, fully occupied

sidai, měnyidai hang out to dry; *těrsidai* hung out to dry

sihat, sehat health

sila, silakan *Skr.* invite (to enter, to begin eating), please, be pleased to; *běrsila* sit cross-legged

silat, běrsilat an exhibition self-defence 'dance' performed by two men, one of them armed with a dagger or, sometimes, a sword

simpan, měnyimpan keep, put away, store

simpang cross-roads

singgah call in at, visit; *singgah-měnyinggah* to call at various places

singgong dig with elbow, knock against

sini here

siram sprinkle with water

sireh betel-vine

situ there

so'al question, query

songkit *kain songkit* cloth with gold threads woven into it

sorok, měnyorok draw back into cover; withdraw into, burrow into; *main sorok-sorok* hide-and-seek

sorong, měnyorongkan push forward, hold out (something) towards (somebody) using both hands

suatu v. *sa-*

sudah completed, finished; has become, is

suka *Skr.* pleasure, delight; *suka hati*, *suka chita* delight, delighted; *měnyukakan hati* to give delight

sukat, měnyukat to measure (capacity)

sumbu wick, fuse

sungai river

sunggoh genuine, true; truly

suntok almost too late, barely enough time left (to do something)

supaya *Skr.* in order that

surah *Ar.* a section of the Kor'an, covering one topic

surat *Ar.* writing, document, letter

surau *Ar.* a small chapel used for Kor'an school, and for services other than the Friday service

suroh tell to do

susah trouble; troubled, difficult

susu breast; milk; *susu gětah* latex of rubber tree

sutěra *Skr.* silk

ta' = *tidak*

tabek greeting. (See Note VII. 22)

tabor, měnabor scatter

tadi just now

tahan restrain; put up with, 'stand' (strain)

tahu know

tahun year

ta' kan = *ta' akan*

takut afraid; *takutkan* afraid of

tali cord, rope, string

tamasha *Pers.* show, spectacle

tambat, těrtambat tethered

tammat *Ar.* ended (esp. of studies)

tanah land, earth; *Tanah Mělayu* Malaya

tanam, měnanam plant, bury; *běrtanam padi* be a padi-planter

tanda sign, mark, indication

tandu a litter; *měnandu* carry (a person) in a litter, or on the shoulders

tangan hand, forearm

tangga ladder, steps, staircase; *rumah tangga* family, home, household

tanggal dropped off; *měnanggalkan* to take off (shoes, clothes)

tangis, měnangis weep

tangkap, měnangkap catch, seize

tanjong cape, promontory

tanya, bĕrtanya ask (a question)

tapak sole of foot, palm of hand

'tapi = *tĕtapi*

tapis strain, filter; *tapisan* a sieve

tarek, mĕnarek pull, draw, drag

tari, mĕnari dance

taukeh *Ch.* Chinese employer of labour

tĕbal thick, fleshy (of fruit)

tĕbĕrau tall wild grasses

tĕbing bank (of river)

teh *Ch.* tea

tĕkan mĕnĕkan press hard on

tĕkat embroider; *bĕrtĕkat* embroidered

tekoh, teko tea-pot

tĕkun diligent application (to work)

tĕlah had, had become, was (replaces *sudah* as an auxiliary in written Malay); *sa-tĕlah* (*conjunction*) after, when

tĕlinga ear, handles (*e.g.* of jar); *bĕrtĕlinga* having handles

tĕlor egg

tĕmbaga *Skr.* brass

tĕmbakau *Hind.* tobacco

tĕmpat place

tempoh *Port.* time within which something is to be done

tĕndang kick

tĕngah middle; *sa-tĕngah* a half; *tĕngah rumah* the living-room of a Malay house

tĕngkolok headkerchief

tengok see, watch, look at

tĕntang opposite; concerning; instance, place, passage (in a book)

tĕntu certain; certainly

tĕpi edge

tĕpok, mĕnĕpok clap, beat lightly, tap

tĕpong flour, paste, dough

tĕrang bright, clear; *tĕrangkan* to explain; *kĕtĕrangan* explanation, exposition

tĕrbang fly

tĕrbit arise, issue

tĕrima, mĕnĕrima to receive; *tĕrima kaseh* thank you

tĕrok serious (of illness), acute (of pain)

tĕrompah, tĕrompak wooden clogs

tĕrus straight through, straight on; *mĕnĕrusi* go through; by way of, via

tĕtap fixed, firm; *tĕtapkan* to fix, make definite

tĕtapi *Skr.* but

tĕtawak gong with boss

tiada v. *tidak*

tiang pole, mast

tiap-tiap each, every

tiba arrive; *tiba-tiba* suddenly, when not expected

tiga three; *kĕtiga* all three

tidak, ta' not; *tiada* is not; is not present

tidor sleep

tikar mat woven from *mĕngkuang* leaves

tilam mattress, flat cushion

timah tin

timbun heap; *bĕrtimbun* in a heap, in heaps

timor east

timpoh, bĕrtimpoh sit on the floor, as Malay women do, with feet to the right

timun cucumber

tindeh lying one on top of another

tinggal be left, remain, live; *tinggalkan* leave, leave behind; *mĕninggal* die (short for *mĕninggalkan dunia*)

tinggi high

tingkap window in a Malay house, *i.e.* a flap shutter with top hinges

tinjau, mĕninjau crane the neck in order to see

to' = *dato'*

tolak, mĕnolak push, push away; *bĕrtolak* set out, start off

tolong, mĕnolong help; 'please'

topekong *Ch.* picture over a Chinese shrine

topi *Hind.* hat; *bĕrtopi* having a hat, wearing a hat

tua old, adult; dark (of colour); *orang tua* father, parents; *orang tua-tua* people of days gone by

tuai, měnuai reap rice with a *tuai* (a small implement of bamboo with a steel cutting-edge, held concealed between palm and fingers in order not to scare the rice-soul)

tuan master, sir; you

tudong cover, covering, lid

tuil, měnuil to prise up with a slight levering movement

tujoh seven

tuju, měnju aim at; *běrsětuju* be in agreement

tukang craftsman, workman, artisan

tulis, měnulis write; *tulisan* writing

tumbang fall over (of trees, posts, cattle)

tumbok, měnumbok to pound

tumpah spill over, be spilt; *těrtumpah* spilt

tumpang, měnumpang to take advantage of help or opportunity afforded, *e.g.* stay at somebody's house, share somebody's umbrella, be a passenger on train or boat; *tumpangkan* leave (something) in somebody's care

tumpul blunt

tunai, měnunaikan to fulfil an obligation, comply with a request

tunggu, měnunggu to watch over, wait

tungku trivet of stones for a cooking-pot

tunjok, měnunjok to point out, show

tuntut, měnuntut to claim one's right, go in search of (learning); *pěnuntut* student

tutor utterance, *tutorkan*, speak, talk

tutup shut

turun go down, come down; fall (of rain); arise (of a storm-wind)

turut, měnurut follow, imitate

ubah, běrubah be different, be altered; *měngubahkan* to alter (something), transplant rice seedlings

ubat drug, cure; 'agent' of any sort, *e.g.* polish for furniture, acid for latex, battery for torch; *běrubat kapada* . . . to take medicine prescribed by . . .; *ta' těrubat* incurable

ubi tuberous root; *ubi kayu* tapioca; *ubi kěntang* potatoes

uchap, měnguchupkan utter, make a speech

udang prawn; *udang galah* crawfish, small lobster

udara *Skr.* atmosphere

ukor, měngukor measure (length or surface)

ular snake

ulas pip (stone and flesh, *e.g.* of durian), section, (*e.g.* of orange)

uli, měnguli to knead

'umor *Ar.* life, age; *běrumor* aged

'umum *Ar.* public, general

unjok, měngunjok offer, hold out, proffer

untong profit; fate, luck, good luck

upah fee for services, or for work done

usah need; *ta' usah* don't (*polite*)

usaha *Skr.* diligence

utara *Skr.* north

wah exclamation of surprise

wajek a sweetmeat made of *pulut* rice and coconut, and cut into diamond-shaped slabs

wakil *Ar.* agent, representative

walau *Ar.* if; *walau* . . . *pun* although

wangi fragrant, scented

wayang theatrical performance

yaani, ya'ni that is to say

yang who, which